POWER PLANETS

POWER PLANETS

A Manual for Human Empowerment

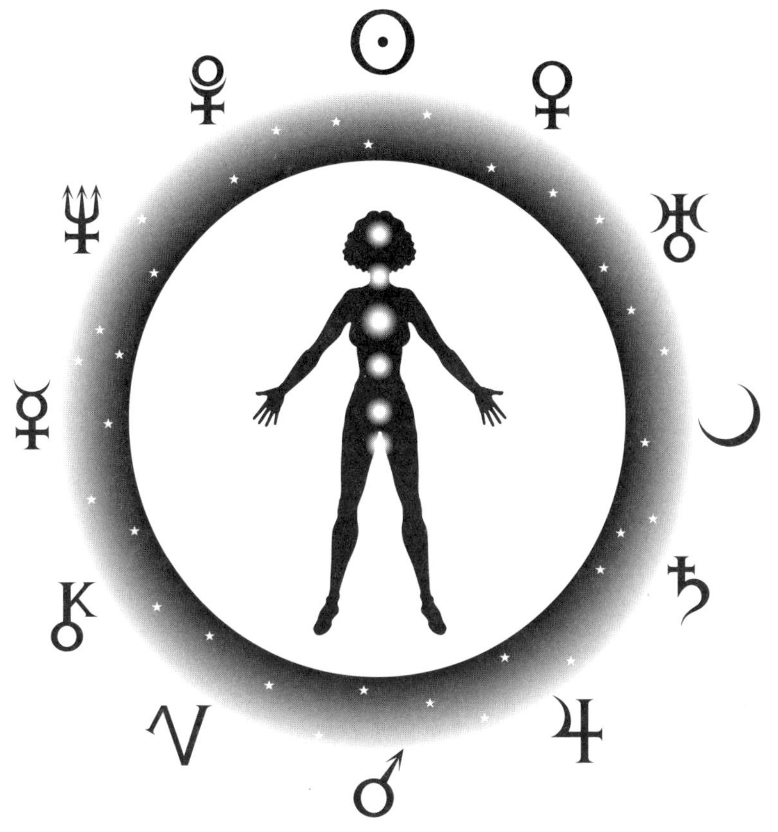

Luisa De La Lama

POWER PLANETS

White Dragon Productions
P.O. Box 68124,
Raleigh, NC 27613
or
STAR*LIFE
1295 South Kihei Rd., Suite 3009
Kihei, Maui, HI 96753

ISBN: 1-883381-20-7
LCCN: 93-60378

I dedicate this book with great love to my husband and Twin Soul, Luis De La Lama; to my long-time friend and teacher, Dolores Ashcroft-Nowicky, who brought us together in this lifetime; to my grandmother, Carmen Marchioness of Villavieja; to my children, Prince Alvin and Princess Ariana Sayn-Wittgenstein-Berleburg and their father, Prince Richard Sayn-Wittgenstein-Berleburg.

I also dedicate this book to the Great Beings Who have guided me along my lifetimes on Earth, especially to the gods and goddeses described in this book.

ACKNOWLEDGEMENTS

I thank my husband Luis for his help in preparing the manuscript and doing the beautiful cover design for this book. I love you, Luis!

I would also like to express my thanks to Bernie Ashman for writing the Foreword and giving me positive feedback. I certainly needed it!

I thank my editor, Myra Parisoff, Ph.D., for her excellent work on the manuscript. Great job, Myra!

My gratitude to my mother, Carmen Escandon, and her friends, Leila and Jaques Bourkin, who are presently recording the inner journeys on tape.

I also thank Marna K. Erech for her encouragement and early work on the manuscript.

And last but not least, I thank the archetypal forces represented by the twelve power planets, who have been so cooperative in revealing themselves when I summoned them.

The Highest, after all, is not to comprehend the Highest, but to do it.

——Soren Kierkegaard

Initiation is a process of developing inclusiveness.

——The Tibetan Master, D.K.

FOREWORD

In my twenty years in the field of Astrology, rarely have I encountered a book as unique as *Power Planets.* I first met Luisa (Lille) De La Lama in 1992 when she came to me for an astrological consultation. She mentioned to me that she was completing her first book. I remember saying to Luisa during the session that her birthchart indicated the potential for a very creative and inspiring writer. I am most happy to see firsthand that my intuitive insights were never truer!

The author challenges us to seek growth. To change. To think. Feel. Understand. To put our intuitive nature into action. This is a book that entices the reader to seek growth. If you have been led to *Power Planets,* it is probably no accident. Your own intuitive forces will guide you, as they did me, to read first the chapters of the planets most desiring your attention. You will soon realize this is a book that goes beyond mere discussion of positive and negative meanings of astrological symbols. *Power Planets* is more than just a valuable contribution to astrology. It is a dynamic experience.

After I began scanning the chapters in *Power Planets,* I remembered the author's initial challenge to the reader in her introduction. She tells us that if we merely desire an "intellectual understanding of the planetary archetypes" then we are "reading the wrong book." The reader is encouraged to go beyond understanding. The author shows through guided imagery and practical exercises how to take the first steps to identify the traps of our personal fears and negative thoughts. The groundwork for helping people to tune into their personal power is masterfully explained. We only need to drink from the knowledge of this book and put it into practice.

Luisa De La Lama has written a book based on her own "inner research." The pages that follow are full of deep messages and mythological references. There is a wisdom in this book that is certain to reach all—those with either a lot or a little astrological expertise. *Power Planets* is about aiding people to respond better to the inner and outer challenges that life is offering. I believe that the author will inspire individuals through this book to find the faith to make needed life changes and to embrace their personal power within.

Bernie Ashman
Durham, North Carolina
April, 1993

Author of *Astrological Games People Play* and *Roadmap to the Future*

CONTENTS

POWER PLANETS

INTRODUCTION

Power Planets is a manual to understand and harness the energies of the planetary archetypes. By connecting with these transpersonal forces represented here as superhuman beings with distinct personalities you will discover your inner power and gain a new sense of aliveness.

I wrote *Power Planets* for the beginner as well as for the more-sophisticated seeker. Its techniques are especially suitable in combination with astrology and cognitive therapies.

However, you do not need to be an astrologer to use this book. You can directly access the power of the planetary archetypes without knowing astrology. Therefore, I have kept the astrological information deliberately brief. For those of you who are not astrologers but become fascinated by astrology and mythology after reading this book, I have included an extensive bibliography as well as the names and addresses of various astrological services who will cast your natal chart for a fee.

I have tried to use as few "esoteric" terms as possible because I want *Power Planets* to be readily understood by everyone. There are some terms, however, I have been unable to avoid. In the Appendix I have included a diagram of the major chakras or energy centers in the human body for those unfamiliar with them.

You may ask why I used planetary archetypes instead of the more commonly used zodiacal signs. The gods and goddesses related to the planets, as opposed to the more abstract and/or animal symbols of the zodiac, can be contacted as if they were actual persons. Clothing archetypes in human form intensifies the contact with them. It gives our subconscious an additional boost by enlisting the etheric power of our physical natures. Is it not much easier to feel connected to and love Apollo or Aphrodite than a lion, a sun disc, a bull, or a scale? Seeing the archetypes as gods and goddesses makes the experience much more intimate and powerful, the contact so intense it becomes almost physical.

Power Planets is also intended to be a workbook for astrologers and their clients. In recent years much has been written about the planets' energies and how they affect a person's life. Although much good and valuable information and explanation has been included in these writings, nevertheless, I feel that now is the time for action.

The natal chart can be seen as a symbolic representation of the personal-energy pattern we chose for ourselves at birth. We must not only analyze, study, understand, and mentally relate the various components of this energy pattern, but it is essential that we take action and start working directly with the energies in question. The easiest way to do this is through contact with the power of the planets.

It is my belief that we must transcend the rather passive attitude of traditional astrology and adopt a more-dynamic approach to the cosmic energies. Rather than simply know their nice and not-so-nice qualities and wait until they affect us, we can contact the archetypes directly and intimately. *Power Planets* shows us the way to avail ourselves of their energy and channel it to fulfill our life's purpose rather than allowing them to appear unexpectedly and cause havoc.

If you merely require an intellectual understanding of the planetary archetypes and are not ready to focus your will to empower your life with action and take charge of your energy, then you are reading the wrong book.

HOW THIS BOOK CAME TO BE

The groundwork for this book was laid as a result of and shortly after my husband Luis and I started STAR*LIFE, Instant Access To Cosmic Energies, a system of initiations for human empowerment.

STAR*LIFE is structured on three levels. The first level introduces the student to the energies of the five Elements. The second level confers the powers of the planetary archetypes in a series of twelve initiations, and the third level connects the student to the stars and constellations.

To help the STAR*LIFE initiates understand the energies they were receiving, we developed a series of manuals to accompany the activations.

While Luis organized STAR*LIFE, did all the artwork, wrote the manuals for the first level, and a set of twelve lessons on healing, I created the practical guides to the planetary initiations.

During my research of each planet I was very fortunate to find an incredible wealth of literature at my disposal. Many of these works contained far-reaching insights that have only recently been incorporated into astrology.

But most important to the emergence of this work was my "inner research. " After pinpointing the "core issue" of each planet, I isolated myself in my meditation room for many days and contacted the archetype associated with the planet in question. I am sharing here some of the techniques I used.

By the time I was through with the twelfth planet I had become a different person. Purified and reborn, I had found a new sense of aliveness, power, and direction I never dreamed possible. Since my own healing journey proved my findings on the power planets were extremely valuable in themselves, we decided to compile the manuals into a book format and adapt the contents to serve the average reader who has not received the STAR*LIFE Cosmic Activations.

I do not claim *Power Planets* to be a complete description of each planetary archetype. Rather, I am elucidating some of the most-controversial and least-understood issues surrounding each archetype. I feel that the obscure themes are the ones that often contain the most power.

The practices described in *Power Planets* are in no way limited to the astrological archetypes, they may be successfully adapted to any other archetype or pantheon. I strongly encourage my readers to do so.

Luisa De La Lama

HOW TO USE THIS BOOK

You can use this book in two ways. The first, and in my opinion, the best way is to read each chapter and work with each power planet in the sequence presented. This will guide you through a gradual and gentle expansion, each energy building on and enhancing the previous one. Go slowly at first. The energies are very powerful and I recommend you not work with more than one planet per week.

The second way is aimed at those versed in astrology or working with an astrologer. Here, after checking your most problematic areas based on your natal chart, you work directly with the corresponding planets. When you have worked to your satisfaction with your natal chart, you may work with the planets transiting the significant areas in your horoscope.

Once you have achieved good conscious contact with at least one of the planetary archetypes, you may work with several consecutively and alter/ adapt the exercises as needed. The power planets are very influential macrocosmic realities equally effective, whether used in conjunction with the natal chart or in the sequence offered in these pages.

Attunement with the archetypal power of the planets . . .

In this section I describe the power of the particular planetary archetype. It is essential that you read it thoroughly to understand the planet's energy and speed up your contact.

As you study and understand the archetypal force of the sun, moon, and each planet, you are greatly expanding your spiritual horizon, building the mental matrix for the ensuing energetic contact. However, you do not need to understand fully each planet before you effect the conscious contact or perform the exercise. In truth, it is doubtful if we will ever be able to claim complete understanding of such vast archetypes as are the planets. They have dimensions within dimensions much too complex and fluid for the human mind to grasp in their entirety. What counts here is knowing as much as we can and focusing our intent on achieving energetic contact with them. Once we have succeeded in integrating their energy through conscious contact, the archetypes will reveal themselves to our awareness in an ongoing process of inner growth and expansion; understanding them and ourselves more deeply will follow naturally.

The god or goddess in mythology and astrology . . .

Power Planets deals with the archetypal energies of the planets of our solar system and their corresponding mythological gods and goddesses, which obviously have been named from Roman and not Greek mythology. Nevertheless, I prefer to use the Greek divinities and myths and, on occasion, even the Egyptian deities to elucidate the archetypal forces represented by these planets. The Greek and Egyptian deities are older and better defined than the Roman. And it is well known that the Romans based their mythology on the Greek, altering it only slightly to suit their purposes and lifestyle.

I am keeping the mythological and astrological aspect of each planet deliberately brief. Although I have synthesized the main characteristics of the gods and goddesses for you, it would be too extensive to describe their legends and attributes further in these pages. With this book you have more than enough to make energetic contact and apply the planet's power to your life. If you wish to learn more about the mythological and astrological aspect of the planets you may do so by reading the books listed in the bibliography.

The inner journey to contact the archetype . . .

To establish your conscious contact with the planetary archetype I have used a form of guided visualization called *inner journey*. Apart from the fulfillment and enlightenment this guided visualization may bring you at the time you use it, it has a lasting effect on your subconscious mind. I recommend you do it regularly. However, do not mix several planetary energies; persevere with a single one until you feel you have contacted and integrated it to your satisfaction.

To perform the inner journey have someone read it to you aloud, if possible; otherwise, record it on tape and play it back. You can also read it yourself until you memorize it, then relax deeply and live through it again, as if it were a real experience.

Before you start the guided visualization make certain that you won't be interrupted. Sit or lie in a comfortable position and begin relaxing by breathing deeply and rhythmically. Then count from ten to zero, allowing your body to relax even more with each count.

Through inner journeying you learn to become a "mediator." The difference between a "mediator" and a "channel" is that the mediator raises consciousness to the subtle realms of manifestation and communicates with the beings that populate those regions *on their own level.* A channel, on the other hand, simply opens him/herself receptively and allows disembodied entities to enter and use his/her body. In channelling, the entity has to descend to the vibration of physicality, but in mediatorship the mediator rises in consciousness to higher realms. The mediator decides where s/he wants to go and whom s/he wants to contact. Opposite most channels, the mediator remains in full awareness and control during the entire process, always able to open, direct, and close the communication at will.

Once you familiarize yourself with inner journeying you may adapt it to contact other gods, goddesses, and transpersonal beings such as saints, masters, and gurus. If you create your own guided visualizations, make certain that you always return the same way you came and that you mark the threshold into the inner realms of consciousness with a door or gate imprinted with a certain symbol related to your goal.

The landscapes I used in the inner journey are not realistic but symbolic. This allows me to weave in any relevant clues that set the correct emotional mood and point your mind toward the intended goal—your contact and integration of the archetype.

In the last part of the inner journey you will ask the god or goddess to give you a personal message. This may be an image you receive telepathically or words you hear clairaudiently. Sometimes you will not receive anything conscious at the first meeting, but the contact will work on your subconscious mind. You will come up with new ideas and a different outlook on life as time goes by. Later, when you have built a strong conscious connection with the archetype, you may ask for more information and even engage in lengthy inner conversations with the gods and goddesses. At this point you will have become a mediator between the gods and humanity.

There is, of course, another effect that will be felt in your everyday life. As you tap into those immense reservoirs of cosmic energy, the radiant power of the archetypes will manifest in your aura. Each time you engage in an activity related to a specific archetype, it will be felt more intensely than under normal conditions, and this will help you experience life to its fullest.

I strongly encourage you to interact with the gods and goddesses as if they were living beings; indeed, on their own level they are very alive. Love them as deeply as you can!

The magical practice . . .

In the magical practice that accompanies each planet you will learn to apply its power to your life. These practices are dynamic and will oriented. You might not understand the deeper implications and symbolism of each at first; however, it is important that you perform them the way they are described.

Whenever you are asked to use a physical object within a magical practice such as a candle, pen, paper, bowl, and so forth, please do so. If you merely perform the practice on a mental level, it will not be as effective.

To show you the correct mental attitude to begin the magical practice, I have compiled a list called "Preliminaries to the Magical Practice." Take these to heart and be honest with yourself.

Most of you have heard by now that one of the best ways to change the quality of your life and environment is first to change yourself. If you attempt directly to influence your environment, you will not progress very far. Since you have not changed the conditions in yourself that brought about the undesired circumstances, you will find yourself again and again unconsciously attracting those same conditions to your life.

If, however, while changing from the inside you also take willful action, that is magical and/or physical, then your progress will indeed be great.

In performing a magical practice to harness, integrate, and apply the planetary power, we are moving forward with our intent, embracing the planet's energy, assimilating and understanding it in a constructive, assertive manner. In this way we avoid being caught unprepared and are, in fact, building suitable channels for the archetype to express its power in ourselves and our environment *according to our will.* And magic has been defined by occultists over the ages to be just that: The art of causing subjective and objective changes in ourselves and our environment at will.

The archetypal power of each planet will tend to express itself in the area and at the level we focus our intent or will. Think of the energy poured into us from and through the planets of the solar system like rainwater running down a steep slope from the higher to the lower areas. If we want to harness its power, we must build a canal and guide it to irrigate those areas needing it most. If we simply let the water flow down the mountain on its own, it will seek a passage through little cracks and crevices and follow the path of least resistance. The water will quench the thirst of the valley all right, but in a general and diffuse manner. Those areas we intend to cultivate might never receive enough water to become as special as we want them to be. They would have to wait until the general humidity caused by the rain eventually made them grow, but the process would be much slower. Therefore, it is important to know and understand the power of each planet and direct it through our focused intent toward the particular area to be empowered.

The energy of the planetary archetypes, if left to run through us unfocused, will express itself in those most-vulnerable and least-resistant areas and levels of our being. If on the contrary, we make a channel, a groove for the energy by our focused intent, then we can use it to empower any other area of our life as well.

Last but not least, we must remember that change is the keynote of these archetypal forces. Even though you are preparing yourself to channel their energies safely, at times they might still appear to you as sudden and explosive. This is normal, first, because the material world–due to the inert qualities of matter in general and humanity in particular–is reluctant to change, preferring to stick to the old patterns that appear safe and predictable; second, more often than not the force of the planetary archetypes has to overcome this inertia before it starts making positive changes. This may be frightening or painful if one is not conscious of it or if one resists change.

When the human aura is empowered by contact with the archetype, everything is energized, the "good" and the "bad." So, at first the "bad" is exacerbated to the point where things may become more chaotic and painful for some time. Learn to accept this inrush of power and direct it to flush away the impurities and clear out that which is stagnant. Do not become distracted or discouraged by the initial reordering of your mind's deep levels. Have faith in your innate ability to be healed and trust that the great archetypes will provide the necessary momentum to carry you over the initial hurdle. If you do not interfere or hinder it, the cleansing process will take care of itself, and eventually you will emerge at the other end of the dark tunnel, clean, pure, and empowered.

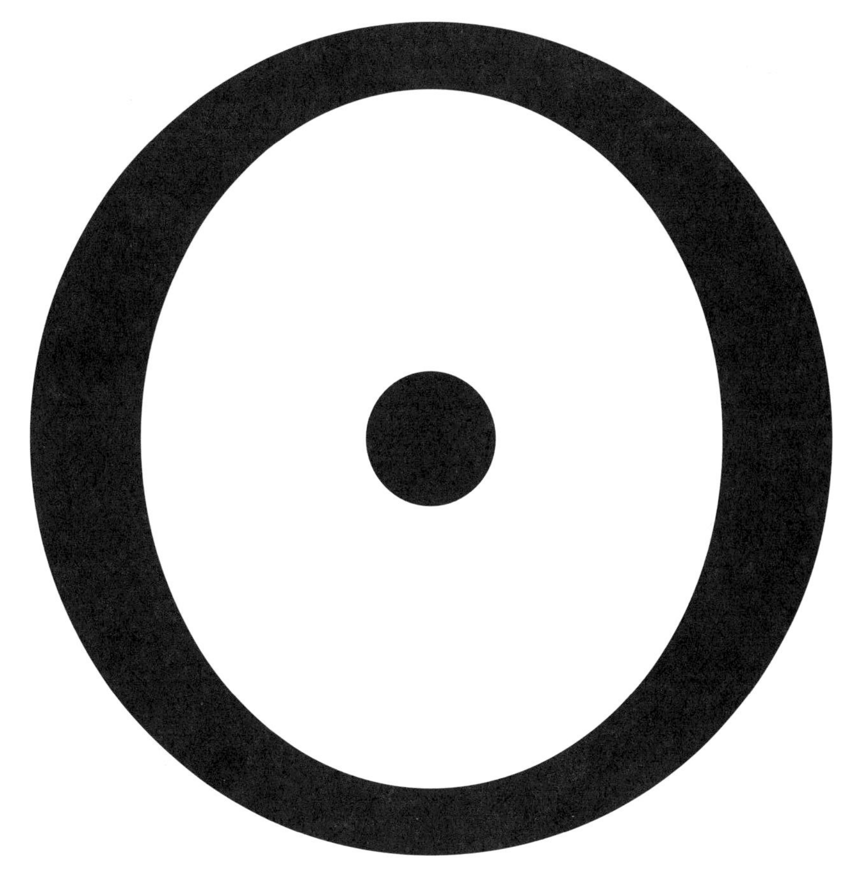

SUN

SUN

Attunement with the Archetypal Power of the Sun

The sun is the source of life for our solar system and spiritually corresponds to our individuality or soul.

Solar energy is healing on all levels. It conveys physical vitality, greatly enhancing the lives of those ready to assimilate its power.

Through attunement with the spiritual power of the sun we can contact the Solar or Guardian Angel, whose influence eases and accelerates our healing and growth.

When we act "solar" we love everything in an unconditional and detached manner. We become like the sun is to our solar system—a source of life, light, and energy to our environment.

"Solar" unconditional love is slightly different from that of Venus. The energy of the sun radiates love in the form of life force and vitality and is more masculine and less subtle than Venus. The latter loves unconditionally, yet in a more-magnetic way. Venus is extremely aware of the effects of her energy on her surroundings; she wishes to evoke in the beloved his most-exquisite qualities, bringing to life his hidden potential through the influence of her magnetic attraction on him. The energy of Venus is powered by the wish to merge with the beloved, be it a person, the environment, or the entire universe. Venus (love) is extremely aware of relationship and polarity, adapting herself to the beloved as needed in eternal fluidity. The sun, on the contrary, is more fixed. He shines (loves) regardless of his effect on the environment, oblivious to those who might absorb his life-giving heat (seed) or be scorched by it.

A strong solar radiance in our personality brings a deep self-confidence which manifests as personal charisma. People are instinctively attracted to charismatic individuals and seek their companionship. They bathe themselves in the powerful aura of those with charisma, to be warmed and enlivened, like cold-blooded creatures in the noonday sun.

Understanding the power of the sun is best gained by meditating on its position and function as nourisher and sustainer of life in the solar system.

The God Apollo in Mythology

The origin of Apollo is uncertain. Some sources state that he is derived from a Hittite god or even related to the Babylonian Sun god Shamash, while others believe he is of Nordic origin due to his association with the Hyperboreans.

Apollo was the son of Zeus and Leto. His twin sister was the goddess Artemis.

Apollo was blonde, blue eyed, and of fair complexion. His attractive looks and irresistible magnetism were legendary.

Like most solar divinities, Apollo was at some point faced by the powers of darkness and had to prove himself against them in battle. For Apollo this confrontation occurred at an early age. For him the forces of darkness were represented by a female dragon, the serpent Python. She was sent by Hera, Zeus's wife, to devour Leto and her offspring.

When only four-days old, Themis fed Apollo nectar and ambrosia which instantly caused him to gain his manly powers. Armed with his famous arrows, he set out to look for a suitable sight on which to erect his sanctuary. During his wanderings he came to the Python's lair in Parnassus and killed the dragon with an arrow. In honor of this confrontation, the place was named Pytho, later changed to Delphi.

Apollo was mainly a sun god, although the sun disk itself was attributed to Helios. His weapon, was the arrow–infallible. He was considered the god and patron of flocks and shepherds, which made him also a rural deity. In Delos and Delphi the first crops of the year were offered to him. Apollo, in his function as sun god, was responsible for ripening the fruits of the earth.

Apollo was also venerated as a divine musician and was said to have brought song and the lyre to men. He was a colonizing and civilizing deity, as are most sun gods.

Apollo fought in many battles, the most famous being the Trojan War, where he protected the Trojans from the Greeks. Of his many loves, the story of Daphne is one of the most famous. As he tried to seduce her, Daphne cried for help to Gaea, Mother Earth, and the earth opened, swallowing her. Because a laurel tree sprang from the ground at that very spot, Apollo made the plant sacred to him.

Apollo was the god of oracles and prophecy as well. The most famous of his oracles was at Delphi, where the priestesses seated on tripods would foretell the future.

In his function as the god of music, Apollo was accompanied by the Muses, nine goddesses of music and poetic inspiration.

The attributes of Apollo are the bow, the quiver, the lyre, and the shepherd's crook. Animals sacred to him are the dolphin, the wolf, the serpent, the hawk, the swan, the crow, the vulture, and the cock. Plants associated with Apollo are the laurel, the olive, the palm, and the tamarisk.

The Sun in Astrology

The sun rules the astrological sign of Leo.

Its natural house is the Fifth House (personal interests, self-expression of one's talents and abilities, risks and speculation, personal pleasure, and love affairs).

Its nature is masculine and positive.

Its astrological symbol is a circle with a dot in the center, symbolizing the Soul with the Divine Spark at its core.

Basic key words describing the influence of the sun are initiative, independence, will, power, individuation, integrity, vitality, health, creativity, leadership, authority, confidence, dignity, generosity, and pride.

The negative attributes of the sun involve: excessive pride, self-centeredness, arrogance, pomposity and cruelty.

A sun that is weakened in the astrological chart by critical aspects with other planets may also bring low vitality, low self-esteem, and difficulty in asserting oneself in life. These aspects may be corrected when working with the sun's energy, bringing a new inner radiance and vitality.

The sun, representing a very masculine energy, stands for the principle of active energy, the source of all life and all motion, symbolizing daylight and consciousness.

To astrologers, the sun is one of the most important elements in the chart since it represents the primary energy of Being.

The basic personality function of the sun in the astrological chart is to define our individuality, integrity, and independence. The sun is the power that lets our own inner light shine out in our own special way. The position of the sun in our chart indicates how our personal universe is illuminated and nourished. It also shows how we overcome limiting environmental conditions.

In the physical body the sun rules over the heart, physical vitality, the back, and the spine.

The day of the sun is obviously Sunday, and its metal is gold.

Inner Journey To Contact the Archetype

Sit or lie in a comfortable position and begin relaxing by breathing deeply and rhythmically. Now count from ten to zero, allowing your body to relax even more with each count.

You are walking downward along the slope of a hill. It is summer and the sun is high in the sky. The air feels warm and softly caresses your skin. Your path winds through rocks and olive trees. The landscape reminds you of the beautiful Greek islands and you feel safe and happy.

After finishing your descent, you arrive at a large golden gate. You recognize the symbol of the sun on its doorknob and confidently pass through.

On the other side of the gate the same landscape surrounds you. But now you perceive shepherds in the distance, sitting in the shade of an olive tree while their animals graze peacefully.

Suddenly, you hear the sound of horses galloping toward you. You become somewhat frightened, not knowing if the riders will see you in your astral body. As they sprint toward you, you notice to your amazement that the beasts are not normal horses with their riders, but half human and half horse. They are centaurs!

Each of these centaurs carries a bow and arrow, and they shoot them playfully at the sun. One of them, who appears to be the strongest and wisest of them all, comes to you and welcomes you warmheartedly. You sigh with relief and reach out to grasp his outstretched hand. He looks so strong and powerful with his horse's hooves and body, yet his human torso and deep-brown eyes seem gentle and wise. At first you are somewhat confused by this blend of animal and man. But he feels so friendly and familiar that trusting him comes naturally to you. The centaur speaks:

"I am Chiron, teacher and healer of many a god and mortal. I have come to guide you to my friend, Apollo. Trust me and you, too, in time will become a healer!" He bids you mount his back, and together you ride off into the distance. You remember his name well, since you know one day that you will learn more about this strange creature and his energy.

After some time you reach a sacred grove. As you approach it, you hear the sweetest music. You are so deeply moved by this sound that you ask Chiron to stop and be silent so that you may absorb into your soul this enchanting tune. There is something so familiar to you in this music, something so pure, as if it were made especially to satisfy your innermost longings . . .

Both of you remain still for awhile, overwhelmed by a feeling of awe and reverence toward this music that so deeply resonates with your own being. Then you proceed to the center of the grove. There, on a small outcropping in the middle of a clearing sits a young man. Apollo! You recognize him instantly.

Apollo appears to you as the epitome of beauty and excellence, more perfect than you would ever have imagined. He is tall and slender, his shoulders wide and strong. A glance from his deep-blue eyes is healing in itself; nothing more is needed, it seems. He is splendid, brilliant, and extremely attractive, as if glowing with beauty and vitality from an inner, unknown source.

He becomes aware of you, sets his instrument aside, and stands up while gracefully shaking his golden locks away from his immaculate face. Immense blue eyes the color of mountain lakes bore themselves questioningly into you, sending a shudder down your spine. You notice he is naked. Powerful muscles cord down his athletic body, broad and wide around his arms and shoulders, long and tapered down to his bare feet. Never before have you seen a man so magnificent, so radiant! He is the countenance of divine beauty and harmony, the very expression of Divinity in human form.

You feel rejuvenated and refreshed, as if the radiance of his presence resonates in each cell of your being, elevating your own vibration to the intense brilliance of Apollo. Shyly you smile back at him, locking your gaze with his for what seems an eternity.

Then Apollo approaches. Taking both of your hands into his, he looks deeply into your eyes again, silently passing something indescribable to you from his depths, something very powerful, soothing, and permanent you will never lose again. From now on Apollo's presence will be deeply in you forever!

As you remain motionless, submerged in your feelings and realizations, purified by this sweet inner glow, Apollo resumes his seat and begins to play his lyre again.

Suddenly it strikes you! Of course you know this heavenly music! It is your very own, the sound of your soul, your individuality. It is the sound, the rhythm of your soul, and the melody of your own essence and growth throughout the ages which Apollo is now playing so beautifully for you. You are so overwhelmed with joy at this realization, that tears run down your cheeks. Never has anything touched you so very personally; never has a sound seemed so powerful to you!

You feel yourself entering a kind of trance, an inner surrender to the forces of good and light. Something burns inside you like a sweet fire, taking you into ever-deeper ecstasy. No part of you is dark; no part of you is shadow. You fear no experience; you withhold nothing from this blazing fire; you are consecrated and one with the Light Divine!

Remain in this state of bliss for some time and open yourself to inner guidance. A message from the sun god may come to you now. Hear how Apollo with his beautiful voice sings your name again and again, accompanied by the lovely music.

After awhile, he stops and approaches you. "You have not yet reached the destination of your journey," he says, calling you by name. "To really understand and know the sun, you must go beyond me; transcend my form and that of all other solar gods. You must soar up past us into the world of abstract thought and Divine Inspiration where the One is the Whole and the Part is not separate anymore, where the human is already Divine and the god is eternally incarnated! You must enter the kingdom that is always Here and Now, yet unseen to the uninitiated. "

Saying this, he takes one of his golden arrows. With the tip he cuts a little cross into your bare chest, exactly over your heart. Then he dips the tip of his arrow into your blood and shoots it towards the sun. "This is you," he says.

You watch the arrow climb toward the sun's disk; when it is finally out of sight, you enter a new dimension.

You feel swiftly lifted higher and higher toward a Great Light. Soon it is so bright that you no longer recognize any forms. All is white; all is pure. You know that you have now reached the center of the sun, not the physical sun, but the spiritual sun. This sun is to be found within each and every one of us; it is the center of our personal "Solar System" and is its basic energy of being, of which all other archetypes are but different expressions.

And, it is also the sun behind the sun, the Heart of the Cosmos. You follow in your mind this chain of suns and centers of being until you can imagine no higher. Then, opening yourself to this White Light, you merge entirely with it.

After a period of resting your inner self in this manner, you begin to sense that you are not alone. You perceive a presence next to you, but you cannot define its form. It feels safe, warm, and pure, but also very familiar. You have experienced this feeling before, but were never quite able to describe it . . . Is it the same presence that was with you when you were a child? Has it appeared to you in times of great distress? Have you sensed it before in a dream? You remember, but cannot define it.

Suddenly, the presence comes closer and you hear it speak to you: "I am your Guardian Angel! I live here in the Great Light, in the Inner Sun. I watch over you in your earthly incarnation because I am really a part of you. I am that part which you have forgotten and left here unattended. I carry the blueprint for your own Divine Will. I am the holder of the perfect plan for you throughout the ages, and am immutable and indestructible. I am the one you visit at times in your dreams when you are troubled and have lost your way. I am the one who brought you comfort and reassurance when you were just an infant and did not quite know how to adapt to physical existence. I was there with you always, although you have forgotten. But behold! There is a reason for this forgetting. Had you remembered too soon, you would not have had the strength and courage to face it. You would have cried and pleaded to return to the Great Center too soon. You would have lost the opportunity to experience existence stretched out against the framework of time, crystallized in the physical world. You would have forsaken your plan and task. So here I am, your faithful companion, guarding and holding carefully in my hands your very destiny, your very being over past, present, and future. Now, since you have come here to meet me face to face, I return it to you; I make you aware of your destiny, of who you really are. Remember now, my beloved! Remember who you are and why you live! Remember your own Divinity, and that part of the Divine Will that is your own and the essence of your existence!"

Saying this, the presence reawakens a golden spark in your heart center that seems to have been dark and dormant for aeons. An immense feeling of happiness and bliss floods your entire being. You feel that you have come home again, that you have found your own true self once more, that you now know your true Inner God.

Remain in this awareness for some time, letting the feelings and words transmitted by the angel flow freely inside you. Identify yourself completely with this inner sun and the angel that dwells in it. Know that you and it are one, always were, and always will be.

When you are ready, gather up your essence again and prepare yourself to leave this place of unity and bliss. You need no guide now to take you back to Apollo, since you have not traveled any farther than to your own soul.

You have now received, through contact with the Guardian Angel, a new impulse for your life, a new meaning and direction. Holding this impulse firmly in your heart, you make a strong intent to return to the worlds of form and to the sacred grove where you left Apollo.

Slowly, forms begin once again to build around you. Apollo is still there, playing with his arrows. As he welcomes you back, you notice that the wound on your chest has healed. Nothing but a small scar is left. He smiles at you reassuringly, and in his eyes you can see that he, too, knows what you experienced only a moment ago. You are not alone; he will remain with you in your heart, always.

You say farewell to the god of light and mount Chiron who awaits you nearby.

After a short ride you return to the golden gate. You say goodbye to your gentle guide and pass through, closing the gate behind you.

The landscape slowly fades away. Gradually, you regain your normal waking consciousness.

The Guardian Angel

Esoteric tradition has it that at the beginning of each cycle of manifestation, God projects the Plan of Creation in the form of His Divine Will. Each of the Divine Sparks that constitute our higher selves or individual spirits are a part of this Divine Will and have a specific task to fulfill in the Great Plan of Creation.

It is said that we humans, on our descent into the worlds of form, have forgotten the part we play in the Divine Plan and have lost our alignment with our inner Divine Will.

Now this is only partially true. It may seem that we have lost our connection to the God within and His Will when we try to find it in our personalities or lower selves. However, as soon as we are able to shift our perception from the merely physical, emotional, and mental viewpoint to the transcendental, we realize that in the inner realms of being, neither time nor space exists and, therefore, we have never lost anything.

It is at this point that we become aware of our true function, our mission to accomplish on earth, as part of the Divine Will that pervades our lives from within as understood by our individuality or soul. The soul is what contains all that we are, were, and will ever be over the ages in one evolutionary cycle. We then realize that what we think of as our personality or self is but a temporary projection of a much greater self, our individuality. This projection is cast into a specific timeframe and place for the sake of a more-detailed experience. This individuality or soul is itself also a part of an even Greater One—the spirit or Monad (our inner God or Divine Spark).

The Guardian Angel is the guardian of our own individual task in the Great Cosmic Plan. He holds the blueprint for our individuality or soul in its purest form and keeps it untainted until we are able to perfect our earthly personality along many incarnations. Then we become aware of the original blueprint and align ourselves with our Individuality. In this case the task of the Holy Guardian Angel will be fulfilled for one evolutionary cycle and he will no longer be perceived as a separate entity. The soul and the Guardian Angel merge as one. In practical terms, the Guardian Angel functions as a mediator between our personalities and our individualities, making us recognize our true mission and inner Divine Will.

On the spiritual path we are told to align ourselves with a Higher Principle or Divine Will and to offer our own small personal will in Divine Sacrifice. This advice is not a sadistic remnant of the Dark Ages, but one of the most important things to accomplish on our way to enlightenment. For if we align ourselves with Divine Will, we gain immense power. We become not only the receptacles for the power of our individuality (which contains in essence the experiences and power of all our other lives), but also the channels of the Divine Power of God coming through our Spirit to us via our Soul!

This power aspect of God and the responsibility that comes with it are often feared and misunderstood by spiritual seekers. Thus, the seekers subconsciously sabotage their alignment with Divine Will by clinging to their little personal wills. The same may be said about false leaders who misguide their followers, making them clutch limiting beliefs that hinder the free flow of Divine Will and blur the link with the soul and indwelling spirit.

The Guardian Angel is often referred to as the Solar Angel. The reason for this term is obvious, since the sun is to the solar system what one's individuality is to human personality.

Magical Use of the Sun

Preliminaries for the magical use of the sun's energy involve the following considerations:

• Be certain you are motivated to contact your Guardian Angel for the benefit of all creation and not just out of curiosity or for selfish motives.

• Beforehand take responsibility for this new awareness and knowledge of your life task this exercise will bring, and commit yourself to using it for the good of all.

• Open yourself without fear to the forces of change; be ready and willing to grow and mature in all aspects of your life.

• Let absolute, unconditional love pervade your work. If you cannot feel this love yet, do the following for several days: Visualize the inner Spiritual Sun of your soul on your heart chakra and meditate on it for as long as you need to feel unconditional love for all creation before proceeding any further.

• Inflame yourself with love and devotion to your Guardian Angel, your individuality, and your life task—even if you do not yet know what they it is in detail.

Magical Practice To Contact the Guardian Angel

This exercise is intended to contact your soul via your Guardian Angel. I am well aware that in other traditions such as the Qabalah, knowledge and conversation with the Holy Guardian Angel are ascribed to another level and not to the sun. It is my experience, however, that some degree of "solar consciousness" is needed to be able to raise one's mind high enough to perceive a broader picture of the Scheme and gain a deeper understanding of our place in the Play of Manifestation and the specific task and mission for which we are called.

Of course, it is always possible to enter into spontaneous contact with the Solar Angel. Although such an experience is extremely important, discernment of the Cosmic Plan and the vision of the inner harmony of creation must be deep enough to bring a lasting understanding of one's inner Divine Will.

To contact the Guardian Angel do the following:

1. Sit in a comfortable position and relax by breathing deeply and rhythmically.

2. State firmly that you want to contact your Guardian Angel in order to know more about your life task and mission for this incarnation.

3. Visualize the astrological symbol of the sun as shown at the beginning of this chapter. Build it up with your inner vision until it is large enough to envelop you completely, creating an energetic bond with the power of the sun.

4. Visualize yourself about two inches high, entering your own body at the throat center. Force yourself to see through the eyes of your little body rather than watching everything from outside as an observer.

5. Imagine that you are carrying an oil lamp. Ascend inside your body in a straight line until you reach the crown.

6. Visualize a Great White Light above your head. Hold your lamp to it and see how it is lit by the Great Light in a sudden effulgence.

7. Descend through the inside of your body with the lamp ablaze with the pure White Light of Spirit until you reach your heart chakra; there you will find a great hall with a golden throne in the center.

8. Stand before the throne and dedicate yourself to the service of the Inner Light. Now, with the lamp in your hand, proceed to illuminate the hall, walking around the throne in a clockwise circle. As you do this, the White Light changes to a soft rose pink and the entire hall glows with unconditional love.

9. Take your seat at the throne and meditate for some time on the responsibility that comes from knowing one's life task. Are you ready for it? If you feel the time has come, then proceed. If the answer is "no," do not feel guilty. Go to step thirteen and continue to close the practice. Remember that this place is in your own heart and that you can return whenever it feels right for you; there is no rush.

10. If the answer is "yes," then still seated at the throne, project a beam of golden-amber light out of your heart (that of your little body in which you are now) to about three feet in front of you. Build it up to the shape of your Guardian Angel, complete with wings and golden locks, if you wish. The actual shape is not important. What matters is to give it as much detail as possible.

11. Now greet the Angel and ask it to show you all about your life task or mission, as far as you are capable of understanding at the moment. While you do this, feel how you inflame yourself with love for this beautiful creature. Let this unconditional love flow through the shaft of light that connects you to the Angel and bring the Angel to life.

12. Remain still for some time in communion with the Angel. You will be shown the next step on your life task. This revelation may occur in the form of a vision, of intuitive knowledge, some form of symbol, or even direct conversation with your Guardian Angel. If you feel that you are not getting a clear message, relax. The contact you are building in this way will lead you to recognize your True Will at a later date.

13. Remain in this position as long as it feels comfortable to you and concentrate on absorbing all that the Angel has to give. Return the gift of the Guardian Angel with your unreserved, unconditional love and blessing. Meditate for a moment on his task and his sacrifice. Then thank the Angel and reabsorb him into your heart.

14. Stand up from the throne and place the lamp on the seat, stating that the Light Divine is to illuminate this Great Hall from now on, and from this Hall it is to spread its Light unconditionally into the entire Cosmos, always.

15. Ascend to the throat center through the straight inner passage and exit your body, resuming normal size.

16. Slowly return to normal consciousness.

You should know that if your psychic abilities are not sufficiently developed, you might not get clear messages; if this is the case, do not feel badly. Ask and you shall be given. The results of the practice will come through more physical and seemingly ordinary events. You will receive what you need to express your potential: a better job, a pleasant environment, open associates, and so forth.

The information about your life is often given in an abstract or general form. In this way you still feel a lot of freedom to develop strategies and fine-tune your objectives. Do not expect life tasks as dramatic as those of Joan d'Arc or Mohammed. Often the life task will be something that seems socially irrelevant, but will bring you the sense of being well-adjusted in life and the satisfaction of acting at your full potential while also being supported by the universe.

MOON

MOON

Attunement with the Archetypal Power of the Moon

The Moon represents the archetype of the eternal feminine force. Her power is that of the Divine Mother. The matrix. The source and origin of physical manifestation.

Lunar power allows us to reach our intuition via our subconscious mind. The moon reflects the sun's rays like a mirror, in the same manner as our subconscious mind reflects our Higher or Divine Self. Usually we cannot access our Higher Self directly. Its influence is filtered into our waking consciousness through the mirror and language of the subconscious mind. Once the channels of communication between our intuitive, subconscious, and conscious minds are clear, we can attain Divine Wisdom.

The moon is associated with the memory of Nature. In the East this memory is referred to as the "Akashic Records," and is said to contain all there was, is, and ever will be. This great informational storehouse may be accessed after thorough purification of the subconscious mind and is also used in divination and the remembrance of past lives.

By attuning ourselves with the moon's power we come to terms with our own femininity. Women find their rightful place in a patriarchal society, while men align with their intuitive and nurturing aspects. Connection with the basic Mother archetype makes us feel nurtured and supported, no matter who we are or what we do. This enables us to mother and nurture others in a pure, nondominating, and unconditional way.

Attunement with the moon and what it symbolizes makes us feel safe and secure by merging with the rhythms of Nature and the cosmos, bringing a wonderful sense of ease and of "swimming with the current."

As the moon's influence is closely connected to the past in all its aspects (personal, racial, and planetary), the work with this archetypal force will most certainly activate emotional links with the past. Long-lost memories of past lives, birth, or childhood experiences may pop up spontaneously.

This allows us to look at such memories in the light of our new knowledge and understanding as well as to integrate them accordingly. The various therapeutic forms of relieving past emotional traumas are strongly related to this lunar archetypal force and are greatly enhanced by proper attunement with her power.

All bodily functions involving the unconscious and the autonomous nervous system are largely influenced by the tides of the sun, the moon, and the planets. By attuning ourselves with the rhythms of nature through the phases of the moon, the changing seasons, and movements of the celestial bodies, we may "ride the tides" as the magicians do, using these powerful forces to our advantage.

The Goddess Isis in Egyptian Mythology

To understand the moon's archetype in its purest form it is most advantageous to step even farther back in time than the ancient Greek forms and study the goddess Isis of Egyptian mythology. She truly represents the Queen of the Night, combining in herself the threefold nature of the Greek goddesses Demeter, Selene, and Hecate. Her name "Isis" means "a throne," and in early days she was depicted with the symbol of a throne as her headdress. Later she was represented with the horns of a cow (or crescents of the waxing and waning moon) on her head and the full moon sustained between them.

In paintings and sculptures she is depicted beside Osiris, whom she helps and protects with her winged arms. Often she is also shown suckling her son, Horus, whom she bore to Osiris—reinforcing her status as Divine Mother.

In Egyptian mythology Isis was the first daughter of the gods Geb (Earth) and Nut (Sky). She is said to have descended from heaven together with her husband/brother, Osiris, to aid in the development of mankind and to rule over the land later called Egypt.

Together with Osiris she civilized Egypt and taught women to grind corn and weave cloth. She was a great healer and magician and instructed her people in these arts. Isis also instituted marriage and domestic life, becoming the symbol of the Universal Woman and the Great Mother—more complete than any other goddess.

In occult tradition the archetype of Isis is said to be divided into three aspects: the White Isis, the Black Isis, and the Rainbow-Colored Isis.

The White Isis is the brilliant transcendent aspect of the Great Mother/Woman/Wife: bright, loving, caring, and nurturing. She is also Sophia or Divine Wisdom.

The Dark or Black Isis is related to the Black Madonna in Christian lore. She represents the Great Mother in her disciplinary and restricting aspect.

The Rainbow-Colored Isis is Mother Nature.

Often Isis is also called the Priestess of the Silver Star, the star being Sothis or Sirius. Her color is deep blue, like the mantle of the Virgin Mary. She is intimately related to the moon, her symbols being the knot or tat (a symbol of fertility), and the sistrum (a musical instrument used in ancient rituals). The cosmic aspect of Isis is the star Sirius.

In Egyptian tradition Sirius is said to be the home or "throne of Isis" from whence the goddess came to earth to teach humanity. This legend reveals that Sirius stands in the same relationship to our solar system as Isis to her son, Horus, the Egyptian sun god. It is said that Isis returned to Sirius long ago and watches over her people from there like a good mother together with her husband, Osiris, often associated with the smaller companion of the bright star, Sirius B.

The Egyptians are not the only people who venerated Sirius. The Dogons, an African tribe, have detailed records of Sirius and its companion Sirius B which date back to antiquity, thousands of years before the first telescope was invented. It is Sirius which holds the key to the mystery of our cosmic past and shows us the ways to our stellar future.

The Moon in Astrology

The moon rules the astrological sign Cancer. Its natural House is the Fourth House (inner emotional security and self-image, the mother, the home, the beginning and end of life). The moon's nature is feminine and receptive. Its astrological symbol, the crescent moon, symbolizes the personality.

Basic key words describing the moon's influence are receptivity, sensitivity, protection, nurturing, emotional response, instinctive actions, moods, habits, the subconscious, good memory, patience, sympathy, cycles, fluctuations, tides, and psychism.

The negative attributes of the moon involve hypersensitivity, emotional instability, worry, moodiness, and over-mothering or "smother-love."

The basic personality function of this celestial body in one's astrological chart stimulates one's automatic response to environmental conditions in a rhythmic and cyclic way, based on the sum total of the conditions of your personal, racial, and planetary past experiences combined with your present personality.

Contrary to its passive and receptive nature, the moon is considered by astrologers to be one of the most-important planets in the astrological chart. Its influence manifests itself spontaneously, ruling a great portion of the personality.

In the physical body the moon presides over the stomach, nutrition and digestion, the breasts, the flow of bodily fluids, the menstrual cycle, and the uterus.

Further, the moon rules over childbirth and motherhood, liquids, water and the tides of the sea, the general public, mobs, and the facial features.

The day of the moon is Monday and its metal is silver.

Inner Journey To Contact the Archetype

Sit or lie in a comfortable position and begin relaxing by breathing deeply. Now count from ten to zero, allowing your body to relax even more with each count.

First, imagine you are walking along a wide, flat, sandy beach. It is night and the full moon is high in the sky. The sand is moist but firm under your bare feet, the air soft; it is the beginning of summer. You know that Sirius must be in the sky, too, but the moon is so bright you cannot find it.

The water feels nice and cool to your toes. You walk leisurely along the shore, submerged in the memories of what you have learned about Isis. After some time a huge silver gate towers before you; you recognize on its door knob the crescent of the moon.

Determined, you walk toward it. You know that you want to cross this gate to learn more about yourself and your subconscious. On the other side you will encounter things that reach far beyond the boundaries of your own psyche and deep into the transcendental world and its archetypes. But are there such boundaries after all?

Confidently, you open the gate and pass to the other side. To your surprise there is no guide waiting for you this time; you are on your own.

Somewhat disappointed, you sit down on the sand, awaiting what might come next.

All is calm around you; the waves play gently with the sand in beautiful rhythm; the moon shines bright and clear; it is almost as bright as daytime. Looking around, you begin to notice that the beach has become magical and symbolical.

You suddenly realize the seashore is that place where your conscious and subconscious minds meet. The waters of the ocean become the symbol of your subconscious, the earth, the conscious and visible aspects of your life. You think of the water—how it is influenced by the moon, coming and going with the tides... You see its darkness, reflecting the moon's silvery light and remember what you heard about the Black Isis. You know that someday you will come to understand her, but it is not yet time.

Then you look down at the sand beneath you and see that it is made of tiny, multicolored gems and crystals—all reflecting the white light of the moon, in turn, reflecting that of the sun making the small crystals shine with the colors of the rainbow. You remember the Rainbow-Colored Isis and are awed by the beauty and perfection of Mother Nature.

You wonder why you have not been aware of this symbolism before, of the magical aspect of your environment, of the ways and language of the inner realms of consciousness. They seem so clear and palpable now!

As you sit on the cool sand, a flood of emotions, thoughts, and realizations wells up from your inner self. You have never had the time or courage to deal with these things before. Some are memories from childhood, others from your adolescent years; some might just be vague feelings and emotions you cannot yet classify. All this is good and normal. You give yourself permission to have these thoughts and emotions and to acknowledge them, without judgment.

After communicating with your subconscious for awhile in this way, you are overcome by a deep longing for someone to guide you and help you understand these past memories and feelings. You feel like a baby learning to walk in this new and uncharted territory. Where is your mother now that you need her most? Why has she never instructed you how to travel the dreamland of your subconscious mind? Carried away in emotional turmoil, you forget you are not a child anymore, but a mature adult, ready and responsible for your own life and development.

You call to her: "Mother! Teach me, guide me, instruct me! Protect me, nurture me, and love me! Show me who I really am!" You wait for several minutes in silence. Then suddenly you feel an answer to your cry come from all around, but most strongly from the moon itself. Its bright light seems to expand, turning everything into a silver mist. As you look up, you cannot perceive the moon anymore, but in its place you see a beautiful young woman walking toward you.

She is young, but her deep-blue eyes reflect the Divine Wisdom of ages past, present, and future. Her body is slim and graceful, her hair long and black, almost bluish in the silvery light. She has the countenance of Divine Purity and Truth, selfless love and understanding. As she approaches, you begin to feel increasingly safe and secure, bathed in the power of her aura like an unborn child in the warmth of its mother's womb. You know who "she" is; she is Isis, Mother Mary, the Great Mother. As she stands in front of you, tall, beautiful, and powerful, she speaks:

"I greet you, my child. I know you have come here to find me, your true Mother, and to learn more about yourself. Place no demands upon your earthly mother; do not reproach her, but know she is, like you, only a creature of the Cosmic Ocean. I, on the contrary, am the Ocean, the Beginning! It is in me you will find for what you search. It is in me you will find your true mother. It is through me you will realize ultimately that I am in you and you are your own mother. "

You feel permeated by love and admiration and overwhelmed by the feeling of having finally "come home" to your own source, your own beginning. You feel deeply accepted, understood, and completely free to be who you are.

Now you approach the goddess and ask her all those questions to which you so eagerly seek answers.

Stand still for a time while absorbing the information. If you do not get anything conscious at this point, the answers will well up from your subconscious at a later time and in a completely natural way.

During your communication with the young woman, your desire to be like her becomes increasingly intense. You want to absorb all her love, her wisdom and understanding, her silent power. You want to be one with her, to be your own mother!

As you feel these wants and fill yourself with a desperate desire to be her, you notice how the Great Mother turns into a luminous gas and enters your body through the area of the heart. The luminosity expands, filling your entire body, consciousness and aura.

You remain motionless for awhile, fusing yourself completely with the Great Mother, Isis, Mary. You feel safe, loved and nurtured, and are one with her.

After a few minutes when you feel ready, you allow the goddess to depart. The luminous gas exits your body at the heart center and builds up again in the form of the Bright Isis in front of you, illuminating everything.

You see that the water has receded far outward toward the ocean. It is low tide now and the sand lies bare, revealing marine creatures which usually live underwater.

Before you say farewell to Isis, you fall into her arms and lean your head against her heart, drawing all the strength from her you can absorb. You know that for the purpose of your future contact with her the crescent moon is most perfectly suited.

Now you say farewell and walk toward the silver gate.

Before going back through it, you see how the figure of Isis slowly fades into the full moon, and all seems normal again. You feel happy and confident, eager to apply your new knowledge to the life that lies ahead. You feel safe and peaceful, one with the Divine Wisdom which guides all creatures great and small.

As you cross through the silver gate alone, the landscape and the beach slowly fade away. Gradually, you regain your normal waking consciousness.

Magical Use of the Moon

Preliminaries for the magical use of the moon's energy involve the following considerations:

- Be responsible for the new awareness and knowledge these exercises will bring, and commit yourself to using them for the good of all.
- Open yourself without fear to the forces of change; be ready and willing to grow and mature in all your life's aspects.
- Let the desire for Divine Wisdom and harmony pervade your work.

The magical application is intended to train your intuition by increasing the clarity of your communication with your own subconscious mind. At first it is best to refrain from judgment about the accuracy of the information and remain open and receptive to the informational flow from the subconscious. This is an area that cannot depend on rationality without stifling the process.

Do not act impulsively on any information you may receive from these exercises. The realm of the subconscious is also the realm of *glamour*, a form of astral illusion that makes things appear more pure, spiritual, and important than they really are by clothing them in flamboyant colors or impressive words. Not that all visions of strong colors are false, but they do have the tendency to delude us. The same goes for words. If you are not well trained in discriminating what constitutes a true intuition or communication from a false one, you may easily be misled. Write down all your experiences in a diary; leave them alone for several days, then recheck and reconsider them. If they still feel right and true, then act, if you will.

To develop intuition we must communicate with our Higher Self via the subconscious. Usually the subconscious is not as pure and as clear a reflective surface as we would like it to be, since it carries all our repressed emotions and fears, among other things. We will most certainly have to clear away emotional and psychic garbage before we can reach the Higher Self. Repressed emotions will surface in this cleansing process, therefore, we must be willing to deal with these feelings.

Magical Practice To Contact the Inner Guide

By practicing the following procedures you will learn to contact your inner guide in full consciousness:

1. Sit in a comfortable position and begin relaxing by breathing deeply and rhythmically. Now count from ten to zero, allowing your body to relax even more with each count.

2. State firmly that you want to know more about yourself and the worlds beyond the rational mind. Express your need for help in these matters to the Divine Mother and then ask to contact your Inner Guide.

3. Visualize the moon's astrological symbol as shown at the beginning of this chapter. Build it up with your inner vision until it is large enough to envelop you completely, creating an energetic bond with the power of the moon.

4. Define the Inner Guide clearly to yourself as someone who will help you travel the Inner Realms of Consciousness safely and easily. Request you be told his/her name.

5. Again relax, this time as deeply as you can, and remain in this state for one or two minutes more. Then visualize a door in front of you with the moon's symbol drawn on it. Do this with as much detail as possible and

remember it well. You will need it in subsequent exercises.

6. See yourself opening the door and walking to the other side. Feel joyful and full of expectation as you are about to meet your Inner Guide! Give total freedom to your imagination at this point. Don't analyze anything.

7. Your Inner Guide will probably appear to greet you. Accept the figure approaching you. Your first impression will be the most important one. Remember it well since it reveals your intuitive feelings about his/her presence before your rational mind starts to analyze and explain.

8. Ask the guide to give you his/her name and to show you the form in which the guide wants you to contact him/her in the future.

9. Pay attention to the guide's particular vibration or frequency and take notice of any feelings s/he evokes in you. After contacting your guide several times, you will recognize him/her instantly by his/her vibration even if you don't "see" him or her.

10. Let the guide take you through a journey in the imagination.

11. When you feel it is time to return, tell him/her so, then come back the way you came. Thank your guide and exit through the gate alone, making certain the guide remains on the far side of the gate. Close the gate after you pass through. Be careful to retrace your steps when returning in your imaginary journey; this is very important to keep the mind in good order.

12. Slowly return to normal consciousness.

Do not do this exercise during the day of the new moon or on the three days before and after it. Those are the times in which the subconscious mind processes, and sometimes casts away, negative material. This procedure may distort your perceptions.

If you do not gain any results the first few times, stop for a few days and reconsider your motives: Are they in line with the purity of Universal Truth and for the good of all? If they are, try again around the period of the full moon. Those who are experimenting along these lines for the first time might have to wait a little longer to have conscious contact with the Inner Guide.

Dreaming

The world of dreams belongs to the subconscious mind, and in your endeavor to expand your consciousness, you can make good use of this realm. We are not concerned with dream interpretation here. What this practice will give you is easy retrieval of dream memories and an intuitive understanding of their meanings. You will begin first by remembering your dreams more clearly and in sequence. After awhile you will begin to understand their language and symbolism. Eventually, from time to time you will find yourself becoming conscious while still in the dream state.

You can learn to interpret the language of your dreams by deciphering the hidden and symbolic meaning of the landscapes, beings, and objects you see there. Make it a habit to record your dreams immediately on awakening. Then, later in the day, you may go back and analyze them in the following ways.

Keep your mind relaxed and attentive while asking yourself about the meaning of the dream images you recall. At this point feelings and intuitive thoughts will flash up before your mind. Be careful to catch them and hold them since they are usually very subtle and last only a short time before the rational mind sets in to "explain away" everything. The true meaning of your dream images will make itself felt in a "gut feeling" that must be trusted when it first appears or else it will vanish just as quickly.

To disclose obscure images from your dreams you may use the following technique: Go back inside your dream in your imagination making it as vivid and real as you possibly can. Then approach the subject in question and imagine that its outer layer is but a mask. Strip away the mask and see what hides beneath it. Repeat this procedure until what you find hidden beneath the layers of masks shows you who the subject is truly representing. Our subconscious uses these masks symbolically so as not to be too direct during sleep and wake us up. I personally find this technique most effective.

If you intend to buy a book on dream symbolism, note that the general interpretations found merely represent guidelines. Your subconscious uses symbols and images from your own life experiences to convey messages to you most effectively in your dreams, mixing and matching them as it pleases. Therefore, any given symbol will mean quite differently to you from the way it does to someone else. Only you can truly know what your symbols represent to you.

Magical Practice To Understand Your Dreams

This practice is intended to make you more conscious of your dreams. Understanding your dreams builds a bridge of communication between your conscious and subconscious minds. By paying attention to your dreams and focusing your will to understand them on a daily basis, you will soon find yourself receiving important clues about upcoming events, decisions, or even personal dangers. No matter how obscure or chaotic some dreams might appear, if you are determined, you will eventually understand them by following this given procedure:

1. Set a note pad and pen by your bedside. Eat lightly or not at all before this practice.

2. Just before going to sleep, firmly state your desire to remember your dream as clearly as possible. If you want the answer to a specific question or problem, formulate it at this time.

3. Visualize the moon's astrological symbol as shown at the beginning of this chapter. Build it up with your inner vision until it is large enough to envelop you completely, creating an energetic bond with the power of the moon.

4. Visualize the full moon in the center of your Third Eye. Affirm that the moon is illuminating the dark recesses of your subconscious and revealing what needs to be brought up into consciousness. State firmly that the power of the full moon will elucidate what wells up from the subconscious, making it clear and understandable to you.

5. Let your last thought before falling asleep be that of reverence for the Great Mother in her aspect as Divine Wisdom or Sophia. Imagine that you are falling asleep at her breast, her love and guidance nurturing and enveloping your entire being, her Divine Wisdom enlightening you and answering your most-difficult questions.

6. Make notes of your dreams immediately upon awakening. If you don't, you will soon forget them.

Magical Practice To Increase Intuition

This practice, intended to give you direct access to your intuition, will be more effective if you already have done some preliminary work exploring and clearing the subconscious of unnecessary emotional debris. If you have already accomplished some preliminary work, then follow the given procedures:

1. Sit or lie in a comfortable position and begin relaxing by breathing deeply and rhythmically. Now count from ten to zero, allowing your body to relax even more with each count.

2. Allow the moon goddess to overshadow you in the following way: Build up in your inner vision an image of the Great Mother standing behind you. Make her body about seven feet high. Feel her great power and aura extending far beyond her body's limits into outer space. Concentrate on your love and admiration for the Great Goddess as well as on your gratitude to her for helping you in this matter. Now allow her to step up as close as possible behind you and concentrate on the overshadowing effect of her aura on yours. Still focused on your love for the Great Mother, allow her to empower you by blending her great aura with your smaller one. Feel how both your energy fields are strengthened and vitalized by the contact. Feel your aura grow in size and power to coincide with that of the goddess. Remain this way for awhile before you proceed to the next step.

3. Ask the moon goddess anything you desire to know and wait attentively. Notice any intuitive feelings, words, or images coming up spontaneously since they will hold the answer. Keep on asking for as long as it seems comfortable.

4. When you feel the time is appropriate, say farewell to the goddess. Allow the Great Mother to depart by having her step back and slowly but thoroughly disengaging your aura from hers. Thank the goddess for her help. Express your love to her and then dissolve her form completely.

5. Relax and slowly return to normal consciousness.

6. Record any answers you may have received immediately in your magical diary.

You may repeat this procedure once a day for three consecutive days. After that allow a week to pass before you contact the goddess in this manner again since it is not good to overdo this practice. The reason for this being that if you allow one archetype to overshadow you too often, it will strongly bias you towards its particular mode of expression, not allowing your individuality to unfold in balance. You may, of course, work directly with your intuition, without the help of a godform, as often as you please.

MERCURY

MERCURY

Attunement with the Archetypal Power of Mercury

The god Mercury, who was Hermes to the Greeks and Thoth to the Egyptians, represents reason and the intellect. It is through the influence of the Mercurial archetype that we develop rationality and abstract thinking, which distinguishes humanity from animals. In Greek and Roman mythology Mercury/Hermes was the divine messenger, moving swiftly on his winged sandals, carrying information between the gods themselves and from the gods to humanity.

Mercury in his highest aspect is a mediator between God and the human race, between the rational mind and the transpersonal realms of consciousness. In his more-common aspect Mercury mediates horizontally between the minds of people in speech, writing, and the exchange of goods for money in commerce. Mercury also mediates within the mind itself, enabling it to reason, learn, organize, classify, and correlate mental concepts.

Ideally the various aspects of Mercury should be in constant connection with each other, allowing the mental processes to flow smoothly. When our mind functions at its best, we become able to grasp transpersonal realities, encode them into a logical sequence of symbols, and then express them through the spoken or written word for the benefit of others. We are also capable of abstracting mental concepts from the occurrences of our daily lives and clustering them into greater abstractions to allow us a better understanding of our world and its Creator.

On the spiritual level Mercury's energy works consciously to connect the soul with the personality through the Antahkarana or Rainbow Bridge. Mercury's inquisitive and exploratory nature reaches up to grasp the "messages" of the abstract mind and intuition and encodes intuitive and transpersonal input into understandable symbols. Then Mercury proceeds to organize, classify, and compare them to already existing concepts, which brings the intuitive realms of spirit "down" to merge with matter.

Mercury empowers us to understand spiritual laws and clusters of abstract concepts such as the "hermetic teachings" and internalize them as part of our personal belief system. He incessantly expands our mental faculties by pushing us to reach farther and farther into the transpersonal realms. Through Mercury the unknown becomes the known.

This process is greatly eased by the study and practice of spiritual and magical teachings and disciplines. They provide the Mercury within us with the symbolic language needed to mediate between our conscious minds, our abstract mind, and our Spiritual Will.

The hermetic teachings are a body of spiritual knowledge which branches out into the Tarot, Alchemy, Western Astrology, and the Qabalah. These teachings were brought to us by the archetypal power of Mercury/Hermes/Thoth in his vertical polarity. Although the Qabalah is said to have been given to humanity by the Archangel Metatron, it is still very much related to Mercury since all paradigms and theoretical models are built by the Mercurial mind.

The legendary founder of the hermetic teachings was Hermes Trismegistus, the "Thrice Greatest Hermes," who is said to have lived in the times when the Egyptian and Greek cultures merged. Hermes Trismegistus recorded the great hermetic axioms in "The Emerald Tablet." It may be possible, however, that his name was only a pseudonym for an entire school of hermetic initiates.

A strong connection between Mercury/Hermes and Venus energy is also hinted at here because the emerald is the stone sacred to Venus. Indeed, in Qabalah the sphere of Venus (Netzach) precedes that of Mercury (Hod), showing that the mind, to function properly, has to be fueled and exalted by the intensity and higher aspiration of Venus. Esoteric astrology also links the mind with Venus. It states that the "Lords of Mind" came from Venus in Atlantean times to fertilize humanity and impel it toward its next step in evolution, i. e. , the building of the concrete and abstract minds. Whether this fertilization was effected purely on a soul level or also on a physical level remains to be determined.

As we have seen, the power of Mercury is twofold, a fact well exemplified in one of the astrological signs he rules, Gemini, the twins. In his highest aspect as Lord of Wisdom he connects us to our soul and spirit via our intuition, encoding abstract and intuitive input into symbols which our rational mind can understand and coordinate. On this level the power of the planet Mercury is best represented by the Egyptian god Thoth.

Thoth is a very ancient deity whose origin is not well defined. He is the Lord of magic, science, and healing. As divine scribe he is also the keeper of time and past deeds. Thoth, as Lord of Wisdom, rules over the Memory of Nature which contains all that ever was, is, or will be.

From the intermingling of the Greek and Egyptian cultures sprang the teachings of the hermetic school, of which the city of Alexandria was the center and hub. In this city lived many philosophers, sages, and magicians of antiquity. The famous library of Alexandria contained the wisdom of the ages encoded in its many volumes, safeguarded, or so it seemed, for future generations. Alas, the fanaticism of early Christians eventually overpowered this center of learning and the library was burned, precipitating the advent of the Dark Ages in the Western world.

Even though the books of Alexandria have been lost, the Memory of Nature, or "Akashic Record" as it is called in the East (see also the chapter on the moon), is still there–immutable and freely accessible to those who would train themselves to reach it. The Memory of Nature gives willingly to those who know how to travel through the "Treasure House of Images" and extract the morsels of truth hidden beneath the layers of astral glamour.

In this Thoth is a most skilled teacher. For he will, through his exacting and thorough training, show us how to link our rational mind to our abstract mind. With his help we organize within our consciousness the symbolic language of the wisdom of the ages. Once understood and allocated to a more-familiar frame of reference (rationality), Mercury/Thoth proceeds to show us the usefulness of our newly gained insights. Mercury in conjunction with the unconditional love of Venus guides us enthusiastically to apply our knowledge for the progress of humanity.

Thoth/Hermes then, in his higher aspect as god of wisdom, is the archetypal teacher of humanity. To connect the personal and transpersonal levels of consciousness and to teach and train the mind are his primary functions.

In his lower aspect, the archetypal energy related to the planet Mercury corresponds more to the Greek god Hermes and the Roman god Mercury, divine messenger, patron of shepherds, travelers, and thieves. He is the divine trickster, the jack-of-all-trades, who cunningly applies his wisdom to attain his goals, ignoring entirely society's code of ethics. He is also the swift messenger of the gods, who with his winged sandals delivers information between the gods themselves and between Olympus and earth.

The divine trickster Hermes/Mercury, although not evil, is mischievous. Lacking moral codes, he takes endless delight in misguiding and trapping the human mind in a self-righteous, dry, lifeless rational labyrinth. Mercury in his aspect of trickster fools the thinker into believing that an emphasis on the rational functions of the mind will finally bring the solution to his mental dilemmas, the synthesis to thesis and antithesis. The truth is that the compulsive thinker is locked into an ever tighter "hermetic" universe which is, given the common deffinition of this term, sealed within itself. As a result the mind of the thinker swims around and around like a fish in a fishbowl, viewing the surrounding truth blurred through the concavity of his own rationality and self-righteousness.

The most-effective escape from this mental gridlock is through the passion and higher mystical inspiration of Venus. Venus, flooding the mind with fresh unstructured energy, shatters the rigid mental structures brick by brick and eventually uncoils the labyrinth, evening out unnecessary folds in the mental hologram.

Mercury gains nothing by his trickery but sheer delight. In fact, it seems that the entire cosmos is but a large playground to this youthful god. From a higher perspective, the hermetic tradition is but an array of very amusing board games which Mercury delights in playing with human manikins. It is not until we have mastered the "board game" of the mind ourselves, at least to some degree, that we can recognize what kind of game he has had us play. By then our abstract mind has most surely been well integrated and we "mind" the playing no more than he, taking ecstatic delight in the mental juggling of entire universes.

Proper attunement with the powers of Mercury and Venus minimizes mental entrapment. Furthermore, with the practices described in this book, you will have the correct tools to clear the mind of unwanted loops and blockages.

Mercury empowers the intellect and cognitive faculties. He brings a swift mind and the ability to see many different points of view without loosing mental balance. Mercury, the divine jester, enjoys shuffling and analyzing ideas and concepts only to resynthesize them with ease.

Computer "wizards" are under a strong and positive Mercurial influence and we have much to thank them for in our present society. Successful business people, stock brokers, and investors are under Mercury's influence as well. They are extremely skilled in translating their intuitive hunches into rational facts, often intuitively anticipating the market's next move.

Mercury promotes an airy emotional detachment combined with a healthy self-confidence, curiosity, and mental involvement. Mercury doesn't care what others think of him, but sells himself, his ideas, and merchandise with great skill and self-assurance. He represents the successful salesperson, corporate leader, and diplomat.

If Mercury is unbalanced, Mercurial detachment turns into "flakiness." However, through proper attunement to Mercury's higher aspect, imbalance is avoided.

On the physical level, Mercury promotes dexterity, social grace, ease of speech and expression in every way. He enhances communication through the spoken and written word and through visual images from television and the movies.

Throughout history we have applied Mercurial formulas and abstractions to build the technology that has allowed humanity at large to move from the mere struggle for survival of the cave people to the sophistication of contemporary society.

Our Western world with its trade, computers, and machines working efficiently for human progress is a good example of the physical level of Mercurial power, its drawbacks being excessive materialism, rationality, and intellectuality.

Mimicry in its positive aspect is also a physical expression of Mercury. It is easily observed in children and youths who learn by copying from their parents, their peers, and their environment. Mimic also helps us learn foreign languages and their correct pronunciation.

To copy or mimic without understanding, however, is an aberration of the Mercurial quality to connect and interrelate. In Egyptian mythology Thoth was accompanied by a monkey, who symbolizes the monkey's faculty to perform seemingly rational deeds by imitating without understanding their meaning. Thoth's monkey is the trickster in his lowest aspect. And most of us have come across somebody who leads us to believe that s/he knows something, whereas, in truth the person is only repeating what was heard or read without truly understanding.

The God Hermes/Mercury in Mythology

Hermes was originally venerated as the god of shepherds. His image was placed at the doors of houses and huts. Later Hermes was replaced in this function by Apollo and became prominent as the guide and protector of travelers instead. To protect people on their voyages, statues of Hermes were placed at crossroads and at intersections. From this guiding function another aspect of Hermes evolved, i. e. , Hermes Psychopompus as the guide or conductor of the souls of the dead. In Egypt this same task was performed by Anubis, the jackal-headed god and "The Opener of the

Ways. " During the Greco-Egyptian era the merging of these two deities gave rise to the cult of Hermanubis.

Hermes was also the god of commerce and profit. And since trade was mostly performed at the marketplace with its lengthy price discussions where the merchant tried to persuade the buyer by his wit and eloquence, Hermes became the god of clever speech and cunning. Lawful merchants as well as thieves fall under this god's protection. His most-prominent function, however, is that of messenger of the gods, and of Zeus in particular.

Hermes is usually portrayed as a young athlete with a slim, muscular body. His youthful and chiseled features are framed by his short blonde curly hair. His most-important attributes are his winged sandals and winged helmet. He also carries a winged staff called a caduceus. With these accoutrements Hermes glides swiftly and gracefully between heaven and earth to deliver his master's missives.

The caduceus is a staff with two intertwined serpents topped by a winged globe. Although it has become the emblem of medical science, in its original sense it represented the perfect flow of the currents of energy within the three main etheric channels of the human body. From another perspective, the two snakes represent the duality of every mental construction: thesis and antithesis, while the staff represents their merging into synthesis. The pine cone or winged globe at its top is the spirit from which everything comes into being.

Hermes is the son of Zeus and Maia. It is said that immediately after his birth he stole Apollo's cattle, openly displaying his cunning and mischievous nature. Soon, however, little Hermes appeased Apollo by giving him the lyre, a musical instrument he had just invented. Since Apollo was delighted, the two gods became friends for life.

Hermes had many love affairs with nymphs and goddesses. Among the goddesses he entertained liaisons with were Aphrodite, Persephone, and Hecate. He had many sons and daughters, Pan and Eros among the most renowned. Although Eros' parentage is not clearly defined, according to some traditions his father was Hermes and his mother Aphrodite, from my viewpoint a most-suitable choice.

Mercury in Astrology

Mercury rules the astrological signs of Gemini and Virgo.

His natural house is the Third House (communications, short journeys, concrete knowledge such as science and mathematics, and the educational years from age seven to fourteen) and the Sixth House (work, health, efficiency, service, servants, clerks, and employees).

Mercury is androgynous. The glyph that represents Mercury is a circle topping an equal-armed cross with a half circle topping the circle. Although this glyph is open to various interpretations, one explains the circle as representing the mind receiving impulses from two directions. The inspirational and intuitive realms of spirit are represented by the semicircle, while the earthly environment is symbolized by the cross.

Basic key words describing the influence of Mercury are reason, communication, activity, analysis, discrimination, versatility, dexterity, cunning, intelligence, alertness, and eloquence.

Mercury's negative attributes are restlessness, flakiness, superficiality, indecision, nit-picking, opportunism, hypercriticality, and nosiness.

The basic function of Mercury in one's astrological chart involves activating the mind and the reasoning faculty to promote knowledge, understanding, communication, and freedom of choice.

In the physical body Mercury rules over memory and the conscious mind, the nervous system, the breathing apparatus, the tongue, hands, and coordination.

Furthermore, Mercury rules over all means of communication through the spoken and written word such as the telephone, mail, books, and computers. He rules over short journeys, education, medicine, and clerical work as well. His day is Wednesday and his metal is, of course, Mercury.

Inner Journey To Contact the Archetype

Sit or lie in a comfortable position and begin relaxing by breathing deeply and rhythmically. Now count from ten to zero, allowing your body to relax even more with each count.

Imagine that your surroundings slowly fade and you find yourself walking along a desert landscape. It is morning. A hot and dry breeze whips your face. Sand is swished up all around in little funnels like miniature tornadoes. You pull the hood of your cloak up around your head to protect you from the dust and walk on, determinedly. With every step you take your feet seem to sink deeper into the sand, and you become tired, almost exhausted. Nevertheless, you continue.

Your path leads you toward two large boulders, and as you approach them, a silvery portal materializes between them. The morning sun glints off the Mercurial gate, enveloping you in an ethereal shimmer. The doorknob, you notice, is in the shape of the astrological symbol of Mercury. You open the gate and pass through.

On the other side you are greeted by a handsome young man, welcoming you with his friendly smile. He is tall and slender, his lean and muscular body showing the training of an athlete. Short blonde locks frame his immaculate features. And clear, sky-blue eyes surrounded by the thickest lashes lock with yours. A roguish smile curls his lips as he speaks:

"Come with me, dear traveler of Cosmos, and I will show you my world." He stretches out his hand in a welcoming gesture and you take it without hesitation. He starts to move swiftly along the path, his feet barely touching the ground. You admire his lithe, muscular body and graceful movements; you also notice his winged sandals, so perfectly fitted for his aristocratic feet. Silently you wish you could also sport such a fine pair of sandals. And before you know it, you are wearing a pair yourself.

Soon you are both lifted up in the air and flying fast toward the planet Mercury. The sun shines brightly and proudly, concealing almost entirely the little planet you are seeking. However, you know you will safely reach your destination, since you are being led gently by no other than Hermes, divine messenger and patron of travelers.

After a short flight, Hermes points ahead to a little sphere that stands out almost black against the sun's blazing face. "That's my home," he says. "Fear not, dear friend, for the sun will cause you no harm. " As soon as he says these words you find yourself landing smoothly on a sandy surface. The sky is blue above and the sun shines brightly. Nothing seems to distinguish this landscape from the desert you just left behind. You lift your questioning eyes to Hermes and he reacts immediately by beckoning you to follow him up to a rocky promontory. From its summit, he says, you may both admire the valley that lies below.

As you reach the top you gasp in awe. Before you lies a field full of people. You see men, women, and children of all ages busily competing at different tasks and games. From their clothing you can see that they seem to come from different historical epochs. Some stem from as far back as Egyptian and Greek times, yet others are dressed in contemporary attire. The field is divided into many different squares through rows of white stones. In each square a different activity is being pursued. To your left young Greek athletes are competing, some running and some jumping. To your right men and women seem to be engrossed in study. They are seated on benches, books and workbooks piled high before them. Some seem to be taking tests as they nervously write on loose sheets of white paper. Others are passing oral exams before a committee of teachers.

In the adjacent field you see men and women clerks and secretaries working busily. And farther to your right you can see a group of philosophers and scientists in heated discussion. On the square behind the athletes, computer tables, screens, monitors, keyboards, and printers have been set up for the computer experts to prove their skills. In the square next to this, men, women, and children are playing card and board games. Many of them, you notice, are playing chess, their brows furrowed in deep concentration.

You walk on, still holding Hermes' hand. He smiles at you over his shoulder, with the self-satisfaction of a satiated feline. "Do you like it?" he asks. "Yes, I do and very much so," you answer honestly. Still following Hermes, you pass many similar squares where people are competing diligently with their Mercurial skills.

At the end of the field there is an elevated platform. A table is set up with a jury and gold medals are being awarded to the winners in each category. From the people's faces you can see how very seriously they are taking their competition—the winners dashing proud and boastful smiles like overblown peacocks and the losers cringing in shame. This you feel as odd and somewhat painful, but quickly disregard the feeling.

The sun gleams off Mercury's helmet almost blinding you, forcing you to shield its light from your eyes with your hands. By now sweat is beading on your face and you wonder how all these people manage to work so obsessively in this scorching heat. So engrossed are they in their pursuits that you and your heavenly guide pass completely unnoticed.

After crossing the plain Hermes leads you up a steep path again. You walk toward a high rocky platform which overlooks the valley directly opposite the place you landed. Soon you reach the top and are again amazed. The view is breathtaking and a soft cool breeze caresses your cheeks. But this is not what strikes you. No. It is what you encounter there that seems at first unsettling. On top of the rocky platform you see, seated on richly carved stone benches, two men very unlike each other. One is young and incredibly handsome, youthful yet athletic. His skin is smooth and his eyes hazel, with hair the color of honey. The other on the contrary is muscular and broad shouldered. His deep-green eyes are piercing and incredibly magnetic, yet his entire body is covered with fur. Two little horns adorn his forehead and a pipe lies on his lap. At the sight of Hermes both stand up and embrace him joyfully. After awhile Hermes turns around to you and says, "May I present my sons, Eros and Pan. " You nod and smile at them while your gaze moves over them in wonder.

Hermes points toward the path that winds up where you stand. And you behold the winners from the valley parading upward, proudly clasping their golden medals. As each one reaches the top, they hand over the trophy to Hermes, their fingers trembling in expectation. Hermes collects the medals with a ceremonious and somewhat mocking bow. Then he throws them high up in the air and starts a happy juggling game with the golden awards. He breaks out in loud laughter that echoes throughout the valley, his joy clearly written across his face for all to see. The divine jester jumps back and forth in sheer delight while skillfully juggling the many medals up and down in circles.

You watch in awe, for the god is not only playing with the people's hard-won trophies, but now he is also shapeshifting. His form changes from that of a young athlete to that of a clown, a jack-of-all-trades, a magician, a beggar, a shepherd, a thief, a philosopher, a computer expert, a clerk, a secretary, a wise old man, a monkey, and then back again into the handsome athletic god Hermes—all the while never loosing the tumbling medals. The winners stand by as if frozen. All life seems to have gone out of them. And suddenly it dawns on you! The people you saw competing on the field are truly aspects of yourself, and the squares they were in, your own mental pigeonholes! This entire show is but for your benefit! And fun, you should have had fun experiencing it!

As if reading your thoughts Mercury replies: "Yes, my friend, you are absolutely right! You should have fun with it, with the mental training and competition, especially since the gold up here has no value except as a symbol of integrity!" With this the divine harlequin throws one gold medal after another over the cliff behind his back. You hear a soft splash as they reach the bottom, as if falling into deep water. After he has thrown the last one, he dashes you an open and honest smile. He speaks: "Dear friend, do what you must do. And remember that I am so close to you that you cannot always see me. 'Tis in playfulness that you will gain the right perspective of your achievements. 'Tis in fun that you find the mastery of every game."

Oh, Mercury! Hermes! Thoth! How you do long to be like him—so commanding, intelligent, and swift, so lighthearted and detached, handsome and appealing! A true winner in every sense, masterfully skilled in word and deed! Suddenly you are overwhelmed by your desire to be like him. You burn with the need to fuse with him, to integrate his divine qualities, to absorb his joy, grace, and ease, to learn from his knowledge and versatility! You know what you must do. Love him, you must love him! And you must love all the aspects of yourself being trained by him.

While you are immersed in these thoughts, the winners seem to return to life. They, together with Hermes, turn into a luminous gas that enters your body through your heart chakra. Once inside, the gas pulsates, expands, and finally explodes, flooding your entire being with a thousand particles of light. You are thrust into sweet ecstasy. And all the while you can feel how the Mercurial fire is expanding, readjusting, and organizing your inner matrix to align it even more closely to Divinity.

You open yourself completely to Hermes, lovingly cradling his divine particles inside yourself, allowing them to work their magic. You gladly accept what is happening and know that from now on you will never be the same again. You ask the god to give you a personal message and allow some time for it to appear.

Remain in fusion with the god for as long as it feels agreeable. Then thank Hermes and open yourself again to allow the god and the winners to depart. See how the luminous gas exits your body through your heart and immediately see how the figure of Hermes and the winners materialize again before you. They all sport the most-winsome smiles and your love flows out to them once more, reaffirming the rapport that remains among all of you.

The winners proceed to walk back down the hill, whistling happily as they go. For your contact and conscious awareness of them has made a great change. They are desperate achievers no more, but have become cheerful players of the cosmic game.

You notice that Hermes has once more changed his attire. He is dressed as a magus now. A tunic of indigo silk embellished with silver and golden stars enwraps his shapely frame. As he points to the sky above with a crystal wand, the sun fades and gives way to a breathtaking starry night.

He moves his wand again, this time to the ground, materializing an imposing white-marble throne before you. But this is not all. Out of the starry sky a beautiful woman appears, gliding slowly down to earth. She reaches out to Hermes and they fall into each other's arms in a passionate embrace. Her beauty and magnetism leave no doubt about her identity; she is Aphrodite, goddess of love.

Hermes, his left arm around the goddess' waist, points down at the field with his wand, bathing the players and their accoutrements in a blazing light. Pan picks up his pipe and plays a happy song. Hermes and Aphrodite laugh heartily in response, and gazing deeply into each other's eyes, they start to dance gracefully around the rocky platform. You watch the couple with admiration and tap your foot to the beat of Pan's inviting tune.

After awhile Hermes lifts his wand to heaven. And while still dancing with his beloved, he swings his wand around and around, causing the stars to shoot and pour their light onto you. While you are flooded with the brilliance and warmth of heaven, stars flash all around like fireworks on New Year's Eve. You experience a joy so great, it threatens to tear you apart. All is light; all is warmth and bliss. And suddenly you know it. This is Mercury no more, but with his help and his magic you have pierced right through him and reached into the heart of the sun.

You remain on the spot for a while longer, eagerly absorbing the light. Then, so as not to disturb the dancing couple you silently make your descent toward home. You are not afraid to travel alone because you know that you must only focus your mind on your destination and you will safely reach it. However, Eros, too familiar with his parents' love display to be entertained by it any longer, eagerly offers himself as guide. You take his outstretched hand willingly and slowly walk back along the path you came. You look at the rocky mount once more and see Aphrodite seated on her marble throne with Hermes and Pan at her feet happily immersed in a heated discussion.

Soon you are high up in the sky again and heading toward earth. You land gently before the Mercurial door. You thank your handsome guide and say farewell. Then you open the gate and pass through, closing it tightly behind you. You feel refreshed and rejuvenated, happy, light, and inspired. Then the landscape slowly fades away while you gradually regain your normal waking consciousness.

Magical Use of Mercury

Preliminaries for the magical use of Mercury's energy involve the following considerations:

• Open yourself without fear to the forces of change; be ready and willing to grow and mature in all aspects of your life.

• Take responsibility for the new awareness and knowledge this exercise will bring.

• Inflame yourself with the desire and dedication to be like Mercury, to expand the realms of your conscious mind and integrate your abstract mind and intuition.

• Aspire to transcend the narrow view and conditioning of human society and existence throughout your work; identify with Divine Wisdom.

• Commit yourself to using the intuitive knowledge and cunning you gain through Mercury for the good of all; balance it carefully with Divine Love and compassion.

• Be honest with yourself.

Magical Practice To Understand Your Personality Assets

This practice will make you aware of all your personal assets. You will make a list of these assets and correlate them with the seven major chakras (your body's energy centers as in appendix A) and their corresponding colors. Then you will write each asset onto graph paper inside a two-inch square, color it in the corresponding color and cut it out. Once you have colored and cut squares for all your assets you will spread them out in a special pattern and meditate on the combination of these assets until you reach an intuitive synthesis of your personality. Through this synthesis you will recognize the way to apply your personality effectively to realize your life purpose in world service. It is said that "God helps those who help themselves." Mercury is the power that shows you what you have available and how to combine it most successfully to achieve your spiritual goal, that is, to build a suitable channel for the divine energies of your spirit.

The key phrase of this practice is, "What am I and how can I apply what I am to the Divine Plan?"

Before you start, familiarize yourself with the colors, attributes, and levels of expression of each of the seven chakras as shown below. I have chosen to use a system of seven chakras, although other authors use more.

The color correlations I use are the ones given in the STAR*LIFE system. They have worked best for me. Other authors and traditions use different color attributions, which is all right. You may use the one you are more familiar with if it is different from this one. The practice will work regardless.

It is very important that you do the entire practice, coloring and cutting the individual squares. If you only write down your assets but don't do the entire practice, you are merely performing an intellectual exercise, missing the point entirely. The power of encoding concepts in colors is similar to extracting their essences. So when you play around with the colored squares, it is as if you were shuffling the essential frequencies that make up each asset, then laying them out into a "mandala" or harmonious picture of yourself and the universe. Colors connect your subconscious, conscious, and transpersonal levels most efficiently. Just find out for yourself! Be imaginative and play with the colored squares after you have finished the exercise on the fourteenth day. Combine them in patterns; always be aware that they represent the essences of your inner qualities.

The following list will give you an idea of which personal assets relate to which chakra. I strongly encourage you to add as many assets as you can. Do not worry if you cannot determine the exact chakra allocation of your asset. Use the chakra you feel is best.

The higher chakras are related to more-abstract, wider concepts, whereas, the lower chakras are connected to more-specific, detailed assets. Therefore, to gain a more-realistic picture you should give yourself more than one square for assets related to the higher chakras, particularly to the crown chakra (up to five squares seems reasonable here). And I also suggest that you give yourself more than one square for those assets about which you feel particularly strong. Use your own judgment.

First chakra: assets related to your physical expression, the color red. Ask yourself: How is my physical health? My job? My financial situation? My willpower? Do I move around physically? How is my material well-being, stamina, strength? Am I physically attractive? Am I realistic, practical? Am I bold and courageous? Independent? Do I have material resources? Do I feel well grounded?

Second chakra: sexual area; color orange. Assets related to your emotional/instinctive/creative expression. Note that the specific qualities of this chakra are felt somewhat differently for men than for women. Ask yourself: Am I creative? If a man: How is my self expression? If a woman: Am I nurturing? For both: Do I attract what I need? Do I enjoy life? Am I sexually fulfilled? Do I flow with the rhythms of nature? Do I feel emotionally connected to nature? Can I give and receive love freely? Do I get along well with people on an every day level? Men tend to express their love actively with the first and second chakra and are receptive, containing, and nurturing with the heart; whereas, women naturally receive, nurture, and contain love with the second chakra and actively express love with the heart chakra.

Third chakra: solar plexus and abdominal area; color yellow. Assets that relate to your conscious passions, desires, and your ability to accomplish what you want. This chakra is also related to the lower mind, although its attributions overlap partly with those of the Third Eye. Ask yourself: Which positive emotional drives do I have? Am I persevering? Courageous in a self-centered way? Do I accomplish what I want? Am I in touch with my subconscious mind by following up on hunches and gut feelings? Do I have leadership qualities? Ambition? An imposing presence? Do I recover easily from emotional blows? Do I have a healthy self-esteem? Am I empathic? Do I feel bonded to family and social groups? Am I psychic? Am I passionate about life?

Fourth chakra: the heart; color emerald or mint green. Assets that relate to unconditional love, generosity, joy, bliss, compassion, mystical experience, and group consciousness. Ask yourself: Do I love? Do I express love? Do I nurture and contain my beloved? Do I love unconditionally? Do I love all creation? Am I joyful? Am I happy? Enthusiastic? Easy-going? Have I experienced bliss? Am I compassionate? Am I humanistic? Idealistic? Am I generous? Do I have family and group consciousness? Am I a mystical person? Have I had significant mystical experiences I can share? Am I loyal? Devotional? Do I sustain deep friendships? Do I have faith?

Fifth chakra: the throat; color sky blue. Assets that relate to higher creative self-expression. Ask yourself: Do I express myself creatively? In writing? In art? Through music? With my voice? Do I speak my truth? Do I express my true self to others in any other way? Am I resourceful? Inventive? Versatile? Adaptable?

Sixth chakra: the Third Eye; color indigo blue. Assets that relate to your mental focus, foresight, insight, and materializing power. Ask yourself: Am I intuitive? Am I mentally focused? Am I a free thinker? Do I have high executive abilities? A talent for organization? Do I have a clear definition of my goals and a vision of what I want to be and accomplish? Do I have a broad perspective of things? Do I learn and reason with ease? Is my memory good? Do I grasp abstract concepts and philosophical truths easily? Do I have good forethought and planning abilities? Do I have good analytical and synthesizing skills? Can I pinpoint what I want and achieve it easily? Do I have good strategic skills?

Seventh chakra: the crown; color purple. Assets related to spiritual enlightenment and cosmic consciousness. Ask yourself: Am I spiritually enlightened? Do I possess cosmic consciousness? Am I aware of the transpersonal realms of the universe? Have I experienced universal unity? Have I experienced direct knowing? Do I have a sense of mission in my life?

Here again some assets might overlap with the mystical experiences related to the heart. However, the experiences related to the crown chakra are more wisdom oriented while the ones related to the heart more feeling oriented.

Note that some of the assets related to the crown are in the past tense. The spiritual experiences related to the crown chakra are not easy to achieve. They are permanently established only in very advanced individuals. Those fortunate enough to count these assets as a permanent part of their personality will most probably not need this magical practice any more.

Before you start the practice, secure a white candle and matches, a pair of scissors, a blue ballpoint pen, a notebook, graph paper with one-inch squares, and seven markers with the colors red, orange, yellow, green, sky blue, indigo, and purple.

Starting on the day of the new moon and ending the day of the full moon, practice the following procedures:

1. Sit or lie in a comfortable position and begin relaxing by breathing deeply and rhythmically. Now count from ten to zero, allowing your body to relax even more with each count.

2. Attune yourself with Divine Wisdom as manifested through the energy of Mercury. State firmly that you want to know more about yourself and are willing to change. State your desire to analyze and understand your personal assets and bring them together in a synthetic whole. Ask Mercury to help you in this task.

3. Visualize Mercury's astrological symbol as shown at the beginning of this chapter. Build it up with your inner vision until it is large enough to envelop you completely, creating an energetic bond with the power of the Mercury.

4. Imagine the energy of Mercury spreading all around you until it envelops your entire aura like a cocoon. Feel it vibrating and pulsating with power. Inflame yourself with love and desire to be like Mercury. Feel how the power of Mercury enlivens each of your chakras, making them spin in full power and speed.

5. Now ask yourself the questions provided on the previous page which relate only to your first chakra. Add as many other additional first-chakra assets as you can. Do this by taking a mental inventory of all your good qualities related to your physical body, life, and environment. Meditate on them for a few minutes, focusing and highlighting their potential and actual goodness and usefulness for the Divine Plan. Men-

tally imprint all these assets related to the first chakra with the color red. After about ten minutes of meditation, write down your findings with the red marker.

6. On the following day repeat procedures one to four. Then repeat the procedure described under number five using only the second-chakra questions. This time write down your assets with the orange marker. Concentrate on one chakra each day, starting with the first chakra on the first day, and moving up to the seventh on the seventh day. Write down the assets related to each chakra on a fresh page of your notebook with the marker of the corresponding color. Then copy all assets to your graph paper with the blue ballpoint pen (blue stands for royalty), writing each asset inside a two-inch square. Color each square with the corresponding color. Then proceed to cut out the little colored squares, keeping those of the same color together. At the end of the first seven days you should have seven piles of assets in seven different colors.

7. On the eighth day take your seven piles of assets and sit down on the floor. Proceed to build a circle around you with the colored two-inch squares, using up all the squares of one color before you add the next. Start with the red, then orange, yellow and so forth, until the last purple square rests adjacent to the first red one. Make the circle big enough for you to sit or lie in it comfortably.

8. Put the white candle inside the circle, light it, and take your meditation position; then repeat procedures one to four.

9. Now look around at the little squares and let their colors engrave themselves deeply in you. Which are predominant? Which lacking? What does this signify? Analyze the color configuration of your personal assets for some time, then fantasize how the color created by blending them would look. After that, imagine the essence of these colors swirling up from the papers creating a beautiful marbleized effect. Then let them combine themselves and synthesize into a small sphere, and bring this sphere into your Third Eye.

10. Ask yourself, "If I could condense all these assets and the energy they represent into one symbol, what would it be?" Allow some time for a symbol to appear before your inner eye.

11. Remain this way for awhile, absorbing the essence of your own assets in this abstract way, then meditate on the following for ten minutes or more, "What am I and how can I best serve the Divine Plan?"

12. After at least ten minutes, close down the practice and blow out the candle. Collect the colored squares and keep them in a safe place away from the sight and touch of other people until the next day. Finish by recording your findings and impressions in your notebook.

13. Repeat this process for six more days, which should give fourteen in all and end with the day of the full moon. On this day experiment with the squares, laying them out in different patterns. What do you see? What do you feel?

14. On the day of the full moon, if not before, you should have achieved a fairly clear idea of what your life purpose is and how best to apply all your personal assets to fulfill it. Remember that your purpose will evolve as will your assets. You may repeat the practice the following month, adding or subtracting squares as needed. If your wish to repeat the practice after three months, you should color and cut a new set of squares.

You may ask yourself what all this analyzing, cataloging, and shuffling of concepts is all about. Find out for yourself. The least you will achieve, however, is a crisp idea of the value of your personal assets and how to combine them appealingly. You will also gain intuitive insight about your own essence and the piece that you are in the great patchwork quilt of creation.

VENUS

VENUS

Attunement with the Archetypal Power of Venus

Venus represents the binding force of creation on all levels of existence, which is love in its many dimensions. The highest love of Venus knows no possessiveness or jealousy, but rejoices in the joy and bliss of another. She represents the love of the Creator who eternally gives of Himself for the Universe to exist. Never exhausting itself, remaining eternally fluid, Divine Unconditional Love is unbound by the parameters of time and space.

Through attunement with Venus we experience a joyful state of pure being and complete fluidity where Unconditional Love radiates its full power, joy, and beauty from our entire being.

One of the most-ecstatic and life-transforming Venusian experiences available to a human being is his/her encounter with the Twin Soul in physical form. This experience is so intense it eclipses almost everything else.

In reuniting the Twin Souls Venus brings together the separate units and combines them into a greater harmonious whole where the parts complement each other in a perfect dance. In their union the Twin Souls release the tremendous energy that was bound in their separation, propelling themselves into ever-higher peaks of experience.

With the power of Venus on the spiritual level we see a dream and hold it, as irrational and fantastic as it might seem and no matter what adversities we encounter. This dream may be one of peace and unconditional love, of a better world full of abundance and happiness, of harmony between the races, or of meeting our Twin Soul. And it is through the inspiration of these "crazy" dreams that the world is eventually made a better place. The spiritual power of Venus drives us incessantly and passionately to seek and express the beauty, love, and harmony hidden beneath the layers of rationality and practicality.

When we act upon a true prompting of our heart, which is Venus on the spiritual plane, we will be deeply rewarded by a feeling of "doing the right thing," even though rationally it might not appear to be so. This "feeling right" about an action should be taken most seriously since it is one of the strongest intuitive prompts we ever get about being on the "right track."

If in doubt about a decision and when our heart is not aligned with our mind, we should always follow our heart. The heart is our access to the soul and the Divine. The mind, on the contrary, is most often biased and clouded by rationality.

In my own life, when my mind seemed most painfully opposed to my heart, I was wise enough to follow my heart. Against the rational warnings of my mind that kept telling me I was completely crazy and indecent, I wrote my Qabalah teacher—whom I knew only by correspondence—that I loved him more than anything, even myself. Still after reading his denial of his feelings about me, I went on and told him by letter that I believed he was my Twin Soul and that we would marry! I did this without knowing his age or physical appearance. I knew only that he came from a social background totally opposite mine. However, my heart told me to tell him and that whatever his response to me, he had a right to know my feelings.

I went through months of agony. For a long time nothing happened that would reflect the rightness of my heart. Suddenly, however, everything changed. We met at a workshop and recognized each other instantly as what we are—Twin Souls.

We moved together and married. We have been together ever since. Later I realized that if I had not followed my heart and held onto my dream, things might have turned out quite differently. We might never have met—or met much later. He was not as clear about the dream of meeting the Twin Soul as I was. He was not in touch with his emotions, as most men aren't. I could have waited forever for him to make the first move because he could not feel his heart well enough to understand its promptings. Luckily for both of us, I dared to make a fool of myself and told him. This changed our lives forever. These events are described in depth in my book, *Twin Soul.*

In our achievement-oriented society it is most difficult indeed simply to "follow our heart." Yet I advise you to meditate on this because it will clarify many issues.

Venus might seem an insignificant and harmless little planet to modern astrologers, but let me tell you that her force is great. She not only works behind the scenes, but she also is most powerful on her spiritual level.

According to esoteric lore the Lords of Mind, who "reside" in Venus, came to propel civilization on earth. The controversial Lucifer—devil, fallen Archangel, and Light Bearer all in one—is said to come from Venus. And so is Melchizedek, "spiritual father," King of Salem, friend of King Solomon, and spiritual guide of many great esoteric orders.

Venus' power is all the greater for being hidden. In today's patriarchal society her power has been largely neglected and misunderstood. She has been degraded mainly because her power is so subtle and subjective. The famous "woman's touch" so much needed in men's lives, cannot be rationally measured. In fact, rationality works directly against Venus. Even if you were to call your Twin Soul in ritual and succeed in having him or her enter your physical life, rationality would explain it away as coincidence and foolishness. Sadly, from the rational perspective every influence of Venus can be classified as unnecessary, wasteful, and foolish. But then if we don't give in to some measure of foolishness, if we don't dare to dream and be romantic, we will never experience our own Divinity and its creative genius and bliss. Ultimately, rationality makes a cold bedtime companion as does pride.

Truly to contact Venus on the spiritual plane we must be humble and crazy all at once. We must dare to dream of the ideal partner and ideal life circumstances. We must be crazy enough to imagine the irrational, delicious Divine Life we so long for and believe that we deserve. We must have faith that it is somewhere waiting for us, even if no rational clue points to its existence. Then, having seen the dream, we must nurture it always and never lose our faith.

Our rational mind will fight that dream and repeatedly tear it to pieces. But we must still hang on with all our heart, regardless of the coldness of our rationality. And eventually, like the sun's rays breaking through heavy storm clouds, a way will clear for us.

It is usually more difficult for men to bypass their rationality. They often fail to reach the spiritual realms of Venus, getting sidetracked by her physical and emotional aspects. But then again, women do, too.

Women are the binders. They focus on the emotions and easily reach the spirituality behind them. Women build, hold, and remember the great dream. Men actualize it.

When the Twin Souls work together, they complement each other so perfectly that efficiency as well as ecstasy is brought to peak. The human potential is then truly actualized and both partners are fulfilled.

On the mental level Venus' cohesive force of love brings separate concepts together to form a more complete whole, expressed in a kind of beauty not only aesthetic, but also functional because it is in accordance with the forces of nature and evolution. Venus represents balance in polarity. She attracts the polar opposites to each other, then combines and fuses them in harmony. Venus brings the necessary mental fluidity for intuitive insight and creative inspiration. Mental images, when properly empowered with desire, form the foundation of physical existence. If these images are built under Venus' influence, they will reflect her love, beauty, and harmony.

Through Venus we contact, feel, and understand our inner countersexual image which helps us to know ourselves and our inner polarity and thus to integrate it into our lives. To encounter our Soulmate or Twin Soul in physical life some preliminary work is needed. We must work thoroughly with the animus or anima and come to a deep understanding of masculinity and femininity. Indeed, we must be firm in our own self before we find our Twin lest we completely lose our balance in the experience.

On the emotional level Venus provides the passion that evokes the act of creation. She promotes romantic love, personal charm, magnetism, elegance, and artistic sensibility. Venus' influence enlivens and brightens everything, especially relationships because she flowers in polarity.

Venus fires the artist with the desire to create beauty and harmony in his or her works. Venus brings the passion of materializing the vision, the personal dream. In her highest emotional expression Venus makes us transcend negative attachments, possessiveness, and jealousy. Through her desire for love and fusion, she focuses us on the important task of materializing our dream rather than losing our creative power in petty jealousies. With Venus's help we materialize our soul's desire through a divine act of creation. Under her influence all is achieved in harmony and we need not overpower our opponent to succeed. With her aid our goals are accomplished magically and mysteriously so that everyone is a winner.

The emotional energy of Venus, which is love, promotes the raw power to materialize anything we need. It empowers our dream and makes us thrive in the beauty and fulfillment of actualizing it, no matter what the circumstances. This can be seen in all those stories where love wins against all odds.

Furthermore, Venus energy subtly changes our etheric field, making our physical bodies appear more graceful, beautiful, and magnetic. The positive and cumulative aspect of the influence of Venus will gradually expand beyond our bodies' limits, permeating our environment, bringing harmony, love, beauty, and comfort to our physical surroundings.

Venus energy may be applied to any act of creation where separate elements are combined to form a more-perfect whole, often revealing aspects not formerly apparent in the separate components. This happens in science, art, business, literature, architecture, decoration and design, as well as by beautifying the physical body with flattering clothes, make up, and hairstyle.

And last but not least, Venusian power can be used not only to find a fulfilling love relationship, but also a harmonious friendship with either gender. However, to find a truly fulfilling relationship, we must include in our aspiration mental and spiritual ideals besides the obvious physical and emotional ones. Otherwise the relationship will soon feel shallow and, moreover, cause unwanted karmic ties to individuals with whom we are not truly compatible.

If Venus is sought on a purely physical or sexual level, she will lead us into shallow attempts at happiness through repeated physical unions with spiritually unsuitable partners. This will limit our mating to the lowest level, leaving our higher natures painfully unfulfilled.

The latter is a sad occurrence indeed and should be taken much more seriously. I highly recommend Dion Fortune's book, *The Esoteric Philosophy of Love and Marriage.* Although she might appear somewhat old-fashioned, there is much truth in her writings. Unfortunately, it is not until you are quite far along your spiritual path that you realize the value and power of spiritual compatibility, true commitment, and monogamy in a love relationship.

The Goddess Aphrodite/Venus in Mythology

According to Homer, Aphrodite was the daughter of Zeus and Dione, a goddess with a rather undefined personality about whom little is known. Another and more-popular source states that Aphrodite was born out of the sea. The legend tells us that when Cronus severed the genitals of his father Uranus he cast them into the sea. When the last drops of Uranus' divine seed touched the water, they formed a white foam (*aphros*) from which Aphrodite was born.

Aphrodite corresponds to the goddess Venus in the Roman tradition, to Freya in the Norse, to Ishtar in Assyro-Babylonian, to Tara in the Tibetan, and to many more figures in other traditions around the world.

Aphrodite was seen as the archetypal symbol of sex and love, though her power is much greater than that. She was depicted with long, full, blonde hair, blue-green eyes, and a well-formed sensual body. She was said to arouse passion in anyone she desired. No god, hero, or mortal could escape her powers, with the exception of Hestia, Artemis, and Athena.

Aphrodite was married to Hephæstus, the lame smith god, whose Roman equivalent is Vulcan. He was the god of the forge, ugly, but hard-working. This marriage could obviously not fully satisfy the goddess of love, who entertained various liaisons with other gods of Olympus. She also mingled with heroes and mortals, sending them on the strangest adventures as a result of the passion and desire she aroused in them.

One of her lovers was Ares, god of war, to whom she bore three children: Phobos and Deimos (fear and terror), who accompanied their father in battle, and a daughter, Harmonia, who perfectly represents the harmony that occurs when the two polar opposites are united and fused in balance.

With the god Hermes she also had a son, Hermaphroditus, who is said to have had no specific gender, yet was of both genders. Here again we have an offspring created by a fusion of two opposite but complementary poles that contains both, yet is, nevertheless, a separate entity in its own right—a new whole, one-in-itself. According to some traditions Aphrodite also bore Hermes, the god Eros, who became the personification of romantic love.

The best-known characters of the retinue of Aphrodite are Eros and the Graces. Eros originated as a symbol of cosmic force, the power of love that brings order and cohesion to Chaos, but was later degraded into a naughty winged child flying around with bow, arrows, and quiver. The divine child Eros delighted himself by shooting at unwary gods and mortals, making them fall hopelessly in love. He is the Cupid of Valentine's Day. The god Eros, however, represents much more than that.

The Graces were three: Thalia, Euphrosyne, and Aglaia. As Aphrodite's attendants they accompanied her on her adventures. They were happy and pleasant deities who brought sweetness and joy wherever they appeared.

The occult symbols of Aphrodite are the rose and the girdle, the latter said to be strong enough even to tie the thunderbolts of Zeus, signifying love as the ultimate power in the universe.

Venus in Astrology

Venus rules the astrological signs of Taurus and Libra.

Her natural houses are the Second House (substance, material and objective goals, money, and possessions) and the Seventh House (relationships with partners).

Her nature is feminine and receptive.

Her astrological symbol is a circle with an equal-armed cross attached beneath signifying spirit overcoming matter.

Basic key words describing the influence of Venus are love, passion, desire, beauty, artistic sensibility, sociability, cooperation, harmony, refinement, arranging things and relationships pleasantly, affection, magnetism, and responsiveness.

Venus' negative attributes are self indulgence, shallowness, laziness, and self centeredness.

The basic influence of this planet on your astrological chart increases your awareness of others in your life as well as consciousness of your environment.

Venus is not considered a strong planet in astrology; it is easily influenced by planets, houses, signs, and aspects in the chart.

In the physical body Venus rules over the throat, internal reproductive organs, kidneys, and blood circulation in the capillaries.

Furthermore, she presides over the voice, music, jewelry, art, and movable possessions. Her metal is copper; her day is Friday.

Venus uses her subtle charm, magnetic persuasion, and the power of love to attract to herself what she wants. Mars, on the contrary, would rather reach out and take what he needs and desires. For this reason in our modern society the astrological symbol for Mars (which shows energy thrusting out of a circle) has come to represent men and that of Venus (which indicates energy being drawn toward a circle) to represent women.

The love force of Venus is what makes us aware of and connects us to others. She inspires us to beautify ourselves, our homes and our environments. It is her sense of beauty and harmony that makes us appreciate nice things, art, music, and literature. However, when we fail to connect to Venus' power on her highest level of expression which is unconditional love, we become possessive and fearful of losing the ones we love or our valued belongings.

Inner Journey To Contact the Archetype

Sit or lie in a comfortable position and begin relaxing by breathing deeply and rhythmically. Now count from ten to zero, allowing your body to relax even more with each count.

Imagine you are walking along a sandy beach. The waves roll gently to the shore and all is calm. It is early morning and the sun has not yet risen. You feel happy and full of expectation about this new and wonderful day. The excitement of adventure bubbles inside you like French champagne. The planet Venus, the "Morning Star" as it is often called, hangs low over the horizon, heralding the sun's first appearance. The atmosphere is permeated by the characteristic serenity of dawn. At this time you recall the reason for your journey, and as in answer to your thoughts, you feel a friendly welcome emanate from this star-like planet.

As you walk on you see a large copper gate appear in front of you. The symbol of Venus is carved on its doorknob. The gate flings open and you pass without questioning.

On the other side someone is already expecting you—a very handsome young man about twenty years of age. He is tall and slender, yet well-built. He is almost naked, except for a white loincloth draped around his lean hips. Sinewy muscles cord down his arms and legs. Long, honey-colored curls frame his chiseled face and his large hazel eyes meet yours defiantly. An impish smile curves his sensuous mouth, revealing immaculate white teeth. And behind his tanned torso a pair of angel's wings stir languidly in the morning sun. He greets you with a nod, his gaze moving over you appreciatively.

It is pure pleasure to watch him; his aura is so magnetic, it draws you irresistibly to him. Despite his slightly arrogant demeanor, you get the distinct impression that universal love in its purest countenance is staring at you through his eyes. They reflect the age-old wisdom of cosmos expressed through eternal youth. Flapping his wings in anticipation, he introduces himself as Eros and you eagerly grasp his outstretched hand. Trusting him comes easily because there is something so lovely and familiar about him, you feel as if you have always known each other.

He takes you with him, flying swiftly over the beach. Hand in hand, you rise higher and higher above earth. Soon you are traveling through outer space toward Venus. As you approach the planet you are able to see clearly through its atmosphere. It is covered with lush vegetation and crystal-clear blue lakes surrounded by shores of light sand, much like a tropical island.

Guided by Eros, you land on the beach of one of the lakes. The sand is made of tiny multicolored gems and crystals, especially emerald and jade. You seat yourself on the warm sand and wait. Eros positions himself beside you and speaks:

"People on earth have lost the real meaning of love. They have reduced me to a little winged and spoiled infant who delights in wounding people randomly with his arrows, causing havoc and mischief. Think about this for a moment! In reality, I Am Love Supreme, the very essence that holds the cosmos together! Were it not for me, all would disintegrate and return to the unorganized state from whence it came! I am the one who brings order to Chaos. I am Divine Love and love is the underlying force of evolution; it drives us incessantly to an ever-greater encompassing within cosmos, until finally, one great day we all are one again. The symbol people have given me nowadays is an exact representation of how love's energy has been repressed and denigrated in modern times. Love has been returned to the nursery, making it seem foolish and childish to love and "falling in love" a mere chance happening. Well, it is not! Love is the very force that holds us together. Love must be brought to its rightful position in life, cared for, and nurtured! The rewards will be magnificent indeed!"

He pauses a moment as if to give weight to his words. Then he continues: "I am happy to teach you more, if you wish. You now know where to find me. "

You thank Eros for his advice and make a mental commitment to meditate on love. Then you hear soft voices and laughter approaching from the woods that skirt the lake. Four beautiful women emerge from the foliage. One of them stands out through her extraordinary grace, beauty, and magnetism. Her golden hair falls in thick curls down to her slender waist. Skin smooth as ivory stretches softly over her graceful, naked, and deliciously curved body. Piercing emerald cat-like eyes lock their gaze with yours. As she moves slowly toward you with the sensual grace of a feline, she holds out her arms to welcome you. She greets you by name with the most-melodious voice you have ever heard. You recognize her immediately: She is Aphrodite, goddess of love!

Willingly you fall into her outstretched arms. You remain silent and motionless for a few moments. Drinking in her essence, relishing her touch, eagerly absorbing the divine strength and beauty she offers so willingly, you return the greeting and tell her the reason for your visit. She nods in agreement and you are rewarded by a powerful energetic outpouring from her heart that instantly surrounds your entire being, enveloping you in unconditional love. The entire universe lies at your feet at this very moment! You are love, pure love, at one with creation.

Remain this way for awhile. If you have a special question to ask her, do so now. Then remain in silent expectation for a minute or two to allow the archetype to communicate with you.

Now looking straight at the goddess, state that you want to absorb into your consciousness and entire being all her qualities as well as those of Eros and the Three Graces.

See how Aphrodite, Eros, and the Three Graces turn into a luminous gas and enter your body through the area of the heart. Feel how the luminosity expands, filling your entire body, consciousness, and aura. Again, you remain in this manner for some time, absorbing all that Aphrodite and the Graces are. If the exercise is successful, you might suddenly feel you are one of them. If you are a man, don't panic; this exercise will not make you change your sexual preferences. It will, however, help you express all the Venusian traits together with an understanding of the ways of women.

When you feel ready, allow the deities to depart. Watch the luminous gas exit your body through the same spot and build up the forms of Aphrodite, Eros, and the Three Graces before you again.

You thank Aphrodite, Eros, and the Graces and say farewell. Eros returns to your side and takes your hand. He gently pulls you up and away from the ground, urging you to fly higher and higher. Hand in hand you soar high into outer space, heading back to planet earth.

As you approach earth, you are overwhelmed by unconditional love for your dear planet and are eager to share with your fellow human beings what you have learned. Before you know it, you are back at the copper gate. You say farewell to your dear companion, knowing that soon you will meet again. Parting is not so difficult anymore because you have changed; now you are stronger, more confident, and know that part of him and his mother Aphrodite will always remain with you.

You pass through the copper gate alone. The landscape and the beach slowly fade away while you gradually regain your normal waking consciousness.

The Countersexual Image

During the first half of this century, the Swiss psychologist, Carl Gustav Jung, set forth the theory that, even though on the physical plane we are obviously conditioned and limited by the gender with which we are born, on the subtler realms of consciousness our psyche has both masculine and feminine elements. This theory means that with proper training and awareness we can draw from the qualities of either form of expression and manifest it at will. Jung called the countersexual aspect of the psyche *anima* for a woman and *animus* for a man.

There is always a reason (even if it is still occult to us) for being born a certain gender. It is essential, therefore, that we come to terms with our own gender first before venturing to integrate fully our countersexual image. We must accept ourselves as what we are now, either man or woman.

Our goal should be to become whole, *One-in-Ourselves*, with all the psychic aspects of our inner self functioning under our will.

A good way to understand the countersexual image is to look at the traditionally feminine and masculine traits and then examine ourselves and our lives to see what we are and what we might be repressing. A word of caution here: Contrary to popular belief, a woman truly expressing her animus does not imitate men, their power, assertiveness, and dominance. No. She will use her inner masculine energies to express her inherent femininity more assertively. The same goes for the opposite sex. Men in sync with their anima do not become soft, over-emotional wimps, but apply their inner femininity to develop intuition, spirituality, nurturing, and compassion. In so doing they don't give up their masculinity but enhance it!

If we repress the animus or anima aspect, we deny a vital part of ourselves without which we will feel lifeless and empty. Eventually this repression will seek expression by whatever means available, usually in some form of distortion, most often making us compulsive and/or depressed, creating fears and anxieties, among other problems. To fill the void we have created by our own repressions, we will start searching for these missing aspects in whoever is nearby and suitable, expecting this individual to personify what we ourselves lack. By creating this projection we are giving away our power over ourselves and our lives to another, and so become dependent on someone else for our well-being!

This projection will satisfy us temporarily, yet sooner or later we will again recognize our emptiness and seek somebody or something else to carry our projection, making this a painful and endless game.

True love is the union of two separate and utterly independent souls who are one in themselves. These souls have chosen to be together because of a shared dream, unconditional love, likeness, and sympathy—not because they expect the other to live out their own incompetencies and fill the gap of their own repressed natures! They choose to be together anew, day after day, every instant because they so will and not because they are chained to each other by mutual projections.

In true love both partners may choose to complement each other, one performing the seemingly masculine things and the other the traditionally feminine. They have chosen to play the role that comes easier to each of them for the sake of efficiency. Their choice is made by focusing their *will* and *courage* on their goal and shared dream, not from their inability to make it on their own.

Man and woman complementing each other in their tasks is good and natural, but projection (although it cannot be justly termed as unhealthy), serves only a temporary function. This function is to protect and cover the weaker partner until s/he is able to develop his/her disowned qualities. Once this is accomplished and the individual has regained wholeness, i. e., has brought in more of the soul, projection is no longer needed.

When man and woman are in true complement, a woman uses her outgoing masculine or animus qualities to provide the etheric essence for the materialization of the dream. She spins the golden cocoon that clothes their shared dream, like the womb protects and feeds the male's seed. She, through her feminine power and intuition, sees their combined highest potential and guides him toward their shared dream. She keeps the dream safely in her heart. She feeds and nurtures it, spinning an etheric matrix around it with her love as the basis for its materialization. He, in turn, materializes the dream with his work. In so doing he is daily encoding his dream into his genes and then, on a more physical arch of the spiral, through the act of physical union, he implants it back into his woman through his seed. And the process begins once more.

Although this entire cycle often goes unnoticed, men and women perceive it intuitively. When one of them loves another outside of the relationship, they sense an unexplainable energetic leakage, they loose trust in their partner, and eventually the dream is shattered. This inner disintegration usually occurs long before the partners split on a physical level.

Personally, I am a firm believer in monogamy because one woman can spin only one man's dream at one particular time, in the same manner that once she is physically pregnant she cannot conceive another man's baby, although she may do so for several in the course of her life. A man, on the other hand, if he seeds more than one woman, will not have his dream shown and reflected to him. The physical personalities of several women, no matter how spiritual they may be, will conflict with each other energetically. The result will be that the man might be greatly admired and his ego satisfied, but he will be completely on his own to find his dream, hold it, and spin it (and by "spinning" I mean building the energetic matrix for it to materialize, not an easy task to say the least).

On a smaller scale this cycle also is at work between our masculine and feminine selves. When our inner masculine and feminine work together and are "in love," we reach our peak performance and greatest well-being, regardless if we are outwardly engaged in a romantic relationship or not. Apart from making us feel good and right inside, the love and integration of our countersexual image reflects itself on our environment, attracting to us a more-fulfilling life and more-meaningful relationships.

Actually, in truth, the magic of polarity between the sexes and its reflection within the human being is so complex that it is impossible to cover it entirely in these few pages. In fact, however, I am devoting my entire life to its study and mastery. My next book, *Twin Soul*, on which I am presently working, explains this most-sacred magic in detail.

I strongly advise the reader to study extensively the teachings of Tantra and apply them to his/her life as much as possible. For those who do not have a suitable partner, the sexual practices described in Tantric literature can be adapted and used in guided meditations with your countersexual image. Herein lies a secret and a power, the extent of which I can only hint at in these pages. But let me state my opinion: To me Love is sacred in all its manifestations, and that most certainly includes its physical expression as well. Apart from exalting a physical union to divine ecstasy, we can pull down the evolutionary thrust of Divinity, the sacred creative act of God itself into our most-physical encounter with our beloved, be this a physical lover or a spiritual/imaginary one.

Magical Use of Venus

Preliminaries for the magical use of Venus' energy involve the following considerations:

• Be certain that what you want is based on the principles of Universal Love, Beauty, and Harmony.

• Make yourself responsible for all the changes the desired result will bring to your life.

• Open yourself without fear to the forces of change; be ready and willing to stop being what you are; detach yourself from past events or future outcome.

• Let joy pervade your work.

Magical Practice To Love and Integrate the Countersexual Image

In this practice the power of Venus will be directed to love and understand your countersexual image. If you do it consistently, it will soon bring into your life a special person with whom you can establish a meaningful and fulfilling relationship. If you are fortunate enough to find yourself in such an alliance, then this practice will further strengthen and deepen the relationship.

We must first establish the ideals we seek in the relationship with our partner in the relationship that exists within ourselves. For this purpose, the work with the countersexual image is very useful and includes the following procedures:

1. Sit in a comfortable position and relax by breathing deeply and rhythmically.

2. Attune yourself with Divine Love as manifested through the power of Venus. State firmly that you want to regain your wholeness and power and are willing to change.

3. Visualize Venus' astrological symbol as shown at the beginning of this chapter. Build it up with your inner vision until it is large enough to envelop you completely, creating an energetic bond with the power of Venus.

4. Meditate on the specific characteristics your ideal mate would have: spiritual, mental, emotional, and physical. Think about what your perfect complement would be, a person who would bring out the best in you, and you in that person. One who loves you unconditionally as you are now, and to whom you return love in the same way.

5. Feel how the energy of Venus permeates each cell of your entire body and expands into your aura, making it glow with love and the desire to express this love unconditionally to someone of your opposite sex. You feel so much love and bliss inside that you are burning to share it.

6. Concentrate this love and desire in three centers of your body: the heart, the solar plexus (region of the stomach), and the genitals.

7. Visualize a luminous gas emanating from these three areas simultaneously and slowly building into a human figure that remains attached to your body by a thin silvery cord. If you are a man, you will make this figure into a woman, your anima; if you are a woman, visualize your animus in front of you. At this point, the figure is not yet well defined.

8. Now transfer to your anima or animus all the attributes of your ideal counterpart, making him/her come alive in all the details: hear him/her breathing, smell his/her perfume, feel his/her skin, but keep him/her attached to you through the silver cord.

9. Concentrate on your love for your animus or anima and have it ask you, "What am I to you?" Then answer this question on all the levels of your understanding, from the most-physical attraction to the highest, most-spiritual communion. Take your time and be thorough. This interaction will clarify many things for you.

10. Adore this figure as the most-exquisite and divine representation of the opposite sex, your true complement. At the same time, always remain conscious that the anima or animus is still an essential part of yourself and that the eyes looking at you are also your own.

11. Ask the animus or anima to give you advice on how to integrate and express it better in your life. Wait quietly for a moment to receive an answer or a symbol.

12. Now feel how love flows as an energy current back and forth between you and your countersexual image. Allow this current to flow around at least ten times. Let your imagination run free and play with him/her in true unconditional love. Make love to your animus or anima. Immerse yourself in your ecstasy for each other!

13. Join in love and at the moment of greatest ecstasy, see how your bodies are fused and how the figure with the luminous gas is instantly reabsorbed into your body, creating an explosion of love and bliss, a feeling of wholeness, power, and total acceptance.

14. Remain in this feeling of wholeness and bliss for some time; decree that it is your will and your right to live in this exalted state for as long as possible.

15. Slowly return to normal consciousness.

Be open and communicate with this element of your psyche beyond the time frame of this exercise, but never give him/her a separate name; to do so might produce too much of a separate identity in your countersexual image, splitting you apart rather than integrating you.

Once you familiarize yourself with your animus or anima through this exercise, you can take it a step farther and learn to see in it your own inherent Divinity, not only as a vital aspect of your psyche, but as a manifestation of your God Within as represented by the opposite sex. The teachings of Tantra are based on the same principle of identifying the beloved with the universal principles you want to incorporate into yourself. Again, we encourage you to study along these lines.

Years after I wrote this exercise, revealed to me intuitively, Loretta Ferrier wrote a book called *Dance of the Selves,* which is entirely devoted to this subject (see Bibliography).

Venus and the Experience of the Twin Soul

It is said in esoteric astrology that Venus is the Twin Soul of earth. The practical application of this, symbolically speaking, is that through Venus each of us may access his/her Twin Soul. As stated previously but bears repeating, I have had far-reaching and life-transforming experiences in this matter and am currently working on my book, *Twin Soul*, which deals extensively with this issue.

The Twin Soul experience is based on the science of polarity and right relationship coupled with an unreserved dedication to the divine and total commitment to the partner. Without this total commitment it is impossible to pull oneself through the experience and the effect is diminished before it rises to its full power. Venusian magnetism, when experienced on the spiritual plane, will draw to you that which you need most. On a spiritual level this is fusion with God and the encounter and mystical union with the Twin Soul, who is in one sense a physical and personal manifestation of the Divine.

Even if you are not conscious of the need to find the Twin Soul, it's there inside you. Folklore from every culture tells how the princess meets the prince, how they marry and live happily ever after. There is no denying that in the deepest recesses of our being we all long for the perfect partner—the loving, understanding, courageous other who knows us almost better than we know ourselves. The Twin Soul who fulfills our every dream, who satisfies our every longing by his/her mere presence. The one and only who makes us feel utterly safe; in whose arms we finally feel we have at last come home. Twin Souls not only share the same dream, but they represent the dream of One Spirit or Monad, materialized in two opposite and complementary halves.

To encounter the Twin Soul in physical existence much preliminary housecleaning is needed. For as blissful and exquisite as it is, it's also a most-challenging experience! We must be thoroughly prepared and utterly pure to meet the Twin Soul in physical body because s/he will not only bring out the best in us, but also the worst! The Twin will exacerbate our every fault to the maximum. It will take years of loving discipline and inner work to harmonize with the Twin Soul should we be fortunate enough to meet him/her in our physical existence.

The meeting with the Twin Soul and the power that will run through you as a result of it, completely uproots your life. You might be forced to grow and improve in areas that you never even dreamed existed. You will be hit by the sheer impact of the Cosmic Ray of Power as it pours down from your One Monad, hits your Twin Souls, and through them your physical personas. You will be shaken and stretched to the limit for a long time until you finally reach some measure of equilibrium in your newly combined self. The power that comes with the union of the Twins is immeasurable, but the force and discipline that is called upon to bridle and channel this force into constructive avenues is also vast. When the Twins meet, all is multiplied. If the increased power is not correctly handled, the damage is great indeed. Only the most courageous and disciplined should seek this venture. In fact, it is not all that difficult to call upon Venus' influence on the spiritual level; however, to bring her influence down to the material level successfully, great integrity is needed.

Luckily, to contact him/her on the astral level or in dreams is much easier. It can be done with little previous training. The power of Venus on the spiritual plane will draw us to our Twin Soul in one way or another. However, if you feel the need to call him/her down all the way into physical manifestation, then be very certain that you are ready, or you will find yourself with more than you can handle.

MARS

MARS

Attunement with the Archetypal Power of Mars

Mars epitomizes the energy of survival, will power, and individuality. He stands for the force of change and the forward-striving energies of evolution. Mars represents the power to overcome obstacles, and is the embodiment of virility, vitality, courage, originality, initiative, willpower, male sexuality, and war. Martial energy is the driving power that enables us to grow and expand our personal boundaries on all levels of our multidimensional existence.

The power of Mars is most useful in those areas of our lives where there is a need to break old structures. He will tend to tear down those no longer useful so that evolution can proceed unhindered. We should welcome this process as necessary and refreshing. The old temple must be torn down first before we start to build a new one on the same sight!

The energy of Mars is self centered and individualistic. A strong Mars influence will push us to choose our individual and unique approach to life, providing the initiative and originality necessary to overcome inertia and start new adventures. Mars makes us trailblazers.

The power of Mars is radiant rather than magnetic, making us define and maintain our individuality in the face of outside pressures and adversity. Mars energy, when allowed to run through the emotions in a constructive manner, will promote self-confidence, the thrill of competition, emotional independence, and self-reliance.

The power of Mars is the self expressive quality of love that complements the merging quality of the love of Venus. Both energies are needed to create sexual passion, and ideally both partners should have Venusian, merging qualities as well as Martial, self-expressive ones. Although the harmonious interplay of these energies is what is most difficult to achieve in a sexual relationship, it is necessary for true fulfillment.

Traditionally, Mars is said to be ruthless or even cruel in achieving victory, and, therefore, often feared. However, as we understand and work with Mars on a conscious level and befriend ourselves of his energy, the negative aspects of his influence will lessen while the positive ones will gain in strength.

Physically Mars brings vital energy, stamina, ease in athletic performances and physical activity in general. His energy has a cleansing influence on the etheric channels of our body which allows the life forces to flow with full intensity. Mars also strengthens the immune system.

The God Mars/Ares in Mythology

Ares is said to have been worshipped first in Thrace. Some sources state that he was originally honored as a god of fertility, but in general it is believed that to the Greeks his role was quite limited. He was simply the god of war, blind violence, courage, and slaughter.

Ares was depicted as a very handsome young warrior with helmet and spear, clad in bronze armor, and mounted on a chariot drawn by fast horses. He was well built, agile, and swift. Ares was said to spend most of his day roaming over battlefields, striking down enemies left and right, accompanied by his squires Phobos (Fright), Deimos (Fear), and Eris (Strife).

Even though Ares was feared by the Greeks more than any other god, he still was one of the Olympians, which shows the sacredness and importance of his power when correctly used.

Ares was Aphrodite's lover. Together they had a daughter named Harmonia. Aphrodite's marriage to Hephæstus on the other hand was barren. This shows how the union and fusion through love and desire of the two opposite poles (symbolized by Ares and Aphrodite) culminates in and produces divine harmony, a sure sign of the importance of acknowledging our own Martial traits and incorporating them into our whole conscious being. Although our belligerent aspects appear to be crude and unspiritual, they also hold our vitality, power, and courage. Without a sane measure of them we are useless on the spiritual path, incapable of conquering new levels of consciousness and upholding them in the face of adversity. Without the power of Ares we would succumb to self-pity and drown mercilessly in our own tears.

The warrior-goddess Athena as the daughter of Zeus with her wisdom and cool intelligent courage in battle, was the eternal opponent of Ares. Often they encountered each other when fighting on the plains of Greece; usually the very sight of Athena set Ares into a rage.

Mars in Roman mythology was a slightly different character. He was much more important to the Romans than Ares ever was to the Greeks. Tradition says that he was the father of the twins Romulus and Remus, founders of Rome.

In ancient times Mars was the god of fertility and vegetation, also presiding over the fertility of cattle. Later Mars also became the god of war. The woodpecker, horse, and wolf were sacred to him. It was a she-wolf who suckled Romulus and Remus. His sacred plants were the dogwood, laurel, fig, oak, and bean.

The Romans celebrated Mars' most-important festivals in spring. This reinforced his status as god of agriculture and fertility. Only later were these attributes passed on to the goddess Ceres, while Mars became mainly the god of war, battle, and conquest. Before every military expedition and combat sacrifices were offered to him. In battle he was said to be seen accompanied by the two warrior goddesses Bellona and Vacuna, by Pavor and Pallor to terrify the enemy, by Honos and Virtus who filled the Romans with honor and courage, and after victory also by Vitula and Victoria.

Already in this relatively short period of history we can see how the archetype of the god of war has evolved from being a crude, ruthless, and rather brainless macho to a more-honorable and protective deity. Mars uses his power in battle to conquer more territory for his people and enable their growth (evolution) and not simply for the pleasure of strife. Have the forces of Mars undergone another transformation through our own human evolution since Roman and Greek times? Meditation on this subject will be well worth your while.

Mars in Astrology

Mars rules the astrological sign of Aries. His natural house is the First House (physical body, self-awareness, and the personality).

His nature is masculine and positive.

The astrological symbol of Mars is a circle with an arrow extending outward to the upper right. It signifies spirit expanding into matter as well as the self expanding outward and upward along the line of evolution.

Basic key words describing the influence of Mars are courage, initiative, energy, desire, activity, originality, power, virility, passion, and determination.

Negative attributes of Mars are arrogance, impatience, selfishness, impulsiveness, aggression, and cruelty.

The basic function of this planet in your astrological chart is to propel your personality to action. Mars will provide the courage necessary to remove obstacles on your path and to find new ways of self-expression.

Mars in astrology is called the "lesser malefic" (after Saturn, the "greater malefic") because his influence often brings disruption. However, life must flow; it cannot remain static. If we foolishly believe that life can be frozen in time to make it safe and predictable, we will soon be going backward and against the current. The more open we are to change and to the natural flow of evolution, the less friction we will encounter in our daily lives. We should learn to take advantage of the tremendous energy of Mars and use it for our own goals, instead of waiting for Mars to push us forward more or less violently.

In the physical body Mars rules over vigor and vitality, muscular energy, the red blood cells, and the iron they contain (which gives blood its color), the adrenal glands, irritation, inflammation, and fever.

Mars also rules over the male gender, the military, iron, steel (especially machinery and tools made from these metals), weapons, sharp instruments, heat, and wounds. His color is red; his day is Tuesday.

The situation (house and sign) of Mars in the astrological chart will indicate into what area the individual will channel his/her initiative and energy. Mars is the energy of survival and individuality on all levels, from the most-basic animal-survival instincts to the highest striving of the soul and spirit to express actively its individuality and unique qualities.

Inner Journey To Contact the Archetype

Sit or lie in a comfortable position and begin relaxing by breathing deeply and rhythmically. Now count from ten to zero, allowing your body to relax even more with each count.

Imagine yourself drifting away from your room and slowly landing in a desert. It is before sunrise and you can see thousands of stars overhead. One of them, the one twinkling with a reddish-orange light, you know to be the planet Mars. Since there is no moon tonight, you are able to see into the depths of space. Will mankind ever reach those magnificent bodies of light? You wonder, but in your heart you somehow know it will.

Not a creature is stirring as you walk. The sun rises slowly, and as you look up from the sandy path, you see a large iron door before you. You notice its doorknob has the shape of the symbol of Mars.

You know that you must eventually pass through the door, but are you ready? You pause for a moment to rethink your life. You ask yourself: Do I really want to move on? Do I feel ready to change and grow?

Once you pass through this gate, you enter the influence of Mars, and if you are not yet ready for innovation, you will suffer. It is all right if you wish to remain where you are. You can return at a later date when you feel stronger. Remember though that because life is change, we will all have to pass into the sphere of Mars' influence again and again, that is, if we want to remain alive and grow to our full potential.

Suddenly a feeling of determination overwhelms you; your entire being vibrates with one impulse: "Yes! I want to change! I want to move on and grow! I want to discover new potentials!" You are uncertain as to where this will take you, but are confident change will be for the better.

Now as the large iron door before you opens to your silent command, you walk through. A beautiful winged woman is already waiting for you on the other side. She wears a helmet, Roman tunic, and sandals. In one hand she holds a flaming sword. Even though she seems to be in her early twenties, her entire presence emanates the power of a winner and leader.

She introduces herself as Victoria, one of Mars's companions in victory. As her deep-green eyes rest on yours for a moment, you recognize again that familiar feeling, as if you had met before, as if you were of the same blood. Already this short meeting had a tremendous effect on you. Gone are all your doubts and fears! Now the thrill of adventure and the drive to new conquests has replaced them.

Confident and secure you follow her. The landscape has faded and you find yourself surrounded by a warm reddish mist. She bids you into her chariot and off you fly toward Mars, drawn swiftly by a black and a white stallion.

You fly together for some time; then the planet Mars appears in the distance. The sky is clear now and the warm sun shines on the chariot and armor of Victoria, making all gleam like gold.

Softly you land on Mars. The surroundings resemble a desert, but much different from any desert you have known on earth. As you follow your beautiful guide, you notice the sand is reddish in color as are the huge rocks that line the path. The sun is high in the sky now and very hot. All is dry and rocky; water is nowhere to be seen. On some of the rocks you observe huge lizards warming their scaly bodies in the noonday sun. Some of them slither away swiftly as you pass; others remain still.

Victoria points to a lizard that is just about to swallow a smaller individual of its same kind. "This is a symbol of how Martial energies are used on their most-primitive reptilian level—for survival of the strongest," she explains calmly. She further insists: "It is cruel, yes, but as much a part of creation as you and me. Without this energy, you would never have grown into the sensitive and refined individual you are now. At this point in human evolution you can choose how to use these survival instincts. " She walks on, untouched by the distress of the dying animal.

As you continue on your path, the rocks give way to a great plain. Here you see thousands of warriors from all epochs of history training for battle. Some of them wear familiar attires from the past, such as those worn by Greek and Roman soldiers, by Viking warriors, by Native American Indians, and many more. As you walk on, contemporary soldiers are added to these, all training in military discipline. The air is hot and dry, charged with the energy of masculine activity, heavy with the anticipation of battle.

In the center of the great plain a huge volcanic rock towers up before you. A narrow path leads straight up its steep slope. Victoria, oblivious to the dangers, sets a firm foot on the precipitous trail. You must follow now since there is no turning back at this point. Besides, you need to quench your thirst, since there is no water on the plains .

As you reach the top you are overwhelmed and awestruck. Before you, in the shade of a silken tent, stands Ares, the god of war himself, surrounded by his best warriors and most-faithful friends. You are speechless; for a moment all is motionless, except for the warm desert breeze that plays joyfully with the tent's fabric, making its fiery color billow like flames in the wind.

He breaks the silence with a warm welcome and a charming smile. He is truly the most-handsome man you have ever seen. Now you understand why Aphrodite fell in love with him! Tall, with broad, muscular shoulders and narrow hips, thick black hair, and irresistible brown eyes, he is the countenance of power, valor, and righteousness—the very incarnation of the masculine ideal.

To your surprise Ares is not as terrible as you thought. On the contrary, you feel incredibly attracted to him, safe, and guarded by his aura of power. You realize that his energy is only terrible if misunderstood and used for selfish purposes. He, as you, is also subordinated to Divine Cosmic Will and Power. In truth, he is only the great officer of the Divine

Forces of evolution. You understand now that if you learn to approach him with the correct attitude, he will become your greatest ally, helping and protecting you always.

You reciprocate his salute and take a seat before him, absorbing the powerful emanation of his presence. Now looking straight into his eyes you tell him the reason for your visit and ask for his help.

Remain in silence for awhile, feeling the interchange of energy and information. Even if you do not feel a definite telepathic contact or message at this moment, the rapport will have been established. You will perceive the effect in your life sooner or later.

Still looking him in the eyes, you are filled with the desire to be like him, to overcome all obstacles in your life, to be a winner for the good! Tell him that you wish to be like him, to absorb his essence! Inflame yourself with the desire to be him! As you feel your desire burning in you, you watch how his figure slowly turns into a luminous orange-red gas and enters your body at the heart area. In you it expands and augments, filling you entirely with the attributes of the god. You are now invincible, strong and powerful, courageous and heroic! No obstacle is too big for you, no task too great.

Feel the ecstasy of the Divine Power of spirit; rejoice in its purity! Then immerse yourself in communion with the archetype as long as you feel comfortable. Decree that you will always subordinate your personal power to Divine Power and Will, and never forget this feeling.

After a few minutes of being one with Ares, you allow him to depart again. You see how the luminous gas contracts and leaves your body at the heart center. It builds up in front of you into the god's shape. You thank him and say farewell with a warm embrace. But now you are not the same person anymore; you have changed. Ares has activated something in you that had been dormant for ages, but is now yours to use.

Victoria takes you by the hand and you walk back down the hill and through the plains. The warriors interrupt their practices to congratulate you as you pass. You see their cheerful faces and rejoice. They are more numerous now, and among them are the heroes of all the ages: Hercules, Aeneas, Siegfried, King Arthur, El Cid, and many more. You feel honored by their presence, but in some strange way you also feel that you belong with them.

As you round the rocks where the lizards rested, you see a male mounting a female. Victoria passes them with a smile.

Soon you are in the chariot heading back for earth. As you approach our planet, you are filled with Spiritual Will and Power, eager to share this love and all you have learned about Mars with your fellow human beings on earth. Before you know it, you are back at the iron gate. You must say farewell to your dear companion, knowing that soon you will meet again. Parting is not so difficult anymore because you are changed, are stronger and more confident. You know that part of Victoria and Ares will always remain with you.

As you pass through the iron door alone, it closes behind you. The landscape and the desert slowly fade away. Gradually you regain your normal waking consciousness.

Victim and Victor

A great many problems we experience in our lives today are due to victim patterns. We have given away our personal power and authority over our lives to other people, institutions, and outside circumstances. We are quick to project the blame for our problems and shortcomings on our environment. We make everything and everyone else responsible for our predicament, then wonder why we feel like powerless victims.

Victims never act on their environment; they are acted upon. They cannot make changes or influence anything because they are powerless and at the mercy of other people, of destiny, or of "luck."

A victim will never live up to his/her full human potential because his/her happiness depends on the generosity of others. To what are you a victim? What holds you back in your growth and fulfillment? Some common excuses include: "I am stuck in my life, and it is the fault of my parents, a difficult childhood, my physical body (that is, I'm too fat/ugly/short/weak), the wrong job, my boss, my doctor, my husband, wife, partner, children, education, the country I live in, the lack of money, the IRS," and so forth.

Consider this. To use the energy of Mars effectively you must be willing to move on and away from your victim patterns, to stop being a loser and become a winner in every aspect of your life. This you do by first assuming responsibility for your entire life as it is now, with the good and the bad, accusing neither anyone else nor blaming anything for your present situation. Retract the blame and victimization you have projected onto outside circumstances. Recognize that the conditions of your present life are entirely of your own making and understand that they have a purpose. What exactly that purpose is, only you may decipher.

Mars will help you step beyond your victim patterns into those of victor, at least for a time until you become truly able to transcend them both, and ultimately resolve them on a higher level. Mars's influence alone will not suffice to elevate you entirely above the victim/oppressor dynamic should this be present in your life. True liberation from that pattern can only be achieved by balancing and integrating the two opposite poles of Mars and Venus on a higher level. Greek mythology exemplifies this integration by Ares and Aphrodite parenting a beautiful daughter they named "Harmonia."

You might ask: "Will this transformation make me cruel and ruthless, victimizing anyone else?" No! There is infinite power and good in the universe, more than enough for everyone. It is not the fault of the universe if we cut ourselves off from its eternal supply by our own erroneous belief system. Let's change it now! Believe me, we can be true winners without ever trampling on or victimizing anyone else.

If everyone were to change their limited beliefs simultaneously, an enormous amount of light and good would be attracted toward our planet, raising the quality of all life. On the contrary, our limited thoughts and attitudes keep us victims and losers and bind us to the mass beliefs of a negative society.

Magical Use of Mars

Preliminaries for the magical use of Mars's energy involve the following considerations:

• Be certain what you want is also part of the Divine Plan and that your practice is not aimed at any one person. Focus on abstract principles rather than on little details or specific individuals when removing obstacles. You are working with very powerful Universal Forces here, and you will reap the fruits of your actions, so think carefully before you act.

• Take responsibility beforehand for all changes the desired result will bring into your life and that of others.

• Open yourself without fear to the forces of change. Be ready and willing to stop being what you are; detach yourself from past events or future outcome.

• Feel Divine Power as you work.

Magical Practice To Burn Away Victim Patterns

This practice will show you how to become aware of your victim patterns. By allowing Mars to overshadow you and burn away the victim patterns, you will replace them with those of a winner. To accomplish this, proceed in the following manner:

1. Take a pen and notebook. Sit in a comfortable position and relax by breathing deeply and rhythmically.

2. Attune yourself with Divine Will as manifested through the energy of Mars. State firmly that you want to know more about yourself and are willing to change.

3. Visualize Mars's astrological symbol as shown at the beginning of this chapter. Build it up with your inner vision until it is large enough to envelop you completely, creating an energetic bond with the power of Mars.

4. Meditate on your life for twenty minutes. Discover all areas in your life where you feel stuck and would like to move on. It doesn't matter if you do not know how to change them yet, the important thing is that you should become aware of them and be willing to change.

If you have trouble finding the stagnant areas, go through your life backwards, visualizing it before you like a movie. You will soon stumble on some uncomfortable event. This is probably an area of friction that needs to be looked at more closely. For example, you could have come to the conclusion that you are a victim of your parents' values and judgments in this way: "I cannot get a job because I am not good enough, or I'm too stupid, or too lazy. But why do I think this? Because I have been told so! By whom? By my parents. " Another common one is: "I have to be nice to everyone and let people walk all over me because spiritual people are always supposed to be nice. Therefore, I am a victim of the spiritual path." Have you ever questioned this attitude and its usefulness in your life? Have you ever thought about that important aspect of God called Divine Justice? Have you reflected upon the lives of the famous knights of history who were also deeply spiritual?

5. Make yourself aware that all victim patterns are rooted in distorted beliefs. Beliefs are thoughts, and thoughts can be changed. You now have the power to become aware of the negative patterns and change them. You have freedom of choice.

6. Do this meditation for five days in a row. After each session make a detailed record of what you want to change in yourself. Rest for two days before you go on to the second part of the practice.

7. On the eighth day prepare a fireproof plate or bowl and a white candle. Light the candle and center yourself on your purpose to become a winner. On this day you do not need to meditate prior to the practice, although you may do so if you wish.

8. Proceed to make a clear and precise list of all the areas in which you feel powerless and victimized. Make another list stating the opposite, that is, what you want to be instead of what you are now, for example: "I am the master of my own life and I free myself of other people's judgment" or "I am a winner on the spiritual path and I have the courage and power to stand up for my own rights," and so forth.

9. Draw the astrological symbol of Mars on the list of victim patterns, preferably with a red marker and covering the entire paper.

10. Stand up and place the list of victim patterns on the floor before you.

11. Now allow Mars to overshadow you in the following way: Build up with your inner vision the image of the great warrior-god standing behind you; make his body about seven-feet high. Feel his great power and aura extending far beyond his body's limits into outer space. Concentrate on your love and admiration for Mars, as well as on your gratitude to him for helping you in this matter. Now allow him to step as close as possible behind you and concentrate on the overshadowing effect of his aura on yours. Still focused on your love for Mars, allow him to empower you by blending his great aura with your smaller one. Feel how both your energy fields are strengthened and vitalized by the contact. Feel your aura grow in size and power to coincide with that of the god. Remain this way for awhile before your proceed to the next step.

12. Focus on the tremendous buildup of power and Divine Will for a moment, then extend your hands over the list with the victim patterns. Visualize a lightning flash of Martial energy pouring out of your hands and hitting the paper. See with your mind's eye the list and all the patterns it represents exploding into nothingness. Remember that the lightning flash of energy you are blasting on the list is Divine Will of pure spirit.

13. Light the victim list in the fire of the candle and let it burn completely in the fireproof bowl.

14. Now, still standing in communion with Mars, feel how his power and yours are one, how Divine Will pervades your entire being.

Acknowledge the new control over the circumstances of your life that pulsates through your veins! Become one with the Divine Will of your spirit. Decree your willingness to change and be a winner in all areas of your life.

15. Read aloud, if possible, the statements of your winner list. Fill yourself with the burning desire to materialize these assertions in your life, then feel how Mars's energy implants these new qualities firmly in your being. Remain in silence for some time.

16. Then allow Mars to depart by having him step back and slowly but thoroughly disengae your aura from his. Thank Mars for his help, express your love to him, then dissolve his form completely.

17. Relax again and slowly return to normal consciousness.

18. Keep the winner list with you and look at it whenever you have a quiet moment. Change and improve it as needed.

JUPITER

JUPITER

Attunement with the Archetypal Power of Jupiter

Jupiter's energy is happy, abundant, fertilizing, expansive, and wise. His power allows a high, broad perspective on life, showing us our special place in the Cosmic Scheme. We see where we want to go and what steps need to be taken to get there successfully. We realize that we are the progenitors of our own universe, that we can achieve almost anything as long as it is in line with our Divine Self, serving our highest good, and that of others. We merge more and more with our Divine creative power and learn to apply it wisely and actively in the physical world.

With Jupiter's help we see that the universe is already infinitely abundant, that the essence of most things and qualities we desire are already within our grasp. We must make only the correct mental shift to recognize them and understand that we deserve them. By this, Jupiter teaches us a lesson in loving ourselves. Our self-love is the channel through which the universe provides us with what we long for. If we don't love ourselves enough to grant us what we want when the opportunity arises, then nobody else will.

Jupiter's wisdom brings us the clarity necessary to manifest abundance. We learn to discern between those qualities and things essential to our highest good and those which would only be a burden if they were to appear. Jupiter enables us to rise above the short-sightedness of immediate and often conflicting desires; he helps us plot out a big scheme for our life that brings joy and fulfillment, satisfaction and bliss. It's obvious that we cannot achieve satisfying results in manifesting abundance while we hold a blurred picture or vague impression of what we want.

Once we know what we truly want, we must desire it with all our heart in order to manifest it. And Jupiter, with his characteristic enthusiasm, joy, and love of life, provides us with the necessary emotional fuel to do just that.

Our new life plan under Jupiter's influence—based on spiritual love, wisdom, understanding, and aligned with Divine Will—allows us to savor every bit and enjoy each new step along our journey. Jupiter is said to rule over long journeys, but the journey to find our Inner Godhead is the longest and most beautiful of them all.

The God Zeus/Jupiter in Mythology

Zeus was the son of Cronus and Rhea. It is said that Cronus swallowed all his children at birth, but when it came to Zeus, his wife gave him a stone wrapped in swaddling clothes. This he ate, mistaking it for his son. Young Zeus, to escape this terrible fate, hid in the forests of Ida where he grew strong, nursed by the legendary goat Amaltheia.

In the early days Zeus was the god of the heavens and all atmospheric phenomena such as storms, thunder, lightning, clouds, and rain. He was said to live in the ether and on high mountain tops, especially Mount Olympus. Later Zeus became more of a moral god, taking on a sovereign and all-mighty personality. He became the supreme god and father figure, incorporating in himself all attributes of divinity.

Zeus was said to see and know everything; therefore, he was considered to be the supreme source of all divination. Dodona was his most celebrated oracle and sanctuary where people came from all over the country to consult his sacred oak tree. This famous oak was said to impart his very words when it whispered and murmured in the wind.

Zeus was married to his sister, the goddess Hera. Zeus, however, was not renowned for the tranquility of his domestic life with Hera, but rather for his frequent escapades into the arms of various goddesses and mortal women. By them he fathered countless children who became gods, heroes, kings, and famous mortals.

One of the most-important functions of Zeus as an All-Father figure was that of procreation. Before he married his sister Hera he was married to several other goddesses. His first wife was Metis (Wisdom), whom he swallowed as she was about to give birth to Athena, goddess of Wisdom. His next wife was Themis, who was considered to be the Law, both in a physical and a moral sense. Together they produced the Horae or Seasons, as well as the Morae or Fates. With Mnemosyne he had nine daughters known as the Muses. By Demeter he fathered Kore, or Persephone as she was later called. With Eurynome he begat the Three Graces.

From these accounts we can see clearly the two most-important attributes associated with the archetype of Zeus, namely, his function (1) as All-Father or cosmic fertilizer of the feminine and receptive principle in the traditional sense, and (2) his function as begetter and bringer of growth, abundance, and all cnnsidered "good" in the world of gods and men, as well as his role as wise, just ruler. It is significant to realize, moreover, that Zeus expresses those qualities best when working in polarity with the feminine principle.

Hera's notorious rages and retaliations as she learned of her spouse's love affairs may be interpreted as the growth-and-expansion-controlling forces in ourselves represented by our assimilation of establishment values.

The symbols of Zeus were the scepter, the eagle, and, of course, the thunder and deadly lightning bolts.

Jupiter in Astrology

Jupiter rules the astrological sign Sagittarius and is co-ruler of Pisces. He is associated with the Ninth House (the higher mind and cultural perspective, religion, philosophy, law, and long physical or mental journeys) as well as with the Twelfth House (Karma, confinement, unity with humanity and God).

His nature is masculine and positive.

His astrological symbol is an equally armed cross with a crescent set on its left arm, facing outward, as seen at the beginning of this chapter.

Basic key words describing the influence of Jupiter are expansion, growth, abundance, opulence, breadth of experience, and wisdom through understanding, opportunity, enthusiasm, optimism, learning, social consciousness (philosophical, ethical, and moral), wise rulership and leadership qualities, tolerance, and cultural integration as opposed to submission. Furthermore, Jupiter is related to banking and financial dealing with far countries as well as to higher education.

The negative attributes of Jupiter are opportunism, excess, arrogance, bigotry, wastefulness, indulgence, fanaticism, gluttony, pride, opinionatedness, and sloppiness.

The basic function of this planet in your astrological chart is to stimulate growth and expansion on all levels of your personality. Traditionally, Jupiter was considered the bringer of success, achievement, and good luck. However, if you want to make the best use of Jupiter's energy, you must focus it on the specific areas you wish to expand. If you let it run through you unchecked, it will enlarge the areas of least resistance, which are not necessarily the ones you want expanded.

Expansion and growth of your own sphere of influence are important, but if you expand indiscriminately, your personal universe might suddenly become too big to handle and burst like an over-inflated balloon. To prevent this rupture and consequent loss of power, you are given the limiting and concentrating influence of Saturn. Using Saturn's energy wisely, you will achieve integration of both energies. This polarity is, like all others we have and will encounter during our studies, part of the basic rhythm of manifestation, i. e., one pole being as necessary for true evolution as its opposite.

If you are constantly struggling to lose weight, remember: Jupiterian energy tends towards continuous expansion. If you do not make room for inner growth, it will most probably start to expand your physical body, making you gain weight.

In the physical body Jupiter rules over the liver, glycogen production, pancreas, insulin, hips, thighs, cell growth, and tumors.

Jupiter also presides over legal affairs, government, kings, the benevolent father figure, foreign affairs, long-distance travel, books, printing, and publishing.

The day of Jupiter is Thursday and his metal is tin.

Inner Journey To Contact the Archetype

Sit or lie in a comfortable position and begin relaxing by breathing deeply and rhythmically. Now count from ten to zero, allowing your body to relax even more with each count.

Imagine that you are walking along a country road. The air is hot and humid, it is the middle of summer. The early afternoon sky is overcast and a breeze is stirring. Big dark clouds gather quickly above your head heralding a thunderstorm. You feel happy about the coming rain, since the land has been afflicted by a long drought.

Just as the first lightning strikes the earth beside you and the rain begins suddenly with one big downpour, you see a tall grey gate in front of you.

Its doorknob is shaped in the symbol of Jupiter, and as you come closer you notice it is made of tin.

Before you pass through it, you mentally review the reason for your journey. It is true growth and expansion you seek, growth aligned with Divine Will. You remember also that growth and expansion call for responsibility. As you affirm this, the gate opens silently and you pass through it.

On the other side the view is entirely different. The sky is clear and blue. You find yourself at the top of a high mountain looking down over the land. Only now do you realize how long you have been wandering on that windy road in the valley of your own being. It is time to leave it and climb the heights of your own potential! You have learned enough in theory; practical application is what is needed now!

You feel confident in your ability to handle your own growth, and from this mountaintop you have a better perspective of your life and evolution. You not only can see what is available, but also what potentials wait to be developed. Overwhelmed by the wonder of it all, you sense a new, surging power over your own life and destiny. Now you can clearly see the intensity and beauty of the grand scheme you have set yourself to fulfill in this lifetime.

Sit there for awhile overlooking the land. It is your own land, your inner land with all its inhabitants and resources. You can see the little path in the valley far away, where you were walking just a minute ago... it is drenched in rain now. As you reflect on this you are filled with the same joy that overwhelms the little plants growing on the wayside as they happily absorb the life-giving summer rain.

After some time you realize you are not alone. A beautiful woman is sitting next to you, ever so quietly and gently. At first you do not understand what she is doing alone on this mountain peak, but then you remember your journey and immediately associate her with Zeus.

Her skin is fair, her hair blonde and styled elaborately in the Greek fashion. Her voice is soft and friendly as she speaks:

"I am Hera. I have come here to show you the way to my husband. Before we leave this mountain peak, I would like to ask you: Do you know me? Do you know what I stand for? Do you know my importance and my place in the Great Dance of Creation?" She pauses for a few minutes and then proceeds: "In these modern and fast-moving days, people seem to have lost the meaning of my role. I am the divine wife; I am the nurturing background from which Zeus derives his identity and power. I am the solid ground beneath his feet that carries him faithfully."

"Because I am so steady and dependable, so predictable and solid, people have called me 'the establishment.' Whenever my husband's infinite power of growth and expansion encounters a restriction, I am always blamed. It is my bitter jealousy, they say, that hinders him in his growth and curtails his joy. But you, dear traveler of the soul, must know better."

"Then would it not be wise to preserve and organize what has been incorporated and achieved? Wouldn't the all-fertilizing power of gods and men alike disperse itself in boundless expansion without a stable center? I am the mirror in which Zeus sees his reflection, and through me he achieves integration. It is on my breast that Zeus replenishes himself again before he sets out to dispense the 'golden rain' to the world. I have been much feared and misunderstood, but this matters not, for my role is behind the scenes. "

Now she takes you by the hand, and together you soar high into the sky toward the planet Jupiter. Soon you see the earth beneath you like a small and beautiful ball suspended in space. You can almost see the invisible lines of gravity's force that hold her securely in her orbit. As you look ahead toward Jupiter, you clearly recognize its massive size and famous red spot. Still holding onto Hera's hand, you land gently on the planet's surface.

You find yourself in the center of a large square in a beautiful town. The place is crowded with happy and joyful people going about their work in peace. The wide streets are flanked with tall and luxurious buildings, opulence and magnificence permeating the air. Before you rises a beautiful temple, its entrance supported by rows of white marble columns. Your eyes follow the marble stairs up to the dais, and there you see the great ruler sitting on his throne.

As you approach you feel somewhat nervous. You have heard so much about this sovereign, but never really felt his power closely, nor asked your requests directly. Hera leaves you standing to join her husband, seating herself to his right on the empty throne beside him.

You walk a few steps and then kneel before the king. He comes toward you and bids you stand up, welcoming you with a warm embrace. His warmth and power run through you like a lightning flash, setting your soul ablaze. You shiver with joy and anticipation of the new turn your life will take through this encounter.

Zeus is a tall and handsome man of about forty years. His body is muscular but graceful; his face presents a most-winsome combination of power, love, and mercy. The gaze in his dark-brown eyes is an expression of pure wisdom. His hair is curly and cascades down to his shoulders in long black locks, framing his beautiful face just perfectly. Zeus radiates a peculiar warmth and acceptance that feeds and fertilizes your very soul, that brings life and reassurance to your deepest longings. It feels as if you have never before been so deeply touched by such a masculine figure.

Zeus, still holding you by the shoulders like a loving father, nods reassuringly as you make your request. You speak: "Oh Zeus, king of the gods! I have come here to ask for your help. Let me realize my own potential; let me grow and expand beyond the limitations I have set for myself through the ignorance of my little human mind. Let me understand that there is abundance for all in the universe, that true abundance, true opulence is now to be found already within my own spirit. Oh, Divine Father of the gods! Open my eyes that I may see my destiny! Guide me on my path of inner growth, and help me overcome all those limiting beliefs I am struggling so diligently to break. Grant me thy wisdom so that I may learn to funnel this sacred energy of yours into the right channels and bring abundance and joy to all. Forgive me, oh Zeus, for often I have contacted you unknowingly and wasted your precious power. Come to me now and become a part of me so that I may never lose you again!"

As you speak, you notice how your surroundings—the buildings, the street, the entire town—turn into a blue luminous gas. Finally, the king and queen become part of this gas, too, which pulsates with the sheer joy and bliss of abundance. The gas becomes thicker and heavier, gathering around you like clouds in a storm. Slowly they form a huge funnel that points to your heart center.

You are overwhelmed by the intense feeling of this ethereal mist; it is pure life force in movement. You love it so much, you adore it! Where has this divine fertility been all these years? Where had you lost this joy of living, this feeling of eternal universal abundance? You cannot be separated from this wonderful energy any longer and surrender, throwing your heart chakra wide open with one big burst, allowing the power of Jupiter to enter.

The gas enters and expands like a hurricane, impregnating every atom of your being. You almost lose consciousness for a moment, but you do not care. You feel safe in the midst of this turmoil. Before you know it, you are being stretched and stretched farther and farther beyond the limits of your perceptions, toward the outer realms of the universe. You become all-conscious and realize that you are already all. You understand that all those things which you wish to achieve, accomplish, feel, and experience are already within you, part of you, for you are at this level one with the universe.

You remain in silence for awhile, internalizing these feelings and realizations. Never again will you lose this wide perspective, never again will you let your short-sighted beliefs limit and condition you, no matter how fine they appear in the eyes of logic.

After submerging yourself in this bliss and fulfillment as long as it feels comfortable, ask Zeus to give you a personal message. Allow about thirty seconds for this. If you do not get anything, don't worry. You may receive it at a later date when you have become more adept at "seeing" with your inner sight and/or hearing with your inner ear.

You thank the god and goddess and let them depart through your heart chakra. The gas exits slowly and solidifies into forms again.

Allow a few minutes to regain your inner balance, then before you leave ask the god to show you the area of your life which needs his energy the most. Don't worry if you do not receive anything consciously at this moment; it may occur to you later.

Now the time has come to say farewell. Hera is already standing beside you to lead you home. You approach Zeus and give him a warm embrace, thanking him again. He feels even more sympathetic and familiar now. The breadth of his bare chest against your body and the corded muscles of his strong arms as he holds you convey a most-comforting warmth to your soul.

Although sadness overcomes you when you realize you must leave, you immediately compose yourself and remember that a part of Zeus will always remain with you. Silently you take Hera's outstretched hand and, led by the goddess, you fly back to earth. You land before the tin gate that stands ajar.

Now you say goodbye to the goddess and thank her once again. Feeling safe and protected, you pass through the gate alone and close it behind you. You have gained a new certainty and confidence that the universe will always provide you with what you need. As the road and landscape slowly fade away, you gradually regain normal consciousness.

Jupiter and Abundance

The first thing that comes to one's mind is that abundance is to "have a lot of everything. " Stop for a moment and reconsider this notion.

To have a lot of everything is not true abundance. First, true abundance signifies that you have everything you need the moment you need it and abundantly. It does not mean that you have great quantities of things you do not need. Second, true abundance means that there is an endless supply of things you enjoy available to you and that you must never fear its depletion. Third, you will probably realize that true abundance is only meaningful if it comes with positive and agreeable emotions such as joy, happiness, love, bliss, peace, and harmony, namely, if it promotes your higher good and that of others.

If you keep following your thoughts this way, you will soon realize that emotional abundance is even more important and satisfying. From there it will only take a small step to understand that we basically appreciate abundance most when it comes on all four levels of expression, where physical abundance is an expression of the three higher levels of abundance, i. e. , spiritual, mental, and emotional.

Now most of us have been conditioned to believe that the universe is limited and there is not enough to go around. We have been taught to ignore the powers of the creative spirit and mind and be content, or even happy, with what we have. After all, we are told that there are always some even less fortunate than we, such as the starving children in India.

The same creative potential which could be used to bring abundance for everyone on all levels is the very cause of our limited present condition. Many of us have unknowingly been using our creative potential to build around ourselves almost exactly the same limited environment that restricted our parents and grandparents, and have even come to believe that this is the norm.

We must become more aware of our potential to create our environment—abundance or scarcity—according to our beliefs. If we dare not stretch our view of the possible and feasible beyond our present limitations, how will we ever transcend our forefathers?

To manifest this abundance in your life which you so deeply seek, you must realize, once and for all, that you and only you are the designer of your own life, your environment, and all that is related to it. You must own your life and take responsibility for it before you can change it. Realize that all you see around you at this moment, including your physical body, is your own conscious and subconscious creation, and that if you had the power to manifest all this, you must also have the power to change and improve it!

It is of vital importance to realize that your beliefs create the reality in which you live. You are constantly creating and influencing your destiny through your conscious and unconscious beliefs. If you believe that the universe offers an endless supply of riches from which you can draw at any time, then this belief will strongly condition your environment to manifest itself physically around you as abundance. This abundance will, in turn, confirm your belief about an abundant universe, reinforcing it more and more.

Sadly, the same mechanism that reflects your positive beliefs to you through your environment, also reflects your limiting beliefs. Ignorance of this fact is the cause of much suffering in the world today. An example of the effects of deeply ingrained negative and limiting beliefs can be easily observed in people who were raised in times of economic depression, crises, or war. These persons were conditioned to believe from their early childhoods that life is a struggle, food scarce, and money difficult to obtain.

They will grow up with the subliminal message that whatever money, abundance, or wealth they manage to create will soon be taken away by some higher uncontrollable force. Some of them will live in constant fear of losing what they have and cling jealously to whatever riches they have managed to accumulate. Others will switch to the opposite attitude of "Why bother? It's useless anyway," not out of true conviction, but from hidden fear of failure. We can also recognize the origin of envy and jealousy insofar as it seems much easier to try to take whatever our neighbor has managed to acquire and drag him/her down to one's own misery than to face one's inner fear of failure and create a better life for oneself—regardless of what everyone else is preaching and believing.

I was born and raised in Europe. Although World War II is now half a century away, its memories are still deeply ingrained in the minds and beliefs of older and middle-aged people. Most of them, however, are not conscious of it, and many live in constant subliminal fear of a Third World War and/or political regime coming to take away all they have worked so diligently to build.

This underlying belief keeps them from relaxing and truly enjoying the money they earn. Many of those who have made large sums of money after the war have done so out of fear rather than pleasure, that is, to cover the insecurity so deeply imbedded in their consciousness.

It is even more remarkable that many of those who didn't endure any scarcity personally, yet have formed beliefs which conditioned the rest of their lives by only hearing about others miseries from their parents, friends, and relatives.

One good example would be of a person growing up in the slums of a big city such as New York, Mexico City, or Hong Kong. Imagine how difficult it would be for such a person to rise above the limiting beliefs of his/her early childhood environment. If the child grows up hearing constant complaints about ill health, food scarcity, unpaid bills, violence, and criminality, its sense that the world is a place full of misery would, indeed, be very difficult to change. Few could successfully transcend such conditioning. Later in life this person might unknowingly reproduce for himself/herself an environment reflecting this unfortunate inheritance: a miserable and unfair world.

Among these limiting beliefs, the feeling of unworthiness is one of the most difficult to identify and eradicate, but also, alas, one of the most common to occur. It is often formed in early childhood when the child internalizes criticism and punishment to an exaggerated degree, not understanding the full context of the situation. The child grows up feeling unloved, dirty, bad, and, therefore, unworthy. Later in life this person will unknowingly sabotage any chances to succeed because deep within s/he will believe himself/herself to be unworthy of success, happiness, and abundance.

These beliefs, formed in the past, as any other limiting beliefs, do not end with the persons concerned, but are passed on from generation to generation down to the present and into the minds of our own little children. This is dangerous largely because it is so subtle, often masquerading as "old truths," or even worse, as pseudo-spiritual truths. We must all become responsible for this negative and limiting conditioning and stop it.

It is extremely important that we become aware of the effects of our beliefs, for not only is our personal destiny affected by them, but also our collective karma! Imagine how wonderful our world would be if every single person would reflect only positive beliefs onto the environment!

Magical Use of Jupiter

Preliminaries for the magical use of Jupiter's energy involve the following considerations:

• Open yourself without fear to the forces of change; be ready and willing to grow and mature in all aspects of your life.

• Be certain what you want is for your own higher good and that of others.

• Realize beforehand your responsibility for the new awareness and knowledge these exercises will bring and commit yourself to using it for the good of all.

• Let Divine Love and the desire to create a more-abundant and fulfilling universe for all pervade your work.

The main focus of Jupiter's power in the following magical application will be to create abundance on all levels of being.

Before you decide to materialize something general such as money, or something more specific such as a new car, a bigger house, or a better job, you must identify the essence of what this object should satisfy in your life. This is very important; if you fail to recognize the basis of your need, then, even though you might succeed at materializing the item in your life, it will not satisfy you because it fails to fulfill your underlying need.

Most things you desire are mere symbols of a deeper need that remains unrecognized. To define the essence or abstract quality of what you want, imagine the item or accomplishment that would make you feel more abundant. Then concentrate on the feelings and experiences you want these things to give you. Is it more freedom, more comfort, more adventure, a sense of aliveness? Is it a feeling of being loved? More security?

You might think that in order to feel more abundant you might want a bigger house. Now what is the essence of this need? Do you want to have more-personal space, more space for friends or children, do you want to express yourself through a different style house or change of location? Is the desire for a bigger house merely symbolic of a new image you want to create? Do you feel confined by your present lifestyle or attitude? Or do you want to show off to friends because you are not able to show your true colors and want a bigger house to do this for you?

Trace all those things you want as far back as possible to your most-abstract need(s). It is much more effective to work directly on these abstractions. For example, many people want more money because they want to accumulate enough to enable them to work fewer hours and spend more free time pursuing their hobbies. So they concentrate on working harder to earn more. Instead of fulfilling their basic need for free time, they are creating the opposite—more work. They might earn more money, but they have less and less time to enjoy the activities more money should have given them.

If free time to pursue more-fulfilling activities is the essence of what these people want, no amount of money in the world will ever satisfy them. They could start gratifying their true need by working less at jobs they do not enjoy and by taking more time off to do the things they truly like. This, in turn, will attract to them more of the things that promote their highest good; then the universe will respond with more money, better opportunities, and more abundance. These people may not increase their earnings immediately, but in the long run they will feel and become more abundant. This change of attitude takes courage because it does not always follow the familiar line of rational and logic thought, but is based on feeling, mutability, intuition, trust, and faith.

Magical Practice To Reinforce Positive Beliefs

You will recognize with Jupiter's help the negative beliefs keeping you from being more abundant and will learn to replace them with positive beliefs by practicing the following procedures:

1. Choose a time that you will not be interrupted for at least half an hour. Take a notebook and pen. Prepare a fireproof bowl and a box of matches. Fill the bowl halfway with clean water. Sit in a comfortable position and relax by breathing deeply and rhythmically.

2. State firmly that you want to know more about yourself and are willing to change. Express your desire for help in these matters to Jupiter, addressing him as a spiritual being.

3. Visualize Jupiter's astrological symbol as shown at the beginning of this chapter. Build it up with your inner vision until it is large enough to envelop you completely, creating an energetic bond with the power of Jupiter.

4. Make a list of the essential needs you want met to feel more abundant. Make another list of the areas of your life in which you already feel abundant and the objects or persons that have contributed to that feeling. Write them all into your notebook for later reference.

5. Now, to uncover your negative beliefs, trace the needs, the desired objects, qualities, or accomplishments you feel you lack, to disclose the underlying beliefs that have prevented you up to now from fulfilling them. For example, you might not have accumulated enough wealth because deep within you believe that rich people are selfish, bad, or lonely. You might not have enough time for leisure because you subconsciously believe that more free time would be selfish, and that if you had more available time you should devote it to your family and friends instead of to your own pleasure. Be extremely honest with yourself. Even those of us who have been working on ourselves for many years still have limiting beliefs, and as we release them, uncover new ones.

Then proceed to do the same for the things that make you feel abundant, disclosing the positive beliefs that brought them into your life.

To become aware of your beliefs, ask yourself the following question: What would a person have to believe to arrive at the situation in which I now find myself? Answer this as honestly and extensively as possible. Keep the list for later reference.

6. Proceed to eliminate these limiting beliefs with the procedure described below.

7. Look at the list of your negative beliefs.

8. Understand their origin and accept them as part of you at the present time. Acknowledge the fact that you created these beliefs and, therefore, are able to replace them as necessary.

9. Forgive yourself for harboring beliefs you feel are damaging or have limited you in the past.

10. Forgive all those persons who helped create the limiting beliefs and release them from your energy field. Later you might want to talk to them in person if it feels right to do so.

11. From your list of negative beliefs single out three beliefs you want to eliminate first. Write down each of these negative beliefs on a separate clear page of your notebook. Make a quick mental call to Jupiter, invoking his help again. Now tear out each of the three pages with the three negative beliefs and proceed to burn them one by one, holding them over the bowl of water. While you burn each paper, concentrate on the power of Cosmic Fire disintegrating and removing this belief once and for all from your personal universe. Make certain the paper burns as thoroughly as possible, letting the ashes fall into the bowl of clean water. Do not do more than three beliefs per session. Allow several days between sessions, since the changes may bring some disruption; if you change too many too quickly, you might even feel alienated.

12. After each belief you eliminate, find a belief that has had a positive effect on your life and development. Concentrate on this positive belief and expand it in even more detail. For example, if you believe "I deserve to be loved," expand it into "I deserve to have the perfect partner who loves and respects me as I am. " In this manner, set a new, positive, expansive, and fulfilling belief after you burn a negative one. Repeat the positive belief with serious intent several times, and commit yourself to act immediately to fulfill the essence of that belief in one way or another. This essence is always already within reach once you become aware of it. The act of granting yourself this essence will inform the universe you are ready and willing to receive what you ask for and are now taking steps to provide it, even if it is just in small measure. In this case, you would give yourself a present as a magical act that the universe is good, loving, and appreciative, a statement that even if you haven't yet found that loving person, you are now taking charge by providing at least part of that love yourself. You will

be amazed how universal energy will follow the direction of your focused intent!

13. Slowly return to normal consciousness.

Work on reinforcing your positive beliefs as often as you wish, especially on the days between the ritualistic disintegration of negative ones. Seek to connect to Jupiter as a spiritual being as often as possible during this period of reconstruction. He will greatly ease the process.

Magical Practice To Materialize What You Want

Once you have uncovered the essence of what you want and have identified the beliefs limiting your abundance, work with both of these for a minimum of two weeks, Remember: It is essential to know exactly what you really need before calling this to yourself. Then you can proceed to materialize what you want in a spiral motion, drawing it from the realms of your own spirit to the physical world as described below:

1. Sit in a comfortable position and relax by breathing deeply and rhythmically.

2. Express to Jupiter your desire for help in this materialization procedure.

3. Visualize the astrological symbol of Jupiter as shown at the beginning of this chapter. Build it up with your inner vision until it is large enough to envelop you completely, creating an energetic bond with the power of Jupiter.

4. Repeat aloud ten times the positive beliefs you want to condition your new life from now on. Feel how they resonate first in yourself, then spread outward to include the entire universe. Break down any limitation you might encounter with the power of sound and lightning. Hear your creative words reverberate throughout cosmos in an ongoing echo, and feel how these beliefs empower your entire being by demanding their fulfillment.

5. Having identified what you want, concentrate its essence in your heart and merge with it. This can be a new belief about yourself, an accomplishment, an abstract quality, or anything else. Work with only one belief per session for the first two weeks.

6. Expand this essence from your heart center into your aura and beyond, totally permeating yourself, your environment, and the universe.

7. Feel how it deeply affects and changes each cell of your body as it expands throughout. Feel how this essence is absorbed by each molecule of the people and things in your environment. Feel how it transforms them as it passes, making them reflect this essence to you from now on. Imagine the abstract quality of the thing you want, expanding it more and more to include all manifestation with equal strength.

8. Now feel how the essence of what you want is already crystallizing itself very subtly in your aura and environment, ready at your command to bridge the final gap between energy and form.

9. With an effort of your concentrated intent, will this essence to take physical form in your life, then mentally let go of it by returning to normal consciousness and switching your attention to some physical task.

SATURN

SATURN

Attunement with the Archetypal Power of Saturn

Saturn is the Lord of Duality, the polar opposite of the Unfolding Light. Saturn binds manifestation to the level of physical existence by holding it captive between the coordinates of time and space, much like a spider catches a fly in her web. Scary? Maybe.

Saturn is said to be the Lord of Karma, who brings just retribution of our acts on earth. On a higher level this same crystallizing power of Saturn is also what actualizes our soul's purpose here on the physical plane.

Most people have problems recognizing what their soul's purpose really is and fall prey to the mass influence of Saturnine energy. Instead of manifesting their own dreams, people work diligently to actualize what they believe they should according to societal consensus. Expression of their true individuality is limited by other peoples' visions of what they should be doing with their lives. They end up being and doing what everybody else does because it is too difficult and painful to break free. This is why Saturn is mostly experienced at first as an outside restriction, something that one's father, family, society, life, destiny, or karma imposes upon them, limiting growth without mercy.

The uninitiated individual experiences Saturn's influence as "harsh reality," the physical, material, objective world "out there" as opposed to the personal subjective "inner" world of dreams and desires.

At the beginning of our journey through the planes of physical manifestation Saturn's restrictive influence is normal and good because it gives the incoming soul a solid structure in the form of social and tribal customs within which to work. This social structure acts as a healthy grounding and binding influence.

Through the merciless and mathematical retribution of karma Saturn forces us to learn the workings of the material world. Under his influence we eventually discover the laws, rules, and regulations that govern the material plane and become proficient in them.

It is my belief that we not only descend into physical manifestation willingly, but we also submit ourselves to karma willingly. As cruel as Saturn might feel to us when dispensing his just punishment to our wrong actions, we should also remember that he is disciplining us wisely so that we may learn to understand and work with the material world to accomplish our soul's purpose in it. Were it not for Saturn, we would probably never become strong and focused enough to make a permanent change for the better in our environment.

To affect matter and redeem it, we must first learn its language, so to speak. Since Saturn is the Great Teacher, the Initiator of this, whatever hardships or experiences he may present us during our earthly lives, we deliberately planned them from a higher level we might not be aware of presently.

I believe that we came to earth to accomplish something, to redeem and enlighten this place, not simply to float around in happiness and bliss. Generally speaking we all came to clear and organize the energy of the three lower levels of manifestation, that is the physical, emotional, and mental. It is by fulfilling that task that happiness and bliss will ensue. Although, these conditions will appear periodically on the Path as indicators that we have conquered a new platform, they are not, however, our final goals.

Which means, in other words, that we must not only concentrate on our personal pleasure, but also focus on the service we came to provide. Personal pleasure will come as a matter of course as we fulfill our purpose. Bliss and ecstasy are already ours and always have been on the level of our spirit, in which we live simultaneously with our earthly incarnation. We have never really lost it; we simply have forgotten their totalistic relationship.

The density of the level into which we have incarnated is the cause for our forgetting, not our stupidity or sinfulness as some might have us think. If we concentrate on the fact that we already have a happy ending to the fairy tale of our existence in our spirit where we truly live happily ever after, we would stop pitying ourselves for the hardships of our lives and would roll up our sleeves to get to work and clean out this place.

The more we gain awareness and assume responsibility for our personal universe, the more we master our own life by starting to internalize and harness powers that are our heritage, including Saturn. When we assume full responsibility for our lives, Saturn starts to work on our side, providing the crystallizing power that actualizes our soul's purpose.

Yes, here some will cry out that the more we crystallize and solidify our dreams, the more we tie down our potential, and the more we die. Yes, this is also true, but in actualizing our soul's mission we die for our own cause and purpose and the higher good of others, not for other peoples' false ideals born of their fears and limitations. Is the actualization of our soul's purpose not why we incarnated? Were we not born here to accomplish certain tasks, to engrave certain things permanently into the memory of humankind and on the body of Mother Earth? Or are we here merely to intellectualize our purpose and never actually manifest our dreams?

Once we take charge of materializing our soul's mission, Saturn starts to work in our favor. We can learn to use him as an ally to shield our purpose like the womb protects the embryo and the eggshell the unborn chick. Saturn will encircle our aura with a strong etheric bubble to shelter and empower our own purpose and ideal until ready to be actualized.

In his aspect as Father Time Saturn is closely associated with death, cutting down life with his scythe. Yet on other occasions Saturn may work in our favor by allowing events to reach their appropriate point of maturity and effectiveness.

The mythological relationship between Saturn and Santa Claus, the nice old man who rewards faithful and well-behaved children, indicates another dimension of Saturn and his association with the just retribution of karma.

The normal level of Saturnian influence works on and through the mass of humanity, that is, collectively. He acts through the limiting influence of the environment, social conditioning, the limitations of time/space, birth and death, and so forth. Most people, not having dealt with these issues in depth, fear Saturn's influence instead of understanding and harnessing his power to their own benefit.

Once we realize that no restriction is eternal and that we are not our body, emotions, or mind but something so limitless it is almost impossible to grasp, then we come from a point of power beyond fear, old age, and death. We transcend the linear view of death as the end of life; we understand it and Saturn as part of the cosmic cycle, a part as useful and appropriate as birth and growth. Anything less results from the narrow understanding of the rational mind which creates most of our fears and restrictions.

The separateness and limitation we experience when focused on the level of the rational mind is necessary insofar as it serves an important function. Should we be open to all energetic and visual input surrounding us at all times, our brains would be overwhelmed and cease to function properly. The selective influence of the brain or rational mind is good and useful as long as we remain well aware that it does not show us all that goes on in our lives at any given moment.

Our brain knows nothing about our soul and its purpose, about Divine Will and its power. The brain believes that what it perceives through the five senses is the only truth and reality. We, who are gods in the making, know better. We must thank our brain for its advice, but gently lead it toward a more-encompassing perspective.

It is time now to take responsibility for our own universe, karma, and environment. We must dare to use all our potential to its fullest—not only our rational mind. We must learn to harness the powers we gave ourselves at the moment of our birth, including Saturn's energy, and bring about the soul's purpose. It is time to make Saturn our ally and friend.

Of course, even though we can greatly change our subjective feelings and experiences about limitations, illness, aging, and death, we cannot eliminate them completely. This is all right as long as we integrate them into our being by understanding their part in the accomplishment of the soul's purpose.

We must take responsibility for the limitations we encounter in life and exert our Divine Will over them as well as we possibly can. We came to this incarnation knowing that the disagreeable aspects of our lives would be part of the whole experience. Still we chose to incarnate and brave them. So let's now understand their ultimate good or use and see how and what exactly our soul was intending to express through these limitations. Let's make the best of this dualistic world, of its manifest polarity, and understand its great potential and power! Let's learn to pair and marry the bad side of each experience with its good and holy purpose, with its deeper, more-sacred meaning and function!

The energy of Saturn is also reflected in Satan, the Tempter, the Lord of the World, and Sanat Kumara (the planetary spirit), the Ancient of Days. He is waiting our recognition of his power to actualize our soul's purpose. So let's take his offer!

Strangely enough, I personally love Saturn deeply. He is the planet I have most looked forward to writing about. Although I have a Sun/Saturn opposition in my chart, Saturn in Scorpio in my Twelfth House, and both part of a Grand Square, or maybe just because of that, I have come to love Saturn. I have worked my entire life on harmonizing, internalizing, and harnessing the powers of this Sun/Saturn opposition. I have suffered many years of personal restriction and am only now slowly emerging from it. However, I am deeply thankful for having Saturn as my personal teacher.

Consider the great responsibility that Saturn has taken upon himself to be the Great Opposer in this solar system, the thrustblock to evolution. The planets are, as you know, live entities, and so are the Seven Cosmic

Rays which they filter and transmit. Consider also how small the restrictions of your personal life are to such a cosmic task.

Saturn, in his highest form is often depicted as the Wise Old Man. The legendary Mexican shaman Don Juan advised his pupil, Carlos Castaneda, to use death as a teacher, and this is directly related to this highest aspect of Saturn. Don Juan taught Carlos to ask himself before starting something: "If I would die tomorrow, would I still do this today?' or, "If I would die tomorrow, what would I do today?" This is an excellent way to check whether what you are planning to do is really part of consummating your soul's purpose or if it is merely something resulting from mass conditioning and belief. Surely, if you had only one more day to live, would you not use it to come as close as possible to manifesting your soul's intention for this incarnation?

Saturn awaits our command to actualize our soul's purpose. He provides the molecular essence of physicality to crystallize our dreams in time and space.

Saturn also brings discrimination. He helps us patiently and carefully to weigh each situation before deciding what to actualize. Saturn provides the limitations that make the experience of our immediate life and environment real.

In the world of Saturn two things cannot occupy the same space at the same time and that defines physicality for most of us. This realization—with the help of logic and rationality built up and encoded in the human brain over generations through the process of trial and error, discrimination, and elimination—is deeply ingrained in our waking consciousness.

However, if we become trapped in Saturn's influence exclusively, then we enter those mental prisons where we become extremely critical and judgmental perfectionists, never seeing anything good in ourselves, others, or our environment, perhaps even falling into deep bitterness and despair. This negative and excessive obsession with Saturn's capacity for discrimination should be eliminated from our lives.

Due to the fact that Saturn helps us separate the necessary from the superfluous, one of his best most-useful traits promotes efficiency. Nowadays, with information bombarding us from the mass media, it is all too easy to get lost in a million mental possibilities. Then, lacking the power of discrimination and concentration, we are overwhelmed. However, this won't happen once we align ourselves properly with Saturn's energy.

Saturn, after helping us discern the best and most-effective ways to actualize our soul's purpose, will give us the concentration, stamina, perseverance, and discipline to follow through, thereby, bringing us the great joy of completion, accomplishment, and of a job well done.

Generally, Saturn by slowing down our emotional responses, provides us with a more-careful and thoughtful attitude. He gives us deep satisfaction with conventional, status-quo experiences, especially those involving our family, environment, possessions, and achievements.

On the physical level Saturn is experienced as the polar opposite of all the other planetary energies because he functions as their anchoring point in physical existence. He works by building, structuring, and solidifying as well as by giving physical form to our bodies and lives.

The God Cronus/Saturn in Mythology

Cronus was the son of Uranus, the primordial Sky Father and Gaea the Earth Mother. When Heaven and earth united they bore the first race of gods known as the Titans, of whom Cronus was the youngest. After the Titans were born, Uranus and Gaea continued to produce offspring, some being monsters. Uranus, horrified at the sight of these children, forced his entire progeny back into his wife's womb.

Gaea, stretched with pain and pressure and overwhelmed with sadness and rage at his rejection, devised a plan to avenge her children. From her body she fashioned a sickle and asked her children to help her castrate their cruel father. None of them was interested in helping, except her youngest and most-ambitious son, Cronus. So it happened that Gaea armed Cronus with the deadly sickle and hid him under her garments. At night, when Uranus was burning with passion and came to lay by his wife, Cronus jumped out of his hiding place and severed his father's genitals.

The plan succeeded: Uranus was castrated and his genitals were thrown into the ocean. From his blood sprang the Furies and from the last drops of divine seed, Aphrodite, the goddess of love, was born. After Uranus was finally cast back into the sky, Cronus took over his throne. He liberated his brothers and sisters, the Titans and Titanesses, and together they formed a new dynasty and continued the work of creation.

From then on Cronus ruled undisturbed for a long and peaceful period, the so-called Golden Age, which lasted up to the birth of his son Zeus, who later would usurp his father's throne.

After some time Cronus took his sister Rhea as his wife. Together they had six children, three sons: Hades, Poseidon, and Zeus; and three daughters: Hestia, Demeter, and Hera.

However, an oracle had predicted that Cronus was to be dethroned by one of his children in a way similar to how he himself had usurped his father's throne. To prevent his future downfall, Cronus decided to swallow each of his children immediately after their birth. When Rhea was about to give birth to Zeus, she desperately sought her parents' advice to save her youngest child. They told her to hide the newborn god and give her husband a stone instead. She followed this advice and hid herself in a cavern to give birth to little Zeus. As soon as Zeus was born, she presented Cronus a stone wrapped in swaddling clothes, which he promptly swallowed.

Zeus grew strong, suckled by the goat Amaltheia. When he was robust enough to face his father, he sought the help of Metis, daughter of Oceanus. The goddess gave Cronus a potion that made him disgorge the stone and all the children he had swallowed, setting the gods and goddesses free.

Afterwards, the powerful Zeus, together with his brothers and sisters, overthrew Cronus and cast him into exile. There is controversy involving how Cronus' exile is to be defined and where he was sent. According to some sources, after his defeat against Zeus Cronus was sent to Tartarus, the Greek version of Hell, and was kept there in chains. However, other versions of the myth state that he became the peaceful ruler of the Elysian Fields, a kind of Heaven where dead heroes lived happily in eternal abundance.

The myths surrounding Cronus are complex. It is difficult to understand them without some previous training involving the significance of the great archetypes as well as a deeper understanding of the shifting levels of interpretation and the cosmic dimensions of which these myths are but vague descriptions. The seeming duality concerning Cronus' destiny is due only to these different levels of interpretation.

If we see Cronus as the great archetypal Father Time and associate him with an endless time, then it is easier to picture him as the benevolent ruler of a Golden Age, our lost paradise, which supposedly still exists somewhere in another dimension such as the Elysian Fields. While we humans are "down here" in practical, limited "physical" time, it is natural that we will perceive eternity as very blissful, but far beyond our present reach. However, if we see Cronus not as the ruler of eternal and abstract time, but as the cruel sovereign of physical existence where all that is born must soon die, then, of course, it is only justifiable to cast this villain deep into Hell as Zeus did in another version. Finally, it is our free will and our own consciousness that determine the value of the fruit from the Tree of Knowledge. We make it good or evil. Universal energy as it works through the great archetypes is impartial; it is only our will that gives it direction and bias. It is up to us to remake the cruel and jealous Cronus into the divine and benevolent ruler he truly. It is aslso our task to return humanity to that Golden Age for which we so deeply long!

Saturn in Astrology

Saturn rules the astrological sign of Capricorn.

His natural house is the Tenth House (profession, career, personal achievements, social status, recognition, money, personal honors, father, and authority figures).

The influence of the planet Saturn is felt as masculine. The glyph representing Saturn, which is a semicircle topped by a cross, symbolizes the personality held down by the cross of matter.

Basic key words describing Saturn's influence are self-discipline, law, limitation, restriction, protection, power, control, patience, perseverance, caution, wisdom, experience, achievement, time, and death.

The negative attributes of Saturn are fear of death and restriction, confinement, sorrow, disappointment, delay, avarice, and rigidity.

Saturn's basic function in the astrological chart is to restrain us, to forge us in the inner fire of discipline so that we may gain the power and wisdom to actualize our soul's purpose.

In the physical body, Saturn rules over the bones, skin, teeth, knees, and ears. Furthermore, he is said to preside over time, karma, death, stones, gates, the biological father, the day Saturday, and the metal lead.

Inner Journey To Contact the Archetype

Sit or lie in a comfortable position and begin relaxing by breathing deeply and rhythmically. Now count from ten to zero, allowing your body to relax even more with each count.

Imagine that you are walking along a dry canyon. The surrounding land seems dead and forlorn. Not a plant grows, not a drop of water is to be found anywhere. The sun has set already and a swift cool breeze blows through the high desert. Left and right the rocky cliffs tower high above your head. The path, which seems to be the bed of a long-dead river, is full of large boulders that seem to have rolled down from the craggy ridge a long time ago. Because it is difficult to discern where the ground is in the dusk, your feet stumble repeatedly. Nevertheless, you walk on, determined to find Saturn.

Suddenly you see a shimmering golden light in the distance. As you approach you notice the figure of a man poised arrogantly on a large boulder. He is superhumanly tall and handsome, the chiseled features of his beardless face so perfect that he looks almost feminine. He has deep-green eyes and long golden locks cascading down his broad shoulders, all the way to his narrow hips. He is naked, and as far as you can see, his body is that of a very virile male. The man is lean and brawny, his movements smooth and swift like those of a large cat. Behind his muscular back you can see large iridescent wings which he flaps playfully in the wind. As you stand before him, he glides down from the large rock with the ease of a mountain lion, his long blonde curls swirling lightly in the evening breeze. To your astonishment you discover that beneath the silken hair a set of horns adorn his forehead. He greets you with an impish smile. "Lucifer is the name," he says with a low, rumbling voice, well aware of the terrible impact his name and appearance must be causing you. You return his greeting and introduce yourself by name.

"It is good that you came," he assures you. "Not many venture this far. Not many dare to understand Saturn. Isn't it much easier to comply and complain than to face the responsibility of knowing the truth, of knowing one's life's work? You must not fear me, dear brother/sister. Even though you might still be shocked by me or by the others you will encounter along this path, it is good that you respect us. Yet you must not fear us, since fear is what keeps you from understanding our mystery. It is time to replace fear with an honest respect as well as a good and healthy curiosity. Until this day your fear protected you from approaching us too soon. It is good not to seek our contact before you feel ready because you must be strong and wise enough to balance our power without stumbling. Therefore, think well before seeking us out on your own. However, should we happen to appear spontaneously in your life or inner vision, do not fear but respect our power! We are a mystery that can take a lifetime or even several to unravel. "

"I am to Earth, to Sanat Kumara, the Ancient of Days, the Lord of the World, what your Twin Soul is to you since I am also Venus, yet after another manner. There will come a time when my presence will not be threatening to you anymore, when my horns will not frighten you. Then you will have understood polarity and the science of relating; you will have grown and strengthened yourself and built a center that is solid and integrated enough to withstand my power. That day I will come again to you and rejoice. I will make my presence felt and lead you into ecstasy, for I am Lucifer, the Light Bearer, and my Twin Brother is Sanat Kumara, the Ancient of Days, the Lord of this World. Be well aware that for the uninitiated we both appear as Satan, the Tempter, and herein lies the danger. However, remember that as such we are also the snake of the Garden of Eden, the Serpent of Wisdom. Together, my brother and I, entwined in eternal love and bliss, adorn the rod of the healer, the caduceus. I am also the Star of the Morning and my home is the planet Venus. Much of what you are on earth has come to you from my people and my abode. One day you will remember. Farewell for now, but we shall meet again. "

With this he points offhandedly to a large leaden gate that stands where the canyon narrows into a gorge. You smile at him shyly, thank him for what he has shared, and then walk ahead toward the gate. The doorknob is engraved with the symbol of Saturn. You open it and pass through.

On the other side the land appears even more desolate and Godforsaken. It is hot and the rocks seem to have closed in above you, leaving no visible sky. Fumes escape from the ground through hidden crevices and all is gray and barren. You hear the rattling of chains and, as you turn to face the sound, you see people chained to each other, toiling like slaves. Some are working the rocks with their bare hands, while others are carrying boulders on their backs in visible agony up along a winding trail.

You are surrounded by constriction, hopelessness, and despair. Pitiful sighs and moans fill the sticky atmosphere. Your heart shrinks at all this sorrow and, unable to walk on, you stand and wait. Suddenly, as if in answer to your feelings, a somber figure steps out of the night, his rolling laughter shattering your last defenses. "Is it me you seek, sweetheart?" he says in a mocking voice.

Frightened, you stop and look up at this intrusion. He is hairy, ugly, and filthy. His body is covered with thick fur and his legs have hooves instead of feet. Big ears and large horns crown his head. His nails are long and sharp, and as the rest of him, dark with grime. In his eyes you can see a mischievous sparkle as if he delights in seeing your disgust. Again, he poses the question, hopping on his hindlegs toward you, "Is it me you are looking for, dear traveler?" as he points the long filthy crooked nail of his index to your nose.

He is so close now that you are almost suffocated by the foul breath escaping his gaping mouth. Nauseated you turn away, but he will not let you go that easily. Before you know it, he grabs your arm and jerks you back to face him. "Tell me, sweet thing!" He asks. "Why are you here and what do you want? I could find good use for a hard worker like you around here."

It is just in time that you remember what you had learned in the lesson—Saturn is also Satan! Yes, he is if we allow him to constrict, bind, and suffocate us. Yes, he is if we believe that physicality is bad and turn away from solid material existence making it the scapegoat for our sorrow instead of the means to our power. Then and only then will the Wise Old Father Saturn turn into the ugly Satan of Christianity, the eternal opposer of God and the tempter of the righteous souls, working tirelessly at filling the caverns of Hell. Our soul's true mission is to redeem, enlighten, and integrate matter into the Divine Scheme, never to separate from it, denigrate, or curse it.

As this realization crosses your mind, you quickly regain your composure and gather your Divine Will within. You answer: "I will not be fooled by you, Satan! I have come to meet Saturn and am not afraid. I will do whatever it takes to achieve my goal, even if I have to cross this Hell on foot. Now get out of my way and let me do what I must. I know that you are but a creation of the created and as such can be dissolved by Divine Will! I am not intimidated by your appearance nor by your pitiful abode. Rather, I feel sorry for all those who have to slave in these stone caverns, although I know that some day they also will be free. I understand why and how you gained your apparent strength over humanity, and although I respect it, I am not fooled by it. I am a free man/woman, and you have no power over me. I am becoming proficient in the workings of polarity and, therefore, I can now eliminate you from my life with the same power with which I allowed you to enter it!"

With these words you extend your right arm in front of you in a gesture of command; instantly the scene changes and gives way to a golden glow. The energy shifts drastically, the rocky walls fade away and you are lifted up into the air. Before you a golden city towers high in the sky. It is surrounded by a magnificent ring of clouds, shimmering in the colors of the rainbow as they catch the sun's light. You walk to it, cross the city gates, and enter the great hall of the palace. Inside you find a king on his throne. It is Sanat Kumara, the Ancient of Days, the Lord of the World. At his side you see a beautiful blonde woman. She reminds you of Venus; however, as you look more closely you recognize Lucifer's eyes. She stands next to the king, gently massaging his shoulders as he glances up at her tenderly. There is obvious affection between the two.

The king bids you step forward and welcomes you with a charming smile. He looks strong and powerful, not old and senile as you might have imagined, given the fact that he is the "Ancient of Days. " He is about forty-years old and the gentleness and power of his aura touch you deeply. Somewhere you have met him before, sometime long ago. Of this you are certain. He feels warm and familiar, but still his commanding presence is awe inspiring. At his sight a flash of relief runs through your body. If our world is ruled by such a gentle but powerful presence, then things cannot be all that bad on our planet. This man seems to know very well what he is doing.

"I have come to seek and understand the power of Saturn, my Lord," you say with reverence. In response a charming smile broadens his handsome face. He speaks: "I am Sanat Kumara, the Lord of the World. You need go no farther to find what you seek. Saturn is everywhere; he is inherent in polarity; he is the force that binds creation in time and space. He weaves Divine Will on the loom made by these coordinates, creating the fabric of life with Divine Love and Wisdom. "

"Saturn is what holds events captive in the succession of time, in the illusion of linearity so that you may become well aware of your actions' effects and understand how to apply your will, power, and wisdom most effectively. He constitutes the solid ground beneath your earthly being. It is he who allows you to integrate chaos and turn it into cosmos. Saturn shows you with the patience of a benevolent father how to transmute the coarser into the more rarified, to make light of the somber, to bring greater ecstasy to the denser worlds. You can find Saturn right here and now, you do not need to escape the earth's atmosphere to see and understand him. He is not like the other planets whose energy is sometimes veiled by the etheric atmosphere of earth. "

Sanat Kumara speaks on: "To harness Saturn's power for your benefit you must understand polarity and learn to integrate it. Only then will you be free. However, the freedom that springs from fusing the two into one and then separating them again at will is not something to be achieved through an external source, but must be accomplished inside yourself. It is the continuous alchemical transmutation that you must learn, 'solve et coagula' as they say. "

"Polarity, its fusion, and subsequent separation only to fuse again in release is the fuel of life. It is the friction of the polar opposites that produces manifestation in its many facets. The fire of friction brings ecstasy when harnessed and bent to Divine Will. Under the Light Divine of the Spirit the polar opposites in the entire creation are continuously brought together in friction. This friction resembles the act of lovemaking, culminating in the energetic fusion of the pair, and the release of power that ignites them in one big ecstatic blaze. "

"Before this cry of rapture reverberates in the depths of cosmos, innumerable other pairs have already encircled each other. Attracted by their love, they are engaged in the friction that will again culminate in fusion and release. This is the law of the alchemy of force and form on all its levels. Therefore, my dear traveler, know that the polar opposites are as vital to manifestation as life itself and must always be recognized as such. You cannot work with one pole exclusively, rejecting the other, for then you are negating life, friction, ecstasy, and creation itself!"

With this the king stands up and turns around to face Lucifer. He puts one hand gently behind her back and the other on her right shoulder. After looking lovingly into her deep-green eyes, he pulls her close in a passionate embrace. Limbs entwined, seeking wholeness, the dark-haired king with his strong dark male body and the fair pliant blonde beauty kiss and seem to melt into each other. Suddenly the entire room is plunged into a golden haze and the atmosphere becomes permeated by a strange purity you have never felt before. It is as if a thousand angels have descended from heaven to bless this union and bestow the grace of God. Lucifer and Sanat Kumara are blending into one being, its two halves circling and chasing each other in a twirling ball of light. For a moment you recognize the ancient symbol of the yin and yang, the masculine and feminine surrounding and containing each other in eternal embrace, encircled in one sacred whole, the Tao.

The two rulers melt into each other more and more until they are but one big sphere of light hovering above the throne. You now know what must be done, and lovingly and willingly open your heart chakra for them to enter you and bestow their blessing. As soon as you open yourself to them, their blazing sphere turns into a luminous rod and enters your heart chakra. With one big ecstatic explosion the power and jubilation extends into your entire body and aura, fusing with you in an energetic orgasm. The polar opposites are one, the separateness forever bridged. You are one with them. You now know their secret and the secret of all creation and they willingly give themselves to you without restraint. Divine Grace descends upon all at this moment, and you know that here and now all is well, has always been well, and will always be. This is the perfection of manifestation, at this very moment.

You remain in deep communion with the power of the two rulers and absorb their essences, reveling in the fusion of the three energies. Then you mentally ask to be given a personal message.

Allow some time for the message to appear, and when you feel that you have absorbed all you need, allow the rod of power to depart through your heart chakra. The energy pulls out of you and forms itself into a shining sphere of light hovering above the throne. You see it slowly unraveling itself; the two halves appear, not dark and light this time, but gold and silver. You do not need to wait for the two figures to regain their human form again because now you are looking at them from another level. Here they are just that—a blazing sphere of gold and silver light, the two colors melting into each other. Deeply moved, you thank them and say farewell.

You retrace your steps to the city's gate. To your relief you recognize that it is the same leaden gate you crossed at the beginning of the journey. Instantly you understand that this time you will not have to cross the Hell through which you came. And maybe, if you apply yourself well, you might never ever have to traverse that Hell again. Relieved and content, you open the gate and pass through it.

On the other side the dry canyon has changed into a lush and green valley with a crystal-clear stream. High up in the sky you sense an angelic presence, watching. You thank him in your heart and proceed home. The landscape slowly fades away, and gradually you regain your normal waking consciousness.

Magical Use of Saturn

Preliminaries for the magical use of Saturn's energy involve the following considerations:

- Take responsibility for the new power you will gain through this exercise and commit yourself to using it for the good of all.
- Open yourself to the forces of change. Be ready to gain more awareness in all aspects of your life and commit yourself to acting on this new knowledge.
- Let the enthusiasm for the Great Work pervade your practices.
- Make a commitment not to become judgmental toward others and feel "above" them because of your new power and insight. Neither judge yourself nor your personal past. Instead, embrace all life with compassion and understanding.

Magical Practice To Stretch Out Time

This practice is intended to manipulate time. It shows you, among other things, that time is not as objective and quantitative as you might think.

It is fun to use Saturn's energy to "stretch" time when you are in the middle of a chore or event that seems too long to be finished at a certain hour. It will also let you experience the great power of the focused mind and unveil the illusion of time.

For example, let's say that you have a three o'clock appointment at the dentist. It is now 2:20 and you are in the middle of ironing a pile of clothes. You would like to finish this before you leave, but the pile is so big it will probably take at least one more hour to finish. With the help of Saturn you can stretch time to accommodate your chore.

When you are in the middle of an event or chore you want to complete earlier than expected, do this following exercise:

1. Sit or lie in a comfortable position and begin relaxing by breathing deeply and rhythmically. Now count from ten to zero, allowing your body to relax even more with each count. Attune yourself with Divine Will as manifested through the energy of Saturn. State firmly that you want to have more control over your life and are willing to change.

2. Visualize the astrological symbol of Saturn as shown at the beginning of this chapter. Build it up with your inner vision until it is large enough to envelop you completely, creating an energetic bond with the power of Saturn.

3. Then, still focusing on the tremendous buildup of power, draw in the air the astrological symbol of Saturn before your Third Eye with the palms of both hands, one overlapping the other, and both facing outward.

4. Concentrate on your first chakra located around the base of your spine and let your energy build up in that area.

5. Pull a shaft of energy from your base chakra up the length of your spine. Feel how it is charged with your pure will as it rises to your Third Eye; then let it rest there for a few seconds.

6. Now project the energy beam outward through your Third Eye and the palms of your hands, (which should still be positioned on your forehead, facing out). Use the full force of your will, stating that you want time to stretch to accommodate your task before a given hour.

7. Feel how the beam of Life Force is projected through your hands like a missile and detaches, running into the space in front of you stretching out time.

8. Return to your task and forget about the procedure for awhile. You may repeat it once more for the same task.

If successfully done, you will feel how time seems to pass more and more slowly. You will go about your task in a relaxed manner and still find that it is done faster than you thought possible, ending exactly on time or even earlier. This technique also works well when you are caught in traffic and need to get to an appointment on time. It has a tendency to smooth out obstacles and accommodate time to personal needs.

Magical Practice To Materialize with Saturn's Help

This practice will show you how to use Saturn's power to materialize a thing or idea you want accomplished.

1. Think of something that you want to manifest. Relax by breathing deeply and rhythmically.

2. Attune yourself to Divine Power as manifested through the energy of Saturn. State firmly that you want to have more control over your life and environment and are willing to change.

3. Visualize Saturn's astrological symbol as shown at the beginning of this chapter. Build it up with your inner vision until it is large enough to envelop you completely, creating an energetic bond with the power of Saturn.

4. Now allow Saturn to overshadow you in the following way:

Build up with your inner vision the image of the Great Wise Man as you imagine him or Sanat Kumara as described in the inner journey, using the one to whom you feel most attracted. Picture him standing behind you; make his body about seven feet high. Feel his great power and aura extending far beyond his body's limits into outer space. Concentrate on your love and admiration for Saturn or Sanat Kumara, as well as on your gratitude to him for helping you in this matter. Now allow him to step up as close as possible behind you and concentrate on the overshadowing effect of his aura on yours. Still focused on your love for him, allow him to empower you by blending his great aura with your smaller one. Feel how both your energy fields are strengthened and vitalized by the contact. Feel your aura grow in size and power to coincide with that of the god. Remain this way for awhile before your proceed to the next step.

5. Concentrate on your first chakra located around the base of the spine and let your energy build up in that area.

6. Pull a shaft of energy up your spine. Feel how it is charged with your pure will as it rises to your Third Eye. Then let it rest there for a few seconds.

7. Now project the energy beam outward through the palms of your hands (which should still be positioned on your forehead, facing out) with the full force of your will. Have it form itself in the image of the thing or idea you want to materialize at a distance of about three feet in front of you.

8. Now concentrate on your first chakra as above and again build up the energy.

9. Pull a shaft of energy up from the base chakra to the Third Eye as above and let it hover there for a few seconds while you collect your will.

10. Now expel the shaft of energy with one big thrust toward the image of the item or idea you had built up. Feel how the beam of Life Force is projected through your hands like a missile and detaches, running into the space in front of you, hitting the thoughtform with the light like a laser beam. See how your laser beam forms itself into the symbol of Saturn as it hits the item or idea, then melts and fuses its power with the image—enlivening and solidifying it at the same time. While the light beam is hitting its target, you must focus your will and intent to materialize this item with all your strength and passion. You must hold it until you feel that the image, your light beam, your will, and the symbol and energy of Saturn have melted and become one.

11. You will feel an inner click when the four ingredients have successfully fused and your vision is duly empowered. At this point detach yourself from the image and the procedure. Return to normal.

12. Should you be uncertain whether you felt a click or not, just hold your focus for another ten to fifteen seconds—then let go.

13. Allow at least two weeks before you repeat the procedure and do not doubt or think about it during this time. Simply trust and be confident that, if it is in accordance with Divine Will, it will be materialized.

Magical Practice To Use Death as Friend and Advisor

This practice should be done in the evening before falling asleep. It is intended to narrow down your soul's purpose to its essence and to help you learn how to describe it in no more than three sentences according to the following procedures:

1. Take a pen and paper. Sit or lie down in a comfortable position and relax.

2. Attune yourself with Divine Wisdom as manifested through the energy of Saturn. State firmly that you want to know more about yourself and are willing to change.

3. Now allow Saturn to overshadow you in the following way:

Build up with your inner vision the image of the Great Wise Man as you imagine him or Sanat Kumara as described in the inner journey, using the one to whom you feel most attracted. Picture him standing behind you, make his body about seven feet high. Feel his great power and aura extending far beyond his body's limits into outer space. Concentrate on your love and admiration for Saturn or Sanat Kumara as well as on your gratitude to him for helping you in this matter. Now allow him to step up as close as possible behind you and concentrate on the overshadowing effect of his aura on yours. Still focused on your love for him, allow him to empower you by blending his great aura with your smaller one. Feel how both your energy fields are strengthened and vitalized by the contact. Feel your aura grow in size and power to coincide with that of the god. Remain this way for awhile before proceeding to the next step.

4. Still focusing on the tremendous buildup of power and Divine Wisdom, ask yourself that if you would die right now, which of the experiences you have had in this life were good, necessary, and important to this incarnation, and which seem to have been superfluous. Meditate on your life and decide what it is you would miss if you should die tonight, and decide what you came to do, but have not yet completed.

5. Describe in three sentences the essence of the experiences you feel you have missed or failed at, then commit yourself to doing them. Write down these three sentences on your paper.

6. Realize how lucky you are not to die at this very moment and how fortunate you are to have the chance to experience these things in the near

future. Thank God for this. Thank death for holding back for some time longer.

7. Pause for awhile then imagine that you might die in one month. Decide which things and experiences you would still want to encounter as part of your soul's purpose. Narrow them down to three sentences, then write them on your paper. Commit yourself to doing them.

8. Decide which experiences are unnecessary to your soul's purpose and are, in fact, holding you back from fulfilling it. Commit yourself to dropping them within the next month or a soon as possible.

9. Thank God and death as above. Pause for awhile.

10. Repeat the practice, but now imagine that you have only a year more to live. Again narrow down your soul's intent for the next year into three sentences and write them down. Consider them well.

11. Thank the God Within and death for their advice. Then finish the practice by emanating a strong energy of love from your heart chakra. Let it envelop your entire being with love and acceptance for yourself. Love and forgive yourself deeply and thoroughly for being who and where you are now, in time and space. Make certain you succeed in loving yourself before you close the practice.

12. Return to normal and ground yourself by drinking a glass of water or having a small snack.

Since this practice involves heavy energies, be prepared to have things stirred up inside you.

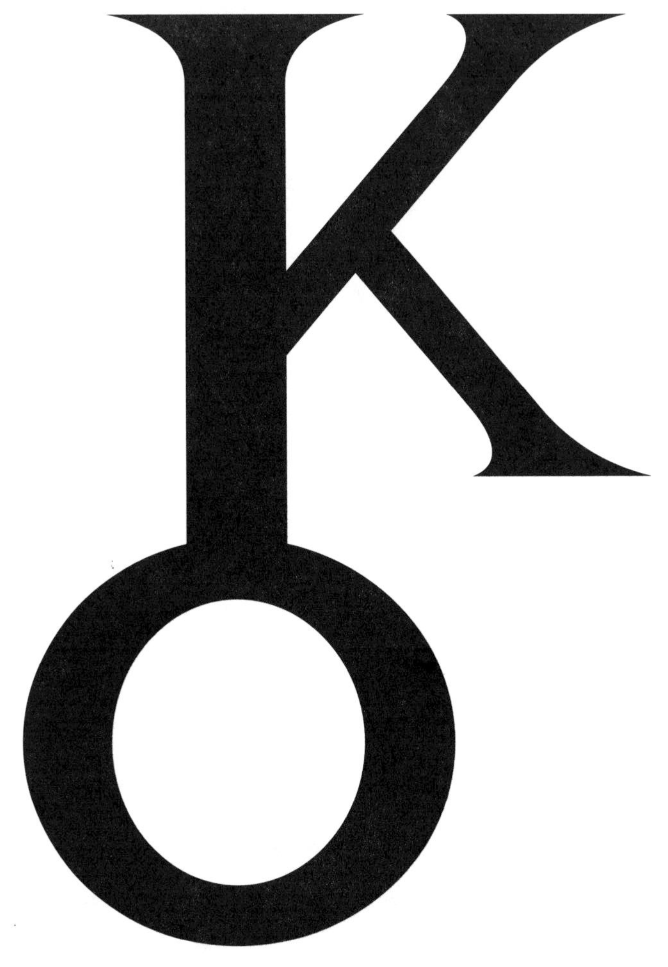

CHIRON

CHIRON

Attunement with the Archetypal Power of Chiron

Since the discovery of the planet Chiron in 1977, this little celestial body has come to represent the archetype of the teacher and wounded healer. The term "wounded healer" means that a healer becomes capable of healing most effectively those areas to which s/he is sensitized through his or her own wounding. The figure of Chiron stems from Greek mythology where he was depicted as a centaur, having a man's head, arms, and torso attached to a horse's body at the waist. The Chiron archetype represents the power that integrates the human and the animal parts of our being into a greater more-harmonious whole. And it is precisely at the solar plexus, around the waist, where animal and human join and where the woundedness caused by a free ethereal soul entering a material body is most noticeable.

The mythological Chiron, as well as his ageless counterpart, the shaman, show us that a true healer must not only be knowledgeable of the "animal" aspects of the human body, but totally attuned and integrated with them as well. At one with his feelings and instincts, Chiron— like the shaman whom he symbolizes— pierces the veil of rationality and directly accesses the healing realms of spirit which lie beyond time and space. He draws from the inner magical worlds at will to instruct and heal those who seek him out.

Since his discovery Chiron has become the symbol for the contemporary healing movement. Weary of the coldness and rationality of orthodox medicine, the modern healer successfully integrates the potential hidden in our animal natures with the ability to heal and empower his/her patients. Like the shaman, the contemporary healer has rediscovered the value of instinct and physicality in achieving wholeness.

The mythological Chiron learned most of his skills from Apollo, which he then passed on to famous heroes-in-the-making: Hercules, Achilles, and Jason, among many others. Ironically, however, it was Hercules who wounded his mentor with a poisoned arrow.

Chiron, being immortal, could not die from the wound inflicted upon him by Hercules. He sought endlessly for a cure to his wound, and in the process learned many new healing techniques. However, while Chiron applied his new skills to his patients, he was unable to remedy his own injury. Eventually, Chiron's wound caused him so much pain that he willingly surrendered his immortality to end the suffering.

If we look at the gods, goddesses, and heroes of mythology as elements of our own psyche, we can interpret Chiron in a new light. First, we are told that Chiron is instructed by the sun-god Apollo, and then becomes a teacher and healer to many solar heroes-in-the-making.

Apollo represents our own soul or Christ consciousness, reaching down to teach our lower self, via Chiron, the shaman. This shows us how the ordinary human, who is usually disconnected from his/her own soul, must seek out the powers of Chiron, the mediator, to reconnect and integrate body and instincts, feelings, and intuition. Eventually, the person is made whole once more and reconnected to his/her own soul. When the ordinary human being merges with the soul, s/he becomes the initiated solar hero/heroine (or perfected personality). After the successful completion of the instruction, the mediator is needed no more, and the hero/heroine is left to continue alone; like Hercules, s/he proceeds to work as a world server, saving humanity from affliction.

At the end of this cycle, however, the solar hero like his mentor must, in turn, sacrifice himself to spirit and die. He must descend into the Underworld, and like Christ after the crucifixion, meet and redeem the Shadow to merge fully with the Divine Self, Spirit, or Monad. Only then does he resurrect triumphant: a human being in full Divine consciousness. Chiron then, like the shaman, is a temporary mediator between the practical and rational worlds and the raw, magical power of our inherent Divinity—working through our bodies and feelings.

The astrological Chiron has been called the rainbow bridge between the inner and outer planets. His power is the connecting link between Saturn's physical and social structure and Uranus' creative, unconventional, and often genial input. One is as necessary as the other for the successful mastery of our physical existence. The inrush of Uranian energy, being the opposite of Saturn's, often causes great pain and shock. However, with Chiron's power we may ease the gap between these two opposing planetary energies. Through Chiron we learn to integrate the personal inner planets with the transpersonal outer ones. As previously mentioned, the entire Chiron theme is centered on an integration of our animal and human parts, as well as the healing resulting from this new wholeness. The part of us which pertains to the animal kingdom obviously involves the body, its feelings, and instincts.

We "human animals" have had to conform to innumerable strict social rules throughout the centuries, being forced to deny many aspects of our animal selves and/or control them by willpower. As a result we have become nicely civilized, but in stifling our animal instincts, we have also lost part of our power. The Chiron theme indicates that there is a certain time during our development when we are civilized and structured enough to reach back safely into our animal nature and free the powers and instincts we have repressed.

Chiron connects us to the spiritual world of the shaman, who reaches beyond rationality and intellectual categories, directly accessing the cosmic and the Divine through his/her various powers. This direct accessing and resultant efficiency is related to the expression of Virgo, the astrological sign to which the newly discovered Chiron has been assigned.

On the personal level the Chiron archetype brings in the will-to-do-good. He focuses our Divine Will on the task at hand. This is, of course, the Great Work to bridge and harmonize the personal realms (represented by the inner planets) with the transpersonal realms (symbolized by the outer planets).

After his descent into the Underworld, the mythological Chiron is turned by Zeus into the constellation Sagittarius. It is said that the arrow of Sagittarius points toward the center of the galaxy. In this same manner Chiron shows us the way to return to Divinity by a full acceptance and integration of our animal selves.

Chiron plays a key role in physical wholeness. He instructs the potential hero or heroine how to reach through the heavy layers of decades of civilization (Saturn) that have greatly stifled his/her energy to reclaim the invigorating and electrifying power of his/her own body and feelings (Uranus and kundalini).

Chiron stresses the inherent divinity of the physical body and its potential for service. He teaches us to accept its faults and restrictions as part of the Divine Plan. With the help of Chiron we learn to make the best of our situation, willingly to bare our woundedness and still be of great service to others. When we let go of our victim patterns and embrace our animal selves we become very powerful!

It is with the help of Chiron that we may finally free ourselves of the dynamic of the wounder/wounded we encountered with Mars. Chiron brings in a third element, the healer, which resolves the two. The healer works regardless of his/her wounds and refuses to dwell in the victim's self-pity. The healer, making the best of a less-than-perfect situation, transcends his woundedness in an act of focused will and love of serving his fellow humans.

Chiron brings compassion as well as an emotional urgency to teach and heal others. It is precisely the suffering of the wounded animal in ourselves that makes us compassionate. And it is this same pain that propels us to learn innumerable healing techniques to alleviate our condition. Then, having achieved some healing ourselves, we feel a deep passion and longing to spare others the same pain, rejection, and shame we felt at the time of our wounding. We become teachers and healers, gathering our inner strength from the joy of sharing what we have learned along our healing journey.

By merging with our animal selves and coming to terms with our own mortality, we unleash an incredible healing force. The acceptance of our selves just the way we are, part animal and part human, has a healing and initiatory effect in itself that is passed on to those around us.

The mythological Chiron lives in a cave, in a natural environment. This symbolizes his closeness to the source of physicality and animal life. Were he to integrate himself fully into civilization, he would succumb to Saturnine constriction and rigidity, losing his power to catalyze. Although we need not permanently live in a cave to become true spiritual healers, periodic seclusion helps us understand and integrate our animal selves and its related power.

Chiron in Mythology

Chiron was the son of Cronus and the nymph Philyra, daughter of Oceanus. When Philyra found out that Cronus was pursuing her, she changed herself into a mare to escape his advances. Cronus then changed himself into a magnificent stallion and mated with the nymph. Eventually, a son, Chiron, was born of their union.

This child was not a normal babe for his lower body was that of a horse. His mother, horrified at the sight of Chiron, abandoned him immediately after birth. Young Chiron, however, was lucky. Found by Apollo who became his foster father, Chiron was instructed by the sun god in the healing arts, the use of weapons and musical instruments, among other things.

Chiron soon became proficient in these disciplines; even the nobility of the times sought him out as instructor to their heirs. As a result Chiron became teacher and mentor to many a famous hero: Jason, Achilles, Hercules, and others.

There were many centaurs besides Chiron, but he was very different from his kin. While they were uncivilized and lecherous, Chiron was a disciplined teacher, healer, musician, and sage. He made the best of his lower animal body and utilized its power and wisdom to heal others. Being the son of a god and a nymph, Chiron was immortal; unfortunately, he was not immune to injury.

One fateful evening, a group of centaurs came to his cave. They got drunk and started a fight. Hercules, who was also present, shot at them with his poisoned arrows. One of these arrows accidentally wounded Chiron in the leg. Since the wound would not heal, Chiron suffered unceasing agony. Being immortal, he could not die, so he searched all over the world for a cure to his affliction. Although his search greatly increased his healing skills, it failed to alleviate his own suffering.

Eventually Chiron found release by sacrificing his immortality in exchange for Prometheus' freedom. The latter had been chained to a rock by Zeus for stealing fire from Olympus. A griffin or eagle ate his liver every day. Since Prometheus was immortal the liver would grow back at night and, of course, the next day the cruel treatment would begin all over again. Prometheus was sentenced to endure such torture until an immortal agreed to die and go to the Underworld in his place.

Hercules, seeing Prometheus' predicament, pleaded Chiron's case before Zeus. The exchange was accepted and Prometheus was freed and allowed to return to Olympus. Chiron died and descended to the Underworld. After nine days Zeus redeemed him and changed him into the constellation Sagittarius for his bravery.

Chiron in Astrology

Since the discovery of Chiron in 1977 many astrologers have successfully incorporated Chiron into their work. They have assigned him diverse attributes, making him the scapegoat as well as the salvation of most afflictions plaguing humanity in our time. I am not too fond of some of these interpretations. However, if we do not get too enthusiastic about this newly discovered little planet, we will find him quite useful.

Chiron is assigned to the astrological sign Virgo.

His natural house is the Sixth House (work, health, and service).

His influence is felt as catalyzing, both wounding and healing at the same time. He contains the paradox of the wounded healer, which states that we can heal best where we are most wounded.

His astrological symbol is a circle topped by a capital "K. "

Basic key words describing the influence of Chiron are the following: wisdom, knowledge, strength, vision, self-sacrifice, transcendence, compassion, dependability, versatility, integrity, intuitive and non-traditional healing methods, animal power, creativity, resourcefulness, unconventionality, and craftiness.

The negative attributes of Chiron are weakness, self-pity, emotional wounding of self or others, shame, isolation, as well as excessive preaching or helping others against their will.

Inner Journey To Contact the Archetype

Sit or lie in a comfortable position and begin relaxing by breathing deeply and rhythmically. Now count from ten to zero, allowing your body to relax even more with each count.

As your surroundings slowly fade, you will find yourself walking alone in the countryside. The sun is high in the sky and the air warm and pleasant. Soon after you enter this sunny landscape, a large gate appears before you. You recognize the symbol of Chiron on its doorknob. Confidently you open the gate and pass through.

On the other side there is no path to guide you. This, however, presents no obstacle because you are determined to find Chiron. You see a large rock formation to your left and walk toward it. As you approach you find the entrance to a cave. Since this is Chiron's private abode you dare not enter without being summoned. So you seat yourself on a nearby rock and wait.

Soon, as if sensing your presence, Chiron's massive form appears at the cave's threshold. He nods to you in recognition. Very aware of the strange effect the sight of him has on you, he says not a word as he approaches. His torso is strong and muscular; his shoulders and arms are those of an athlete. In truth, he is quite handsome, and the large brown eyes that gaze at you are deep and warm. Standing before you, he greets you with a smile.

Only now do you look more closely at his lower body, so enthralled were you by his face. From the waist down he is a black stallion. And you notice that his coat is shiny and clean, his legs powerful. Even though this combination of man and beast looks intimidating and smells distinctly of horse, you feel attracted to him. He emanates an uncommonly strong blend of wisdom, compassion, and understanding. And before you know it, your heart is overflowing with love and admiration for this strange creature who so gracefully accepts his handicap. You take a few steps forward and embrace him.

His soothing aura erasing all traces of past sufferings, he mends the split between your body and mind. You remain in his arms for awhile, basking in the healing force of one who knows your wound. His strength and compassion work like a magic balm on your insecurities so that you feel renewed, rejuvenated, and initiated into a new life.

Then you disengage from his strong arms and he tells you enthusiastically, "Come, I want to show you my abode!" So you follow Chiron into his cave. To your amazement it is very clean and meticulously organized. Shelves with carefully labeled jars containing healing herbs and potions line the walls. In one corner you see a large pallet— his sleeping area, no doubt. In another corner you see a large collection of weapons, all clean and polished. Next to these are musical instruments of every possible size and shape. In awe of the array of things in this rustic dwelling you exclaim: "This is wonderful, Chiron! And so well organized! You must be very knowledgeable indeed to make use of all this. " There is no time for him to answer because someone is standing at the caves's threshold. It is a youth of about fourteen years. He is tall, slender, and quite comely. Chiron excuses himself to embrace the lad. Then, turning again to face you he says: "Meet my friend Achilles. He comes to me for training. Today we will use the bow and arrow. Would you like to watch us? Come along. "

Without waiting for your reply, master and pupil take up their weapons and proceed outside to a large meadow. Eager to watch them, you climb up the rock that covers Chiron's cave and seat yourself on top.

From there you observe how Chiron patiently instructs the lad in archery. There is so much love and caring in Chiron's every gesture that your heart is warmed with pride. Young Achilles seems to be extremely bright. He learns quickly and before you know it, master and pupil are saying their farewells.

As soon as the youth is gone, Chiron canters toward you. He approaches the rock and bids you mount his back. "Come," he insists, "I want to show you yet another side of me. " With this you mount Chiron and together gallop across the meadow.

After awhile you arrive at a small mountain lake. The water is crystal clear and inviting. At Chiron's command you dismount and seat yourself under a large willow tree not far from the water's edge. Chiron tells you to wait there until he returns for you. Then he approaches the shore and lies his massive body down to sleep, or so it seems.

Suddenly, the lake seems to part in the middle and a beautiful water nymph steps gracefully toward the shore. She bends down over Chiron and gently caresses his cheek. Immediately something in Chiron stirs and then he rises. But it is not the Chiron you saw before who now moves to embrace the nymph. What you perceive is the semi-translucent shape of a beautiful blonde man superimposed on the sleeping Chiron.

Chiron, like a fairy prince, steps out of his sleeping body. Leaving it behind like a discarded garment, he rushes to embrace his lady. Together, their bodies entwined in a lovers' embrace, they sink into the blue depths of the lake. You watch it all in astonishment. You understand that Chiron meant to show you that he is not always confined to his horse's body. That the impairment of being neither truly beast nor completely human is but temporary, inherent only in his physical form.

You remain under the shade of the willow, pondering what this experience has to teach you. Then after what seems an eternity, the waters part and the lovers surface again. Their joy and love is written plainly on their faces for all to see, and you cannot help but rejoice with them. After one last passionate embrace, the nymph dives back to her abode while the golden man returns to shore where he swiftly reunites with his sleeping body.

A few seconds later Chiron awakens and jumps to his hoofs. An impish smile curves his lips as he beckons you to re-mount. You accept gladly and seat yourself on his muscular back. While you ride together toward his home he still seems deeply immersed in his thoughts and feelings. You dare not comment on what has happened lest his blissful spell be broken. As you reach the cave he speaks:

"So far I have shown you what I do on earth. Now it is time you know what my greater, more-abstract self accomplishes in the vast and rarified regions of outer space. " With this he climbs the rock formation. As you reach the top he signals you to dismount. He holds your hand and together you fly off into outer space. You note that he leaves his physical body on earth and steps out into the air in his human form.

After quite a long journey you gently land on a small celestial body. Its surface is ragged and cold. Judging from the twilight surrounding you, it must be quite far from the sun. Chiron, still holding your hand, pulls you close in a brotherly embrace. Gladly you lean against this strong being, fully absorbing his power and wisdom. You are overcome with love and tenderness for Chiron and feel very familiar with him. Ah! How you wish you could fuse entirely with him, become one with his wisdom and compassion, integrate his strength and skill! Suddenly, as if in answer to your silent wish, his form begins to dissolve. He turns into a luminous gas that enters your body at your heart center.

While you are being filled with Chiron, you are overcome with ecstasy. It is as if each minute particle of him finds its counterpart in you and merges in a blissful explosion. Once you have incorporated all the luminosity, you seat yourself on the ground and enjoy the blissful communion.

Having Chiron inside you like this summons up strange feelings, memories, and insights. Allow some time for these to rise from your depths, then let them gently slide away. Hear Chiron as he speaks inside your heart:

"Look at the solar system, my friend. Do you see where I, in my planetary form, am at this very moment? I am positioned between Saturn and Uranus! Feel the strain that this position causes on my body. Feel how I am constantly torn by the power my two celestial companions, whose bodies are so much larger than mine, exert on me. Understand the dilemma of balancing Saturn's rigidity and conventionality with Uranus' revolution and creativity. Feel how both join at my waist, pressing my very body into war against itself. But nay, I do not break; I prevail! For I have the wisdom of the ages! I know that no polarity is eternal, that no split is irreparable, that no Abyss remains forever uncrossed! For great is the pioneering spirit of the human race and great is the mending power of its heart! For as powerful an influence as the stifling grip of Saturn has on the creative genius of Uranus, so is also the grounding influence of Saturn vital to give form to Uranus' unbridled genius. One cannot do without the other. To reconcile the opposite poles of these universal powers you, and I the universal healer, have come to be. It is in our bodies where the solidity of Saturn is set against Uranus' fertilizing genius. By appeasing and integrating these warring elements in ourselves, we build the Rainbow Bridge. " He continues:

"God bless you, my fellow healer. And know that it is the very wound you have had to suffer in incarnating into a physical body that holds your power to bridge the greatest of all gaps: the Abyss between physical manifestation and the world of Spirit. "

Before you allow Chiron to depart, you ask him for a personal message. Allow some time for this to appear. Then thank Chiron and allow the luminous gas to depart the way it came. It exits your body and builds itself into Chiron's human form.

Chiron stands before you now and holds a bow and arrow. He takes the arrow, and with its tip, cuts a five-pointed star on your bare chest. He dips the arrow point in your blood, then motions you to shoot it in a specific direction in interstellar space. He speaks: "This arrow symbolizes your focused will, whereas, the blood it contains is your own spirit, eager to reunite itself with the Divine. Shoot it toward the center of the galaxy. The magic this represents you will recognize indeed!"

At his signal you shoot the arrow and watch it disappear in outer space. Realizing what you have just accomplished, tears of longing flood your eyes. Confused yet relieved, you accept Chiron's outstretched arms. Silently but knowingly, you embrace each other for awhile. You both share the same pain of separation from your source and kin.

Then Chiron gently pulls away. He reaches out and grasps your arm and before you know it, you are high in the sky again, heading toward earth.

You land gently on the same rocky formation where you started and climb back down the rock with Chiron, who has now resumed his centaur's body. As you reach the meadow, the large gate appears again before you. You embrace Chiron one last time and say farewell. Confidently, although a little disappointed having to leave your friend, you pass through and close the gate behind you. The landscape slowly fades away, and gradually you regain your normal waking consciousness.

The Wounded Body

As mentioned above, we had to "wound" our body and repress many of our instincts to become civilized and acceptable to society. In the process of controlling our body, we also have forgotten how to read it's messages—a most-regrettable fact indeed—, since it is through our body and feelings that we receive intuitive information and access the realms beyond time and space.

However, our body is a faithful and resilient friend. Even though we have ignored its messages for so long, it still does "talk" to us. For example, when we have a "gut feeling" about something, the body is conveying intuitive information pertaining to a future event or outcome. If we want to enlist the body's wisdom in our quest, we should heed these feelings as much as we do our rational decisions and common sense.

With some practice important events and their outcomes can be traced back to the "hunches" that preceded them. In time the rational mind understands and validates the premonitory feeling, incorporating it into its conscious repertoire for future use. What starts out as an irrational, instinctive feeling of our animal self becomes, thereafter, a valuable tool in conscious decision-making. The communion of body and mind redeems the body and heals the mind.

The Magical Use of Chiron

Preliminaries for the magical use of Chiron's energy involve the following considerations:

• Open yourself without fear to the forces of change; be ready and willing to grow and mature in all aspects of your life. Above all, be extremely honest with yourself.

• Strive to unify your animal, human, and Divine selves into an harmonious whole. Identify with Divine Wisdom and Compassion.

• Take responsibility for the new awareness and knowledge you gain through these exercises.

• Commit yourself to healing your wounds and to using the power gained through your healing for the good of all.

• Commit yourself to applying your intuitive knowledge and healing power in service to humanity with Divine Love, Wisdom, and Compassion.

Magical Practice To Communicate With Your Body

This practice is intended to connect you to your body and communicate with it. By incorporating your body's wisdom into consciousness and learning to work with your body instead of against it, you will heal your inner wounds by doing the following exercise:

1. Sit or lie in a comfortable position and begin relaxing by breathing deeply and rhythmically. Now count from ten to zero, allowing your body to relax even more with each count.

2. Attune yourself with Divine Wisdom as represented through the energy of Chiron. State firmly that you want to know more about yourself and are willing to change and grow.

3. Visualize Chiron's astrological symbol as shown at the beginning of this chapter. Build it up with your inner vision until it is large enough to envelop you completely, creating an energetic bond with the power of Chiron.

4. Encourage your body to express itself to you. Tell it how much you love it and that you are ready and willing to work closely with it. Say something such as: "Dear body, I know that I have abused you many times in the past. I am very sorry for this. I love you and want to know more about you. Please tell me how you feel. Tell me what I can do to make you more comfortable (or powerful, healthy, attractive, etc.), and I will do my best to cooperate with you. Please speak to me."

5. Now allow your body to talk to you. At first it might seem as if you are making up the message. Do not censor or rationalize what comes through, but allow the words to flow unhindered. Soon you will hear astounding truths. The needs and opinions of your body will not always be in sync with the wishes and ideas of your conscious mind, but this is normal.

6. You may continue to talk with your body as long as it feels comfortable. Repeat this practice as often as you wish. In fact, it is most healing if performed daily.

7. When you feel ready to end the practice, return to normal consciousness and write down what you have experienced.

Magical Practice To Reveal Your Woundedness and Heal It

This practice discloses those areas of your body which feel most wounded and helps heal them with Chiron's love and compassion by the following procedures:

1. Sit in a comfortable position and relax by taking several deep breaths. Now count from ten to zero, allowing your body to relax even more with each count.

2. Attune yourself with Divine Love as represented through the energy of Chiron. State firmly that you are willing to change and grow and want to heal yourself.

3. Visualize the astrological symbol of Chiron as shown at the beginning of this chapter. Build it up with your inner vision until it is large enough to envelop you completely, creating an energetic bond with the power of Chiron.

4. Encourage your body to express itself to you. Tell it how much you love it and that you are ready and willing to work closely with it.

5. Now become aware of your body and the area that feels most wounded. Then imagine that your conscious self shrinks to about two inches in height while your body remains unchanged.

6. Transfer your consciousness to your little self and enter your body through the heart chakra. You are carrying a torch and light it with the fire of your soul that burns in your heart chakra.

7. With your flaming torch in hand proceed to the area of your body that feels most wounded. Imagine that the wounded area is hollow inside. Illuminate this cave with your torch and note carefully what you see. The walls may have strange paintings or symbols. You may encounter familiar images inside the cave or even see hurtful past events appear before you as if on a movie screen. Note the form, texture, and color of the inside of your wound. Whatever you encounter in the depth of your wound, pay close attention to it. If it is a symbol, identify it. If you see a person or alien being, ask its reason for being there. Then when you feel ready, proceed to the next step.

8. Make an inner dedication to heal this wound. Then, by an act of will, increase the torch's light until you can see the wound no more. Visualize the blazing white light of the soul cleansing and transmuting the pain and suffering of the wound into health, power, and love.

9. Feel how all images inside the cave are disintegrated by the Spiritual Will, leaving nothing but the pure white light of spirit. Feel how your entire being is regenerated and restored in the healing experience.

10. When you feel that the area has been healed to your satisfaction, travel back to your heart chakra. Then return to normal size and merge with your body.

11. Slowly return to normal consciousness.

The Totem Animal

In many ancient traditions each person has a personal equivalent of the totem animal. This animal represents the raw power of the individual combined with the wisdom of the group soul of the animal's particular species.

In México where the animal spirit is called *nagual*, babies are assigned one at birth. Traditionally, the father of the newborn child spreads flour on the floor outside his dwelling and leaves it there overnight. The next morning he usually finds animal tracks across the flour. The father then identifies the animal and assigns it as *nagual* for the new baby.

In most cultures it is said that you have only one totem animal for your entire life. However, in my experience I have found that you may change animals several times along the path of your spiritual growth. For example, I felt great affinity to the tiger as a child. Then, when I was a teenager, I changed to the dog. Only recently have I changed yet again this time to the panther and the cat.

Now, if I look back over my life, this switch is easy to understand. When I was a child I lived in the country in southern Spain. I was bold and courageous, constantly seeking new physical challenges. Most of the day I spent alone outdoors. The tiger was the perfect totem for me.

Later, however, while I was learning the rules of society, exoteric and esoteric, studying and being a "good mother," my personality was more controlled and resembled that of a dog. Now that I am recovering my inner power, am more myself and less compliant to outside rules, my personality resembles that of a feline once more. Also, when I am in need of protection from other peoples' verbal, emotional, or mental assaults, I feel affinity with the armadillo!

It is not difficult to discover which animals have affinity with what people. In fact, it is an amusing game to match people with their animals. When I was a child I used to play this game with my grandmother. We would ask ourselves the question, "If so-and-so were an animal, what animal would s/he be?"

When you find your *nagual*, interact with it in your imagination. Have it teach you about yourself and your power. Study its body, its way of life, and habitat. What does it feed on? How does it move and catch its prey? Is it a loner or a pack animal? Bold or cautious? Silent or boisterous? Cuddly, fierce, or both? These details will give you a wealth of information about yourself, your behavior, and your ways of power.

Moreover, through your *nagual* you may contact the group soul of your animal's species and draw strength from it. The group soul of a species contains the essence of all of its members combined into one greater whole. It includes their experiences, power, and wisdom.

I would like to mention that Carlos Castaneda used the term *nagual* in his writings about the Mexican sorcerer Don Juan Matus in a very different sense from the way it is used in these pages. The two should not be confused here.

Magical Practice To Contact Your Nagual

This practice is intended to connect you to your *nagual.* Only after working for at least one week with the preceding two practices, should you do the following:

1. Sit or lie in a comfortable position and begin relaxing by breathing deeply and rhythmically. Now count from ten to zero, allowing your body to relax even more with each count.

2. Attune yourself with Divine Power as represented through the energy of Chiron. State firmly that you want to know and contact your *nagual.*

3. Visualize Chiron's astrological symbol as shown at the beginning of this chapter. Build it up with your inner vision until it is large enough to envelop you completely, creating an energetic bond with the power of Chiron.

4. Imagine before you the animals that attract you the most. Observe them for some time; then imagine one of them approaching you. The animal you see moving spontaneously toward you is most probably your present *nagual.*

5. Build up the image of this animal in great detail, while allowing the other animals to fade away from your inner vision. Use all your visualization skills, making the creature as vivid as possible.

6. Look the *nagual* straight in the eyes and talk to it. Ask it about itself and its connection to you. Ask it how you may learn from it and commit yourself to do so. Communicate with it as long as it feels comfortable, then proceed to the next step.

7. Visualize yourself entering the *nagual*'s body at the heart. Once inside stretch yourself so that your shape coincides with the *nagual*'s. Look

out through the animal's eyes as if they were your own. Mentally ask the animal to take you for a stroll around the neighborhood of its natural habitat and carefully note every detail. Then return to where you started and exit the *nagual*'s body.

You may stop the practice at this point and leave the next part for another day, or you may proceed if you feel ready. Both decisions are fine. If you decide to continue, do the following:

8. Reverse the procedure by having the animal enter you through your heart chakra. Once inside you allow the *nagual* to expand until its shape coincides with yours. Now pay close attention to every detail. How does the animal's power combine with yours? Does it feel safe? Familiar? Or is it frightening? Uncontrollable? How would merging with this animal's force improve your life?

9. After your questions have been answered, relax and enjoy merging with this being. Embrace it with your unconditional love. Feel and absorb its raw power, purity, and wisdom. Understand its function in the Great Plan.

10. When you feel ready to end the contact, thank the animal, then allow it to depart the way it came.

11. Slowly return to normal consciousness.

URANUS

URANUS

Attunement with the Archetypal Power of Uranus

Uranus is the archetype of spontaneity and eccentricity. His fertilizing action provides the element of change in the continuity of evolution. He accounts for quantum leaps in the development of any life form on any dimension. Uranus frees us from the tight grip of a Saturnian world and introduces us to the boundless possibilities and infinite dimensions of Neptune which are incorporated into our multifaceted existence by the power of Pluto.

Uranus brings great flashes of intuition, revealing a completely new and revolutionary perspective of life. He connects us to the transpersonal and cosmic aspect of our own spirit, regardless of the effects this might have on our safe, structured personal lives and environments.

Uranus' power exposes new spiritual concepts and ideas, pushing us toward the innovation and freedom necessary for spiritual evolution, showing the way to a more-dynamic life and fuller expression of the Divine Self, illumination, and enlightenment.

Uranus' influence is usually considered by the ordinary person to be uncomfortable if not painful due to his unexpected eruptions into the safe and known. The power of Uranus strikes like a lightning flash, suddenly illuminating our dark and sleepy inner landscape, exposing its features and inhabitants unforgivingly to the harsh realities of bright daylight. Some landscapes, especially the subconscious ones, are at times better left alone and in darkness lest their countenance prove too disrupting to our untrained vision.

Uranus, always sudden and usually harsh, is, nonetheless, extremely effective. It is important to notice that he can be ruthless; his action is indifferent to societal codes or even to our personal understanding of "right living" or spirituality.

Uranian influence surfaces regardless whether it conforms to the traditional views of right and wrong. He is often chaotic and painfully unpredictable. His emergence follows a strange randomly electrical law, which originates in a realm far beyond human comprehension and anticipation. This unpredictability is precisely the reason for his efficiency in shattering the overly rigid, growth-suffocating structures of the safe and known.

On the one hand, although the power of Uranus might unsettle us, it will only hurt us if we resist change by clinging to the stiff patterns of our sheltered, predictable environments. On the other hand, to benefit fully from Uranian power we must also have solid grounding of life experience and spiritual values on which to stand. Otherwise, his influence will not bring regeneration and refreshment, merely chaos.

Indeed, Uranus does have a ruthless side, but to deny it would only diminish his deconditioning, inspiring, and fertilizing effect. However, by learning how to receive and channel his influence effectively, we may utilize his tremendous power to our advantage without harm.

He is a higher octave of the element of air and the planet Mercury. Since he is strongly related to the mental level, he greatly stimulates curiosity and a detached, innovative attitude. He shatters stagnant mental patterns with his sudden electrical inrush and compelling demand for change. He provides a synthesizing quality to the mind by connecting the right, intuitive half of the brain to its left, rational counterpart, thereby making new circuits and crosscurrents that revolutionize our habitual thinking patterns.

Through Uranus we gain emotional detachment from conventionality and the inner freedom to identify with innovative and broader ideals. Under the influence of electrical Uranian energy we are thrilled and delighted at the prospect of novelty and exploration, completely overriding our fear of the unknown so deeply ingrained in the human psyche.

The initiate of Uranus walks freely into the new lands of his creative imagination toward enlightenment, all activated by the Great Cosmic Impulse of which Uranus is the transmitter. S/he takes great and sudden leaps in personal development with an attitude of detachment and carelessness that doesn't cling to outdated views and ways of reacting.

Uranian influence is easily resented by others because they interpret its effects as emotional coldness or even ruthlessness. However, it is necessary to go through a temporary emotional indifference to gather enough energetic momentum to be carried to the next stage of our personal evolution on the crest of the Uranian charge. The more we have allowed our life, energy, flow, inspiration, and vitality to be suffocated by the dictates of society, convention, safety, and predictability, the longer the needed emotional isolation will be.

However, if we don't balance the energy of Uranus with the energies of the seven inner planets, we can fall prey to glamour or astral illusion, the negative aspect of Neptune. We will become deluded into thinking that our new perspective is the only correct one and, consequently, we will over-identify with the new view Uranus is presenting us, often carelessly overthrowing all acquired virtues and values for the sake of some new adventure.

It is easy to see how the effect of Uranus might become chaotic and destructive in the long run, pushing us from one new adventure to the next, without our even finishing the first. We would end up leading fickle and superficial lives, identifying with whatever is new and revolutionary merely for the sake of its inherent emotional thrill and attendant sense of freedom.

Uranian energy clears the chakras and the central channel (or *sushumna*, as it is called in the East) for the ascent of kundalini. When properly contacted he works directly on the nervous system producing an Uranian "surge" of power that activates the entire organism.

The purely astrological influence of Uranus is erratic and intermittent; only through attunement, focused will, and understanding can it be harnessed into a controlled, steadied flow. Nevertheless, even with proper attunement, it is of vital importance to provide safe physical channels and opportunities for the flow of its tremendous creative power and need for freedom. If this is not done properly, the physical manifestation of this power creates considerable tension and restlessness.

On the mundane level, Uranus rules activities related to electrical energy requiring detached, clear thinking involving computers and other technological instruments of this modern age.

The God Uranus in Mythology

According to Greek cosmogony, in the beginning all was dark and infinite Chaos from which sprang Gaea, or earth and material existence. Gaea, in turn, gave birth to Uranus, the starry sky whom she made her equal. Thus, the universe with its polar opposites was formed.

Uranus coupled with his mother Gaea and through their union they created the first race that was to populate this new universe: the Titans. The Titans were twelve in number, six male and six female: Iapetus, Crius, Hyperion, Coeus, Oceanus, and Cronus; and Themis, Thetys, Rhea, Theia, Mnemosyne, and Phoebe.

Later they gave birth to the Cyclopes, three in number, who largely resembled the Titans except for their one large eye in the middle of their foreheads. Then they created three monsters each with one-hundred arms and fifty heads.

Uranus, horrified by his offspring, cast them away by locking them in the depths of their mother's womb. Gaea grieving over the situation for some time, grew increasingly angry and vengeful and created a plan to vindicate her children. Out of her body she fashioned a sickle or "*harpe*" to castrate Uranus with the help of her progeny.

None of her offspring, however, was willing to assist her, except for her youngest son, Cronus. That same evening Uranus came to join his wife as usual, accompanied by Night, daughter of Chaos. Cronus, hiding next to his mother, attacked his father by surprise and castrated him with the sickle. Then Cronus threw his father's severed genitals into the ocean where they transformed themselves into a white foam from which Aphrodite was born. Where Uranus' blood hit the earth several entities were born, among them the Furies and the nymphs of the ash tree.

What we are told here is that Gaea as daughter of Chaos signifies both the cosmic primordial womb and feminine principle as well as material manifestation and "Mother Earth." The marriage of Uranus and Gaea represents the union of the creative mental principle of Uranus with Gaea's material form which grounds his vision.

While Uranus' imagination played freely in the realms of the mind dreaming up a perfect world, he did not realize that his ideas and visions had to clothe themselves in material garments to become manifest reality, and, therefore, coarser and less fluent than his original vision. When he saw his children fully formed and was greatly disappointed by their appearance, he decided to deny his fatherhood by rejecting them.

This rejection caused the rebellion of one of his children, Cronus or Time, who by castrating his father ended the continuity of a timeless eternity. By severing Uranus' genitals, Cronus broke off the direct connection between the creative genius (Uranus here representing the soul and spirit) and its physical vehicle and means of manifestation (Gaea as the physical body and personality). By his action Cronos forced manifestation to the confines of time and space (Cronus and Gaea). This is a clear account of the descent of the spirit into matter along the involutionary arc of manifestation where direct creation through the power of the mind is replaced (temporarily) by procreation on the physical plane; thus, the subsequent reign of Cronus, the Saturn of astrology, and his wife and sister Rhea.

Uranus in Astrology

Uranus rules the astrological sign of Aquarius.

His natural house is the Eleventh House (friends, the abstract mind, intellectual and social relationships with groups and organizations, hopes, wishes, and aspirations).

Uranus is masculine and positive. The glyph that represents Uranus symbolizes our physical being on one side and our spiritual being on the other joined by a cross of matter and topping a circle, designating the sun/soul pressing onward to ever-greater realms of experience and growth.

Basic key words describing the influence of Uranus are originality, creativity, genius, resourcefulness, electricity, awakening, intuition, revolution, unpredictability, eccentricity, innovation, and rebellion.

The negative attributes of Uranus are irresponsibility, chaos, superficiality, fanatical idealism, emotional aloofness, and ruthlessness.

The basic function of Uranus in our astrological chart is to initiate changes wherever necessary in our life and habit patterns. Uranian energy throws us into the unexpected and unknown, forcing us to experience the new and unusual, ever expanding our field of awareness.

In the physical body, Uranus rules over nervous conditions, tension, the lower legs, ankles, and calves. He also rules over the flow of electricity in the body.

Furthermore, Uranus rules over earthquakes, electricity, radio communication, radar, rays, science fiction, inventions, rebellions, revolutions, and space travel.

Inner Journey To Contact the Archetype

Sit or lie in a comfortable position and begin relaxing by breathing deeply and rhythmically. Now count from ten to zero, allowing your body to relax even more with each count.

As your surroundings start to fade slowly, you find yourself on a large rocky platform. While examining this rock formation more closely, you notice that it is really the top of a high mountain. The sun is low on the western horizon, nearly setting. You feel safe in its warm rays and take a seat on the plateau's edge.

Comforted by the warmth of the dark rock under your body, you begin reflecting on your life and yourself. You remember all those past events that have impacted you, perhaps forcing you to take new directions or gently guiding you toward new adventures. You remember all those "rites of passage" you experienced that made you who you are now.

Take some time to let yourself relive all these memories as vividly as possible. Soon you will be able to recognize a pattern of growth, intuition, and Higher Guidance. You should remember exactly the day you first saw this book and link it to the chain of events prompted by your Inner Guidance.

Now that you have organized your life in chronological order and gained a deeper understanding from it, you realize that you are once again facing a turning point, a rite of passage. This, if you succeed, will make you an individual in your own right, helping you break free from conventionalism and conditioned mass behavior.

This time there will be no gentle guide to lead you on your journey. You must go alone. The yawning depth below your feet, as you can now well recognize, is the Abyss. To cross it successfully you must become the Divine Fool and simply jump ahead, regardless of any danger you may encounter. You must feel a deep faith in the universe, God, and yourself, knowing that whatever may happen, even if painful at first, will always be for the better. Like a child, anticipating the thrill of a new adventure, you must disregard momentarily the warning voice of tradition and leap into the unknown.

While these thoughts run through your head, you look down for a moment, and once more you are overcome by fear and doubt; the abysmal depth below your feet looks so very real. You think there is no way to make it down or across safely. What if you fail? What if you fall and die? But soon you pull yourself together. This is only a mind game, after all, and you might as well play it. Now bracing yourself with new courage, you jump into the air and through the symbol of Uranus that has formed itself directly in front of you. You fly away instantly, carried along by a warm ascending summer breeze.

As soon as you are lifted up and away from the hard rock, your perceptions change. You feel nearly weightless now and begin to experience a deep communion with the air that carries you. You feel the wind as a live entity; you can almost touch the electromagnetic waves that permeate its atmosphere. The different frequencies manifest in your new vision as intense colors of unknown hues. You feel the bubbles of gas constituting the atmosphere as if they were highly colored little elementals dancing joyfully in the breeze, caressing your skin as they pass. You perceive how the earth's electromagnetic force field pulls gently on your nearly weightless body, invigorating your entire being. Give yourself some time to feel and understand these elements well. Let them permeate you with their joy of being, their sense of worriless existence and child-like freedom.

Once you feel well saturated with these new feelings, you look up and away from earth. As soon as you decide to experience Uranus, the big blue planet rises majestically in the sky. Instantly you feel a strong attraction and soar up and away from earth to meet him.

As you approach Uranus you are baffled by the way the planet spins around its axis. The motion is so swift you are not quite certain how to land without injuring yourself. Nevertheless, as you come closer, the magnetic attraction becomes so great that, before you realize it, you find yourself standing on its surface.

Not knowing which direction to go, you start to follow a little path that leads straight ahead. As you walk on slowly, images start to rise all around you. They are so intense and realistic that it is very difficult for you to remain calm and recognize them for what they are, merely images.

You see millions of people so set in their ways that terrible earthquakes and other great cataclysms are necessary to change them. They are uprooted and expelled from the safety of their little lives, forced to start all over again. You see accidents that partially mutilate people compelling them to seek new ways of life and expression. You are shown how animals become extinct because they lack the ability to adapt and flow with any changes in global climate and temperature. You see people so afraid of change and innovation that they have totally suffocated the voice of their own intuition, freezing themselves and their environment in time, and even starting to decay... To your great surprise you also recognize your old self among these miserable individuals, that "self" you were just a few minutes ago. Now you realize how deeply you have been affected and conditioned by the Saturnian elements in your life and understand that it is up to you to move ahead.

While these thoughts and realizations build themselves up more and more clearly in your mind, the scenery begins to change. No longer are you surrounded by cataclysms, earthquakes, and suffering people, but by an entirely new world of possibilities opening up before you.

You see images of dreams you had while you were a child, all those things you wished to become when you grew up. They are still here now and very much alive. In fact, they never left you; it was you who "left" them. You were so busy living out what you thought you ought to live that you repressed and forgot what you truly wanted.

Live through all these visions again; allow them all to take form for a few moments and become real in your imagination. Then slowly and gently bring yourself to more-recent wishes and dreams. Allow these to be vivified for a few moments by your creative mind, then let them pass by.

Now look ahead and see how, beyond all these unfulfilled visions, new ones form. These are from the future. Study them carefully because they will show you all the opportunities you will have, all those new ways of living and reacting you will encounter. Live through them also, try them out, assimilate them, make them part of you. Stretch yourself to encompass them all and more! You are infinitely big and powerful here and now! This is the realm of your intuition and your creative mind. Remember: Creativity is limitless!

Let yourself play with all these new possibilities and ideas. Immerse yourself in them; live them as if they were already real! Let these new possibilities touch your innermost essence and watch carefully how each one makes you react. Which one is more energetic, blissful, loving? Continue with this as long as it feels comfortable. When you start to feel saturated with your new visions and ideas, then it will be time to move on and concentrate on the landscape around you.

Before you in the distance stands a magnificent throne. It is empty. This throne radiates a kind of electric blue never seen on earth. The light of the throne feels extremely cold but invigorating, prickly, and effervescent like water from a cold mountain spring. As you approach, you are irresistibly drawn to it and slowly seat yourself.

It is only now that you come to understand what you have just accomplished. You, as a child of earth, are truly one of the Titans buried since time immemorial deep within the womb of Gaea. Now you have risen far above your usual sphere of existence and have reached far beyond the influence of Saturn or "Father Time" to rejoin Father Sky or Uranus in the starry heavens. You have redeemed and completed the myth of Uranus. You have, through your willingness to seek his creative fertilization, restored his genitals and creative potential lost for so long. Here, in truth, you are above and beyond the influence of time. Uranus has never been castrated on this level; it is only to function creatively on earth and in the physical worlds that the power of Uranus needs you to link and mediate, to become his vehicle.

While these thoughts and interpretations rush through your mind for some time, you start growing and growing to the size of a giant. To your amazement you can see another giant figure—your mirror image standing directly in front of you. You recognize it instantly for what it is—the true son or daughter of Uranus and Gaea, your own Titanic self, rejected and locked into dense matter during the process of civilization. You welcome this rejected self, and by holding it in your gigantic arms you reabsorb it lovingly into your present self.

Remain this way for some time and feel the invigorating sense of your giant self merging with your everyday personality. Open yourself to your true Titanic potential and join to this the wisdom acquired through ages of separation from this aspect of yourself. Ready yourself for a new epoch, one of royalty and leadership, of power and inspiration. Assume your new and empowered self! Recognize the infinite fertility of earth, the physical realm when correctly mated to the creativity of mind. Decree that there is no limit to your creativity and its actualization! Once you feel the process of fusion with the Titan if a man or Titaness if a woman is completed, shrink to your normal size, then wait seated on the throne.

You feel happy and strong, ready to embrace the world. Suddenly the sky seems to shake and the stars around you move in a spiral motion, enveloping you in an iridescent haze. The stars circle around you again and again as if searching for a point of rest, covering you with sparkling stardust as they pass.

The entire galaxy seems to be revolving around you now, faster and faster. You cannot discern single stars anymore and are soon entirely submerged in the familiar electric-blue light. You hear a deep masculine voice speak:

"I am Uranus. You cannot see me, for the impact of my form would be too great for you at this point. I cannot enter you and bestow the gift of my fertility unless you ask me. Whenever I come without being asked, I appear to be cruel and destructive. However, my power is only painful to dense and unprepared minds. My impact is so swift and revolutionary that my energy will only be felt as beneficial if you desire it deeply and with all your being."

After having come such a long distance and integrating with your Titanic self, you have lost all fear and willingly open yourself to the god. The electric-blue light turns into a starry mist again, entering your body through the back of your neck just below the skull. You wait patiently until all has entered and see only darkness around you. You feel your mind expanding, with flashes of intuitive insights running through your awareness. You tremble with excitement, feeling tremendously invigorated as the starry particles spread throughout your being and fuse with each tiny cell in your body.

Although you do not necessarily see any clear images of future events at this point, you accept what is happening and know that a permanent change is being effected. You will never be the same again.

Remain in fusion with the god for some time and as long as it feels agreeable. Then, before bidding the god farewell, you ask him for a personal message. Allow some time for this to occur, then open yourself again to allow the god to depart.

Express your thanks to the god as the starry mist exits through the back of your throat chakra. Feel the rapport between you that still remains unchanged. Watch how the surroundings slowly return to their original form. Stand up from the throne and slowly walk back along the path from where you came.

Before you know it, you are high in the sky again and heading toward earth. As you approach the earth's atmosphere you can already see the symbol of Uranus building up in the sky. Confidently you pass through. You land gently on the same rocky mountaintop where you started only a few minutes ago. Nothing has changed here. It is only you who are a different person—newly born, fresh, rejuvenated, and inspired. As the landscape slowly fades away, you gradually regain your normal waking consciousness.

Magical Use of Uranus

Preliminaries for the magical use of Uranus' energy involve the following considerations:

• Remember that the Uranian energy is very powerful and drastic. Check yourself carefully before using it in a magical practice. Be prepared to change completely in exactly those areas which you least expect and which feel most uncomfortable to change. If you are not yet ready for it, all right, but do not invoke Uranus carelessly or experimentally.

• Beforehand take responsibility for the new awareness and knowledge this exercise will bring and commit yourself to using it for the good of all.

• Open yourself without fear to the forces of change; be ready and willing to grow and mature in all aspects of your life. Above all, be extremely honest with yourself.

• Inflame yourself with the desire to revolutionize and transcend the safe and known and to leap into the unknown.

• Let the aspiration to transcend the narrow conditioned view of human society and existence pervade your work. Identify with Divine Wisdom.

• Commit yourself to using the intuitive knowledge and detachment you gain through this practice for the good of all and balancing it carefully with Divine Love and compassion.

Magical Practice To Free Oneself from the "Golden Cage"

To show you which areas of your life feel dead and lifeless and when and how to energize them and invoke change, do the following practice:

1. Sit or lie in a comfortable position and begin relaxing by breathing deeply and rhythmically. Now count from ten to zero, allowing your body to relax even more with each count.

2. Meditate on yourself and your life for forty minutes every day, twenty in the morning and twenty in the evening for a period of three days. Note carefully which areas and activities feel lifeless, stagnant, repetitive, joyless, boring, etc. It is important to recognize your feelings and not be fooled by outer appearances or circumstances.

It is often the case that the life of a particular person seems perfectly fun, happy, luxurious, exciting, and fulfilling to the objective observer, but to the person inside it feels as if s/he were locked in a golden cage with all sense of adventure, spiritual growth, and aliveness lost.

In the worst cases this "death-in-life" syndrome feels so suffocating that one is ready to do whatever is necessary to regain the feeling of being alive. It is precisely this stage that will provide the necessary momentum to accomplish such changes successfully. However, it also carries the danger of being over-enthusiastic about getting out and away from the status quo and jumping head on into whatever promises to be better.

You must be very certain to what extent you can tolerate change and are willing to go with it. It is extremely painful to invoke change and then try to resist it.

3. On the fourth day take a blue marker, pencil, and piece of paper, then write down the areas in your life which feel dead. Describe in detail your personal "golden cage" to yourself. Use your pencil. (Save the blue marker for later.) Then center yourself in your soul or individuality as best you can. Identifying yourself with the sun, become the central sun of your own personal solar system.

4. Still focused on your own soul, meditate on the above issues again for twenty minutes morning and evening on this fourth day.

5. During your meditation pronounce the following sentence at least three times, aloud if possible:

"I am well centered in my soul. I am One with the Solar Angel. I am the Central Spiritual Sun and Creator of my own Personal Universe. I, (your name), am now ready for the next step along the Path of Evolution and assume full responsibility for it. I open my personality to the guidance of my soul and my spirit. "

If you do not receive any specific input during this day, do not worry; just proceed to the next step. The power invoked will manifest regardless of your conscious realizations.

6. On the fifth day take your list, relax, and get into a meditative state. Then pronounce the following words of power:

"I am well centered in my soul. I am One with the Solar Angel. I am the Central Spiritual Sun and Creator of my own Personal Universe. I, (your name) am now ready for the next step along the Path of Evolution and assume full responsibility for it. I now give myself, by the power of the God Within, which I am, the creative impulse that fertilizes, changes, and renovates myself and my personal universe! I, (your name), invoke Uranus to give me his creative and fertilizing thrust. "

7. Take up your list and description of your "golden cage" and draw the astrological symbol of Uranus on the entire list with the blue marker.

8. Stand up and hold the list in your right hand.

9. Now allow Uranus to overshadow you in the following way:

Build up with your inner vision the image of the great sky god standing behind you. Make his body about seven feet high. (Although his features have not been described in the inner journey, you may build up your own image of him. If you cannot see a godform for him, you may chose to use the galaxy as representative of his energy and allow this abstract form to overshadow you.)

Feel his great power and aura extending far beyond his body's limits into outer space. Concentrate on your love and admiration for Uranus as well as on your gratitude to him for helping you in this matter. Now allow him to step up as close as possible behind you and concentrate on the overshadowing effect of his aura on yours. Still focused on your love for Uranus, allow him to empower you by blending his great aura with your smaller one. Feel how both your energy fields are strengthened and vitalized by the contact. Feel your aura grow in size and power to coincide with that of the god. Remain this way for awhile before you proceed to the next step.

10. Hold the list up to your heart chakra and focus on the tremendous Uranian surge of energy and Divine Power. Allow this blazing energy to surround you with a thousand lightning flashes. Feel how the cold fire rushes through your body and aura, revitalizing every cell of it. See how one of the myriad lightning flashes strikes the list and sets it ablaze, burning it in an imaginary white flame.

11. Remain this way for some time, allowing the power of Uranus to roam freely through your body and aura. Watch how after the initial energetic surge following the fusion of both your auras that your energy gradually settles down into a more-predictable rhythm, racing up your spine, then turning at your crown to race down the front of your body. As it hits the soles of your feet it resumes its upward motion along your back. Let it circulate this way for as long as it feels comfortable, but no longer than three minutes.

12. Allow Uranus to depart by having him step back and then slowly, but thoroughly, disengage your aura from his. Thank Uranus for his help, express your love to him, and dissolve his form completely.

13. Slowly return to normal consciousness.

14. The next day pick up your list again. Concentrate on the first issue on the list. Find one area in your home you can relate to that issue (a closet full of clothes, a bookshelf, file cabinet, garage, etc.). Proceed to clean it, throwing away any old unnecessary stuff and reorganizing what is left. This is a ritualistic act, and if performed with the correct attitude, will certainly impact the issue on which you are focusing. Take it seriously. The following day choose another area that corresponds to the next item on the list, and so forth. Do this for three consecutive days and from then on at least once a month.

NEPTUNE

NEPTUNE

Attunement with the Archetypal Power of Neptune

Neptune is illusive, confusing, mystical, and nebulous, yet he is also transcendental, inspiring, and visionary. He represents unconditional love and sacrifice in its highest expression. He shows the essential Oneness and interconnectedness of all Creation, dissolving the "I" and revealing the All.

What practical use does Neptunian experience have on earth apart from obvious escapism? Why would we want to spend time to attune to a power that denies what we are or think we are? A force that throws us out of our "I" and into some nebulous place where the boundaries of ourselves are erased and the "I" is no more? Why do we need that?

The answer to these questions is strange and unexpected: Yes, indeed! When we enter the "Not I" or the All at will, we gain tremendous power! We repossess the All we have lost and with it our creative power. Neptune is our doorway to this experience.

Neptune allows us to grasp the fact we are One with all creation, and, therefore, can claim its power as ours. This connection to the Divine Power of all creation is not done by expanding our consciousness like an overinflated balloon ready to burst at the slightest touch, but by an introspective journey into our inner Central Stillness, the source of that power.

Neptune teaches us to reach back to our own center where everything is already perfect, where all opposites, all struggle, all right and wrong balance and cancel each other. On that level, behind the glamour of physical existence, everything is always right, true, and balanced.

By entering these mystic depths inside ourselves, the realms of our own spirit, our Inner Godhead, we gain a new certainty, that is, the knowledge, that although it is good to strive for the light, to search for spirituality and to work diligently at bettering ourselves, deep within we already are perfect here and now, with all our faults and defects. We are a perfect and integral part of the Great Pattern and all is good and sacred just the way it is.

At this point Neptune will shock us. For we suddenly realize, to our great surprise, that there are really no hard-and-fast rules to this Great Game of Life, other than the ones we arbitrarily agree on among ourselves to live, observe, and experience our existence in the seeming linearity of time and space!

Then, reclaiming our power as true creators of our personal universe, we can *choose* to go ahead and change, to expand and better ourselves even more. We as creators, after seeing the Great Pattern in which the "good" and the "bad" are equally sacred, choose to manifest more Light, not because darkness, stagnation, regression, or whatever else we usually classify as unspiritual are bad, but because evolution and enlightenment represent our path and our choice!

Positively and willingly to accept and benefit from the forces of change we must feel inner certainty to experience choice in our lives. We must have seen, felt, and understood the Great Pattern and the sequence of its unfoldment in order to work with the power of kundalini and not be confused and shattered by it. And this we may see with Neptune's help.

Neptune dissolves the imaginary prisons we create for ourselves with "shoulds" and "musts" or belief systems we have built through social and moral conditioning.

He works subtly and steadily as opposed to Uranus' sudden flashes of intuition. Neptune shifts our values and moral beliefs back and forth between apparent truth and falseness, highlighting their importance in some areas while blurring their meaning in others until finally we see through them and anchor our core self consciously on a new higher level of perception.

Neptune dissolves the emotional barriers and protective armoring we erect between us and our environment. He, acting through our emotions, shows us the interconnectedness of all beings and things. Under his influence we may merge deeply with our surroundings and become one with them, replenishing our strength, beauty, and vision as if drinking from the fountain of youth. In this merging all judgmental thoughts dissipate and we are immersed in the inherent "goodness" of the All. In this state we see how many parallel realities coexist peacefully without competing with each other, in brotherhood and friendship, nourished from the same Great Source where we find inner peace.

Furthermore, Neptune allows us to merge with the Great Artist of All Manifestation (who is also, in a way, our True Self) and experience a deep mystical ecstasy, enveloping our entire being with the great physical and spiritual pleasure of unconditional love.

Like no other energy, Neptune truly blurs the poles of opposites and blends them into beautiful shades of the same Light that sustains our being. He propels our imagination, fueled by the emotion of ecstasy, to transcend all limits and to behold truth, the Great Reality that lies behind and beyond our worldly perceptions where the good and the bad are one beautiful whole. This is Neptune's greatest quality, but also a most-fearsome pitfall for the unprepared.

If only for a while, it is beautiful to be in a world in which all is equally good, all is lovely and peaceful, all is nurtured and sustained in eternal unconditional love, where no distinctions are made, and no choices are necessary.

But for those who glimpse too soon the World of Truth and Beauty accessed through Neptune and do not possess sufficient development of will, reason, and discrimination (or the gifts of Saturn), it can prove a trap. Many are drawn to drugs to reach that Neptunian realm at will, but once there they have a very difficult time returning without assistance to the so-called "normal" world.

To apply Neptune's powers successfully to our work and discipline, to our sense of discretion and discrimination, we must immerse ourselves completely in his mystical ecstasy and unconditional love for awhile, then force ourselves to return through an act of focused will. Only then can we apply what we have gained from the experience to the world of forms as creative inspiration and happiness. To combine and balance the powers of Neptune with Saturn successfully requires the greatest of skills, but it also brings enormous rewards.

Proper attunement with Neptune leads us gently through the rough patches of daily living. He not only reminds us of the beauty and purity of the Truth behind it All, but he also allows us to recognize that the world is not always as serious and rigid as it seems.

Since Neptune is related to projections, illusion, fashion, and fads, he often is involved in projections that reveal themselves as sudden urgent needs for one thing or another—for no apparent reason. Here the lower aspect of Neptune is at work, clouding the real issue giving an illusionary meaning to something truly irrelevant.

On the mundane level Neptunian energies are extremely difficult to deal with. Neptune's delusive qualities may be filtered out through a focused will, strict discipline, and spiritual training, but it can never be completely eradicated. What we perceive as solid reality is, in truth, in constant flux. When we look at all from a Neptunian viewpoint, the world appears ever-changing like the currents and tides of the ocean. This same flow triggers the changes and shifts in our own emotional and mental states. What we experience as true and valid today might not be so tomorrow; Neptune will demand we learn to go with this flow while at the same time try not be swallowed up by it. The choice is ours, but the power, inspiration, love, and ecstasy he provides are unimaginable.

Neptunian energy is essentially non-physical. Its physical effect can best be observed in the creative inspiration of the artist, poet, musician, and spiritual teacher who has a vision, and is then able to bring it down through his/her body and manifest it in some physical form such as new teaching, book, work of art, song, or poem.

If not mediated through an intelligent being, Neptunian energy will, like the ocean's waves, work slowly but consistently on physical structures, eroding them, making them shift and move slowly, turning hard rock into fine gravel. A necessary procedure to allow space for new and better structures to emerge.

Remember: You are the Great Artist of your own existence and are able to tap this powerful energy at will. You can channel it purposefully down and out through your own system to create that great Work of Art as the unfoldment of your own spirit in this present life.

On a purely physical level the effects of Neptune's power is relaxing and soothing to a tense-and-stressed body and comforting to a tight, blocked personality. People who achieve a spontaneous contact with Neptunian force, yet are unfamiliar with its loosening, flowing, shifting, and "spacey" feeling, may feel unsettled at first. This is normal; it just mirrors the fear of letting go.

For those who are not interested in transcendental experiences, Neptune brings artistic inspiration, especially to musicians, poets, and the more-abstract art forms.

The God Neptune/Poseidon in Mythology

Poseidon was the son of Cronus (Saturn) and Rhea. Cronus swallowed all his children at birth and, unfortunately, did not spare Poseidon. Luckily Zeus, Poseidon's youngest brother, who through a trick escaped his father's voracious hunger, gave Cronus a potion to make him vomit all his children, setting Poseidon free.

During the war against the Titans, Poseidon fought at Zeus' side, breaking mountains with his powerful trident and throwing chunks into the ocean to create islands. After the battle with the Giants was over, the world was divided into three parts: Zeus (Jupiter) took the heavens, his brother Hades (Pluto) received the Underworld, and Poseidon (Neptune) was made king of the sea, lakes, and rivers.

Poseidon's wife was Amphitrite, daughter of Oceanus, the god of the primordial waters. She was a gentle and patient deity who symbolizes the feminine principle of the sea. Amphitrite bore Poseidon three children: a son, Triton, and two daughters, Rhode and Benthesicyme.

The strong and handsome sea god was a passionate lover, but often unfaithful to his beautiful wife. Among Poseidon's best-known escapades was his seduction of Medusa inside the temple of Athena, which terribly infuriated his wife Amphitrite. In revenge she turned Medusa's hair into snakes. Later, however, something good was born from this tragedy. When the hero Perseus fought with Medusa and finally cut off her head, the magnificent winged stallion Pegasus was born from her blood. In another affair, Poseidon had a daughter and two sons by Alcyone, one of the Pleiades. One of their sons, Hyrieus, later became the father of the giant Orion.

The most-famous attribute of Poseidon was his trident.

Since there is much mysterious starlore and cosmic knowledge encoded in Greek myth, I encourage you to decipher and correlate them to the psychological and spiritual attributes mentioned above.

Neptune in Astrology

Neptune rules the astrological sign of Pisces.

His natural House is the Twelfth House (karma, selfless service, hidden enemies, confinement, frustrations, and limitations).

The influence of the planet Neptune is felt as feminine and receptive. The glyph that represents Neptune symbolizes the semicircle of the soul pierced by the cross of matter. It is a pictograph of the familiar trident associated with the King of the Sea.

Basic key words describing the influence of Neptune are universal love, vision, sacrifice, dissolution, inspiration, creativity, compassion.

The negative attributes of Neptune are fear, escapism, disillusionment, confusion, delusion, and glamour.

Neptune's basic function in the astrological chart is to dissolve outdated patterns and attachments in order to make room for growth. Neptune also by pointing out false projections and illusions, allows us to reclaim our lost power. Furthermore, he indicates the potential for artistic creativity and inspiration.

In the physical body, Neptune is said to rule the feet. Other things ruled by Neptune are intoxicants of all kinds, hallucinations, drugs and anaesthetics, secret affairs, liquor, spiritualism, psychic research, submarines, the oceans, fog and mist. In essence, Neptune rules water and all water-related activities.

Inner Journey To Contact the Archetype

Sit or lie in a comfortable position and begin relaxing by breathing deeply and rhythmically. Now count from ten to zero, allowing your body to relax even more with each count.

Imagine that your surroundings are slowly fading and you find yourself walking along a beautiful beach. The weather is warm and the landscape resembles the coast of Greece. Ahead of you lies a little peninsula connected to the shore by a stretch of sand. It looks so pure and inviting that you start walking toward it without hesitation.

However, as soon as you approach the peninsula a heavy fog starts to lift from the waters. The fog becomes thicker and thicker as you move on and eventually covers the entire area. You stop, almost paralyzed for a moment, since it has become so heavy you cannot even see your feet. You don't know exactly how close you are to the little peninsula or if the stretch of sand will hold up to the incoming tide. Nevertheless, determined to reach your goal, you walk on.

After taking a few uncertain steps, you look up and, to your great relief, see a huge translucent gate appear in front of you. Its doorknob is formed in the shape of Neptune's symbol. You open it quickly and pass through.

Beyond the gate the weather seems to have cleared up again and you hear splashing sounds in the distance. It is Triton, son of Poseidon, accompanied by sea nymphs and dolphins jumping playfully in the calm waters. Triton approaches you and rises from the sea to give you a wet but warm embrace. He speaks:

"I am Triton, son of Poseidon and Amphitrite. I have come to show you the kingdom of my father. Come and mount my back! I shall take you safely to the king's palace. Fear not the waves for they will cause you no harm."

Only now do you notice that Triton is half human and half fish. His upper body is nicely formed with wide shoulders and well-defined muscles. His face is open and handsome; his bright-green eyes friendly. He smiles at you charmingly, and behind the appearance of a strong man you recognize the playful child hiding inside. You pause to think about the deeper meaning of the shape of his body. Wouldn't it be nice to learn how to swim in life's turbulent waters with the ease of a fish? To make certain you get the point, Triton lifts his massive fish tail and flips it joyfully up and down, soaking you from head to toe.

You laugh with him for awhile, then mount on his back to continue your journey. Within a few seconds you both vanish under the sea's surface. It is soft and warm here under the water, and contrary to your beliefs, in this strange ocean you are able to breathe perfectly. Moreover, your movements are much swifter and more elegant than they were on shore since your body lacks its usual rigidity and weight. Triton, as if reading your mind, responds to your thoughts with a roar of satisfaction.

You must hold tightly to your guide because the water becomes turbulent as you advance. Soon you find yourself alone with Triton in the midst of a terrible storm. Frightened, you close your eyes and lean your head against his neck, willingly surrendering to his lead. After all, he was born and raised in these tempestuous waters; he must know how to navigate them.

A few minutes go by, but just as you are getting used to the wild effervescence of the eddies against your skin, you are propelled out of the waters with one big thrust.

Suddenly you realize you are not on the shore nor in the water anymore, but far away from earth in outer space! The creature carrying you is not Triton anymore; his shape has shifted to that of Pegasus, the white-winged stallion!

Now you remember! You must transcend Neptune's watery realms on planet earth so that you might see and understand real Neptunian truth. While on earth Neptune's energy is almost always illusive, confusing, and shrouded in mystery. Earth is so full of projections and illusions; the "psychic fog" is so thick down there that it becomes extremely difficult to pierce through it voluntarily. Therefore, it is vital to detach from earth for some time and dive into the purity of outer space. There, untainted by the collective mind of the masses, one is more likely to unveil Truth.

Pegasus flies swiftly away from earth and toward the planet Neptune. After a long and beautiful passage, he finally lands gently on the surface of the blue-green globe. You slide down carefully from the horse's back and look around. All is shrouded in mist and a dense fog covers the ground. Nevertheless, the landscape of this remote world is not at all unfriendly, but welcoming and warm. Although you cannot see much ahead, there is an intrinsic feeling of familiarity and safety in the air.

Confidently you walk along a little path that stretches ahead into the mist. You set one foot in front of the other carefully since it is difficult to see the ground. Pegasus follows you faithfully, whinnying reassuringly.

As you examine the patches of fog that pass by, you recognize to your amazement that it does not resemble normal fog, rather it is formed of many beautiful visions of landscapes, people, and events. The colors of these visions are so vivid, much more intense than the ones you are accustomed to seeing on earth. Do these strange visions come from your personal imagination, you wonder? Or are they visible fragments of other realities parallel to yours? It matters not since they are such a joy to contemplate. At first you follow them with your eyes, but soon you are so delighted that they carry you away as they pass. You allow yourself to merge with these visions for a few moments, then walk on along the path into a clearing.

Here the fog has receded and the air is crisp and transparent. A tall handsome man stands before you. He is painting on a very large canvas. As you approach he greets you with a friendly voice. You greet him and introduce yourself by name. In reply the painter answers: "I am the Divine Artist and this is the canvas of your evolution. Welcome to Neptune, my friend!"

The painting is so large, that, as far as you can see, it does not seem to represent anything. What you perceive are merely dots of many shining colors covering the entire canvas in a seemingly random fashion. You reply that it is interesting, but that you do not quite understand its meaning. He answers: "You might not understand at first, but I will soon show you what it is. Please contemplate these colors and let them sink deeply into your being. "

You do what he asks. Then the Great Artist rises from his seat and hands you the painting. As soon as you touch the canvas, it starts to shrink. It becomes smaller and smaller until it is only a fraction of its original size. Or is it you who are growing larger and larger? You cannot really tell. Nevertheless, now that the painting seems to have shrunk, you clearly can see what it is: It is a perfect portrait of you in your most-magnificent celestial body. It is you *perfected*; it is a picture of your soul. All the little colored dots have blended together magically to form a greater and more-perfect whole where each dot is an equally important part of the Great Picture, where the darker areas emphasize the lighter ones, adding to the beauty of the entire creation. Contemplating it you understand: Each dot is necessary to form this beautiful portrait; however, the picture is only visible if you step back and look at its entirety. As long as you are too close, only certain dots will stand out and their significance to the whole Work of Art will be unrecognizable.

You thank the Artist and accept His gift with great reverence. Before you walk away though, the Artist asks you to hold the painting to your heart and let it shrink even more. As you do this the painting becomes smaller and smaller until it becomes a pure-white flame composed of all those luminescent little dots. With one great flash it enters the center of your heart where you will keep it safe forever.

You say farewell to the Artist, thanking him again for this invaluable gift, and walk on determined to find the palace of the sea king. Pegasus is happy to join you and walks by your side.

Still immersed in the beautiful feeling the painting is causing in your heart chakra, namely, the knowledge that in your soul you are already Divine and perfect, you continue ahead, moving your way through the mist. After awhile you reach another clearing. Pegasus is excited, and you can tell from the dancing motion in his steps that you must be very near your destination.

Suddenly the surroundings begin to change and the drifting fog starts to take the shape of a beautiful palace. All the visionary images suspended in the mist now come to life and form themselves into the King and Queen of the Sea and their entourage. As you approach them with respect, the King welcomes you and speaks: "It is not us whom you seek, oh traveler of infinite space! It is that part of you we represent, which you have lost and came to retrieve. Look here and do what you must do!" The King and Queen produce a huge oval mirror and position it between them. It reflects your own image and the misty world in which you find yourself. Recognizing the meaning of this, you proceed to absorb this beautiful effigy.

See how the mirror with all its images slowly moves toward you until its shape coincides exactly with the front of your body. The closer it gets to you, the faster it moves. Soon it is inside you, completely fused with your present self. This fusion brings about an energetic explosion, almost orgasmic. You merge completely with your mirror image, with the projection of yourself, to recapture the energy that was imprisoned in it.

Remain in deepest fusion for as long as it feels comfortable and allow the symbolism of what you are doing to flood your mind with realizations. Connect this experience in your consciousness with past, present, and future, regardless whether you fully understand the deeper implications of this act of fusion. It is sacred and Divine; it will have deep effects on your future life.

Ask Poseidon and Amphitrite, now within you, to give you a personal message. Remain open for awhile and accept what your receive.

When you feel it is time to return, say farewell to the god and goddess and mount Pegasus' back. You do not need to allow the mirror and its images to depart. Just as the painting you received from the Great Artist, they are an intrinsic part you are reclaiming and will keep forever.

Pegasus gallops back along the little path from wnich you came. In the distance you see the Divine Artist bent over a canvas, engrossed in his newest creation. You pass him swiftly and wave your farewell. Then, with one last leap Pegasus spreads his wings and soars up into the sky, away from Neptune, and back to earth.

The passage seems much shorter this time. Before long you both land gently on the little peninsula. You dismount the beautiful Pegasus. He rubs his head affectionately on your shoulder and you say farewell to the white stallion before he vanishes. You then retrace your steps through the translucent gate and walk back to the shore.

The landscape slowly fades away while gradually you regain your normal waking consciousness.

The Central Stillness

The pattern of infinite growth and expansion, the pattern of the Infinite Light Incarnate is contained in the Central Stillness and is accessed through Neptunian power. By consciously reaching the Central Stillness, merging with it, and making its qualities our own, we reconnect ourselves to the Great Cosmic Pattern of creation. From the new depths reached through this process, we may bring forth more light from our innermost recesses and help it to manifest more and more in the form of physical abundance, health, love, wisdom, and so forth.

In the Central Stillness we touch the point of greatest power where the Will of God is known, where there is no structure, simply Divine Will. Paradoxically, although that point has no structure yet, it contains in itself the Great Pattern. In this Sacred Pattern all truths coexist simultaneously. Although in everyday reality all is right action, discrimination, and a choice between the better over the lesser, any polarities are transcended here. All is blended, seen merely as shades of the one brilliant Light ever reflecting itself in its own glow.

The Light, the Power, the Wisdom, and Love of the Central Stillness which is God is limitless because it can recreate itself endlessly, following its own pattern. This it does holographically and each of its parts can do the same. Therefore, we, being one of its parts, have the power to materialize and crystallize Light into abundance endlessly. It is not as many believe that there is a "source" somewhere from which we can draw, but that *we* are the source, One with the Central Stillness that holographically contains the supreme pattern for manifesting.

Neptune makes us aware of the illusions of limitation and lack of power that bind the masses of humanity, letting us see beyond such illusions to find and recognize Divine Truth and to know that we are playing just the right part at the right time in the Great Pattern.

Although Neptune's energy and the conscious contact he may provide with the Central Stillness will not really dissolve the ego, they do serve as tools in the work of the Great Master to unfold His Pattern through us. Neptune's power lifts us beyond the ego as we pierce the veil of our fears, limitations, beliefs, and habits, allowing us to look and experience our naked Essence, the Great Master, God that is One with us at our Innermost Center.

This experience is not weakening, as the word "sacrifice" so often associated with Neptune suggests. On the contrary! It empowers us to the fullest, providing the most sought-after mystical ecstasy that comes from the knowledge and realization of that Great Power that we are! We are refreshed as if drinking from the fountain of youth; we are happy, fulfilled, and eager to make this new experience part of our daily living.

Neptune is the revealer. But to apply Neptune's experience to our daily lives successfully, we must integrate this new vision with the help of all the other planetary influences of the solar system, especially Saturn and the outer, transpersonal ones.

What use would it be to have prolonged contact with the Central Stillness if we could not bring back something into physical life? We would be mystics and dreamers at best, or at worst we would start to feel a great split between our visionary experiences and our physical existence.

Through occasional glimpses of the Central Stillness and a growing understanding of the Unfolding Pattern we can make these experiences an integral part of our day-to-day reality, consciousness, and personal habits. This means reorienting our daily life around the knowledge of that other reality behind the veil, completely restructuring one's life to have available *at will* at least part of the power of that Central Stillness.

Here is where the energy of Pluto comes in, forcing the old self to die and clearing ground for the emergence of the new and empowered self. By raising kundalini Pluto burns away obstructions one by one and forces this birth of Self.

In the Great Central Stillness we see the veil of illusion dissolve; we recognize how the structures of our so-called solid universe are but an infinitely unfolding series of projections and repetitions of the Pattern already contained in the essence of the Central Stillness.

We observe how our entire life, from our experiences and environment to the character of the people we meet and with whom we interact, is but an exact reflection of the growth pattern contained in the Seed of the Central Stillness. No other place is as sacred and special. Visit it as often as possible!

To know our True Self we must utilize the power of Neptune and go within, into the mystic ocean where he rules supreme. We must dive beneath the projections and illusions that form our personal physical existence in time and space (Saturn). We must pierce through them and *beyond* the unfolding Pattern to touch that Central Point that is both our True Self and All simultaneously.

The Power and Use of Projections

I believe that we are the creators and masters of our own universe, therefore, every person, thing, and event that happens "out there" is simply a reflection of what we, our inner selves, want and need to experience.

A common belief among therapists is that if you encounter "bad" events, people, and things in your life, it is because inside you are all messed up. The solution to this, they say, is to clear yourself within in order to attract "better" things to your life. This is partially true if we view all from a linear level of thinking.

This mode of thinking certainly has its place; however, if we want to grow beyond the limits of time and space and connect to The Divine Artist within each of us, we must remember that our personalities, who dwell in the linear world of time and space, can only present us part of the picture. Once we touch the realms of Neptune and what lies beyond we will see that in Divine Truth there is no good or bad, better or worse, clearer or more confused, but only different shades of the same one Light. And that is precisely what makes life so beautiful, this playing with the Light.

When Neptune is contacted at his highest level he shows you that there is no such thing as a "bad" person, event, or thing, but that all is there *for a good reason.* And that, yes, you in your capacity as Cosmic Creator elected to bring it into your life for a specific purpose, and not because you are less than Joe or Susie down the street.

Imagine your entire being in the form of a wheel, with soul at the center and the personality at the periphery (see also the diagram in appendix B). The soul projects its personality into the periphery of its influence (linear time and space) to learn more about what is "out there." The soul's purpose as vehicle of the spirit is to work on its environment to redeem it, bringing order into chaos, light (which stands for a more-encompassing, abundant life) into darkness (which stands for a less-abundant life were individual units are disconnected from each other and the whole), participating in what other aspects of the *one* God like itself are presently doing and creating. The spirit, which is at the core of the soul, is made of the same essence as the spirits of all other creatures "out there," and on its own level is one with all of them.

The way the soul understands and integrates to itself what happens "out there" is by becoming conscious of it. Our consciousness, while in the personality at the periphery of the wheel, is not large enough to encompass and understand all the details. Therefore, our personality projects experiences outward and allows other people, events, and things to play them out for it until consciousness expands enough to realize how these particular issues work. Then the personality can incorporate such into itself and pass it on to the soul as a conscious realization. Once we have properly assimilated and understood an issue, it somehow miraculously vanishes. That is, the new insight will work in our systems by "default" as it were and will not need further attention. *We will at that point regain the energy we used to cause that event to happen in our environment and the energy formerly bound in our friction with that event. Then we can use this new power to shift to a higher energetic level, inadvertently.* This happens all the time in our daily lives, but usually we are not aware of it.

With Neptune's power we can unravel this mechanism and the often complex energetic patterns it includes. We can view the essence of something, understand its use in our development, and then reconnect it to our own essence.

So if you find yourself in conflict with the lady down the street, that is certainly a signal she is acting out something (mostly subconscious, of course) that you need to look at more carefully. Maybe she represents a stage in human development from which you are trying to disengage yourself. Even though you try to do your best to remain calm when in her presence, somehow you always end up defending yourself when she is near. It is almost as if she wields some kind of occult power over you, although she seems to be just a normal person. Sounds familiar? Well, you are most probably projecting your need to be different from what she represents to you into the situation. Recognize your need for what it is and you will see how miraculously things start to even out between the two of you.

Furthermore, this defensiveness she brings out in you is draining some energy you could use for better purposes. Normally a psychologist would tell you that you need to "forgive" that person or whatever she does or evokes in you to be at peace. The problem is that by labeling the issue as something "bad" to be "forgiven," you limit yourself to linear judgmental thinking and, as a result, will never truly be able to incorporate the experience or reclaim your lost power.

To solve the issue you must look at it from another perspective where there is no such thing as good or bad but simply *unity in diversity*, or the Great Artist experiencing more of Himself.

In this case the woman is simply acting the way you were years ago. Inside you are still wrestling with your rigid (or sloppy, boastful, etc.) former ways and trying to perfect your new stage of awareness. With Neptune's power you can get to the heart of the issue. You can understand that her behavior as well as you previous behavious is not better or worse than what you are trying to establish now; it is just *another valid form of expression*. You realize that in the world of time and space within the boundaries of Saturn it is *necessary* to let go of one thing in order to achieve another because here you are moving, thinking, and working at the periphery of the wheel. However, it is not necessary to let the process of discrimination, of moving away from one thing in order to experience another, drain your power.

With Neptune you can regain the power that you left with that issue and reincorporate it by tuning into the center of the imaginary wheel or seat of the soul where all realities are seen as simultaneous and where all experiences will eventually converge.

In this way you won't have to fight against the past and reject it in order to be free to move into the future (or around the wheel) in your personality. Rather, you can re-connect to the issue and reabsorb its power, become one with the past, and finally release the energy previously bound in separation. As you fuse with the essence of the person, event, or thing you have rejected, enormous energy is freed, and after awhile you will be automatically propelled onto the next level of experience.

As your awareness increases, you won't need to project as many issues onto the outside world to learn about them and understand them in detail. You will have more mental ability to work with the issues *inside.* As a result of this, your life will start to run much more smoothly on the outside, and most of the growing pains will be now handled *subjectively.* This does not mean that you will go through fewer crises, but that they will be internalized rather than externalized.

You might also see the process of reclaiming the power of your personal universe and your projections this way: Instead of waiting passively inside your personality and letting events come your way to make you aware of one issue after another, you take control by assuming the role of the soul down here at this point in time where your personality is presently, and start functioning as the soul does after death, that is, by reabsorbing energies it projected outward and restoring its own essence.

Neptune is our way out of linearity, our gateway from the cross of matter into the sea of universal unconditional love.

Magical Use of Neptune

Preliminaries for the magical use of Neptune's energy involve the following considerations:

• Open yourself to the forces of change; be ready to embark on a journey of shifting values and competing truths while doing your best not to loose your grip on reality.

• Commit yourself to using the intuitive knowledge and detachment you gain through this practice for the good of all, and to balancing it carefully with rational, everyday, discriminatory thinking, even though with Neptune this will also appear as illusionary.

• Ground yourself after each use; physical activity is especially good for grounding yourself. Commit yourself to bringing as much as possible into daily reality all the new visions, feelings, and realizations you have gained through Neptune.

• Remember how easy it is to let Neptune's energy degenerate into mere escapism, and how many have fallen into this negative pattern. Check yourself repeatedly for these tendencies.

Magical Practice To View the Essence of Things and Events

With this practice you will view the essence of things, events, and people and understand their true significance in your present life.

Remember: All insights gained under Neptunian influence are essential to being creative, feeling alive and fulfilled. However, be very aware that they are part of a dimension beyond time and space as we know it. To be efficient in our day-to-day living and well grounded as human beings, we must respect and combine both dimensions successfully, a fact that has been the stumbling block of many a great artist and mystic.

To view the essential meaning of a thing, event, or person in your life, do the following:

1. Practice the inner journey of Neptune for three or four days to loosen up your "psychic muscles" before starting.

2. After three or more days of the above, write a list of five things, people, or events that seem to cause friction in your life. Next, write a list of five things you would like very much to have or achieve in the future.

3. Pick up your first list and sit in a comfortable chair. Relax by breathing slowly and rhythmically.

4. Attune yourself with Divine Truth as manifested through the energy of Neptune. State firmly that you want to know more about yourself and are willing to change.

5. Visualize Neptune's astrological symbol as shown at the beginning of this chapter. Build it up with your inner vision until it is large enough to envelop you completely, creating an energetic bond with the power of Neptune.

6. Now, allow Neptune to overshadow you in the following way: Build up with your inner vision the image of Neptune standing behind you. Make his body about seven feet high. Feel his great power and aura extend far beyond his body's limits into outer space. Concentrate on your love and admiration for this god of the ocean as well as on your gratitude to him for helping you in this matter. Now allow him to step up as close as possible

behind you and concentrate on the overshadowing effect of his aura on yours. Still focused on your love for Neptune, allow him to empower you by blending his great aura with your smaller one. Feel how both your energy fields are strengthened and vitalized by the contact. Feel your aura grow in size and power to coincide with that of the god. Remain this way for a few moments before you proceed to the next step.

7. Still focused on the tremendous buildup of power and Divine Truth, position both your hands, palms outward, on your forehead, and draw the astrological symbol of Neptune with both hands in front of your Third Eye. Visualize an intense beam of yellowish-and-aqua-colored light shining forth from your palms.

8. Imagine the first item from your list in front of you at a distance of about five feet. Visualize how the powerful beam of Neptunian light works its way first through layers of mist and fog and then through water, parting it to the sides like Moses divided the Red Sea in the Old Testament. Imagine the air between you and the item thoroughly cleared of all emotions, projections, and beliefs. See the space between you and the item as completely transparent. Watch how the beam of light is keeping the mist and waters standing on both sides.

9. Now while making a conscious effort to see the essence of this item and what it presently stands for in your life, say aloud: "I know I projected you into my life, but I have forgotten the reason. Please reveal this reason to me and show me what you are to me!" Although you can only receive this intuitively and the realization itself might last only a few seconds, this will be enough.

It is also possible that instead of a concept, you may receive a symbol. This is normal since it is difficult for your rational mind to sustain abstract essences for any length of time. To understand them it often must codify those abstract essences into more-concrete symbols.

10. Move your hands down to the area in front of your heart chakra and repeat procedure five and six. Allow the new beam from your heart chakra to reinforce and complement the one from your Third Eye.

11. Assert your will and intent to connect and fuse with the Divine Essence of this item, which is, of course, the same as your own. Recognize and acknowledge its and your own inherent Divinity. Then allow a warm wave of infinite unconditional love to flow out from your heart's depths, along the Neptunian beam of light and directly into the heart of the item, person, or event. As soon as the power of unconditional love hits the heart of the item, feel how your Divine Essence fuses with its Divine Essence, releasing incredible power and love. Feel how this power grows and envelops both of you in one aura of unconditional love.

12. Remain this way for as long as it feels comfortable, then slowly retract your heart beam and the beam from your Third Eye into your own essence.

13. Allow the "ocean" and mist to close over both beams. Press firmly with both hands on your heart chakra as a symbolic gesture to seal the area against energetic leakage. Do the same with your Third Eye. Then slowly return to normal consciousness.

After having practiced this exercise with the items on your "friction list," you can do the same with the items on the second list. However, do no more than one item per day.

PLUTO

PLUTO

Attunement with the Archetypal Power of Pluto

Pluto is the archetype of transmutation and liberation from forms. Classically, his power is described through the basic symbolism of death-resurrection-transcendence on all levels of existence. It is through Pluto's power that we eventually transcend our own limitations and those of our solar system, reclaiming our birthright as multidimensional cosmic beings.

With Pluto's power we are able to reach out to the stars and galaxies that are as much a part of our divine heritage as is our planet earth. Pluto leads us away from linear consciousness into multidimensional existence, freeing our awareness from the narrow coordinates of time and space.

Plutonian energy confers the powers of the rising phoenix, the legendary bird, who after being burned by the inner fire of transmutation, is reborn and rises again from its own ashes. These powers are intimately related to raising the inner fire of kundalini and transmuting the coarser aspects of human nature into the subtler energies characteristic of the spiritually liberated.

Traditionally the planet Pluto in astrology and the god Pluto/Hades in mythology are often interpreted as rather somber and disagreeable; great emphasis is given to the problems stirred up by the energy they represent.I do not deny how Pluto's seamy side may trip the unwary. This denial would only diminish his transmuting and liberating capacities. However, by attuning ourselves with Pluto's power we may befriend ourselves of this powerful god and harness his energy to kindle our inner fire for our own personal good and that of the planet.

The basic influence of Pluto involves the crisis of transition, often experienced as a confrontation and subsequent integration of the dark side of the personality. This darker self is the so-called "Dweller on the Threshold" or Shadow. Successful contact with and integration of our dark self results in transmutation and spiritual liberation through the different stages of the raising of kundalini, the inner fire.

The raising of the inner fire is often experienced as a sun swirling upward along our spine, its rays cutting through blockages like sharp blades. This inner sun will gradually expel everything not compatible with our true self. In time as our outer appearance and aura subtly change, we become more powerful, magnetic, and charismatic while feeling vibrant, light, and whole.

Pluto gives emotional detachment and aloofness, which is extreemly important to regaining our power. Because dwelling on sins and wounds of the past lowers our energy considerably, it is counterproductive to our unfoldment as Divine Beings. Pluto shows us that now is the time to recover our lost divinity. He motivates us to rise beyond our present condition and feel committed to doing so, no matter how high the price.

Through Pluto's influence we experience a healthy pride in our own individuality and potential as a "god-in- the-making. " He kindles in us a deep desire to realize our Divine Self and to transcend the limiting beliefs and indoctrinations of the Age of Pisces, which were colored by a dualistic view of the universe in which we must always chose between opposing forces. With Pluto on our side we know that can handle any change that comes our way.

Pluto's power expands our awareness beyond the narrowness of personality and unfolds before us the cosmic dimension and potential of our own spirit. In revealing the realms of duality, Pluto shows us how to go beyond them to achieve integration and illumination. His power forces our innermost fears to surface and helps us to recognize their source since he is, as the Dweller on the Threshold, the key to our own liberation.

Pluto's energy, together with the raising of kundalini, uncovers all those things in our lives that should be discarded, such as attitudes, beliefs, people, and objects, because they no longer serve our higher purpose.

Once Pluto has worked successfully on our three lower levels (physical, emotional, and mental), then he induces our spiritual rebirth and liberates us from subjective time and space. Through the free flow of kundalini we are integrated into one whole being.

Along the many stages of our spiritual rebirth we acquire a great deal of power. Most of this new power comes from integrating the dual nature of the Dweller on the Threshold. Our Shadow is not only composed of negative, repressed aspects, but it also exhibits positive forces, such as personal power in the form of unrealized potential crying out to be expressed and actualized.

The God Hades/Pluto in Mythology

Hades, son of Rhea and Cronus, was the god of the Underworld where he reigned supreme. Hades was not part of the Olympians, although he still played a major role in Greek mythology. His kingdom, flat and somber, was said to exist beneath the earth's surface. This underworld was connected to our earth through a number of pathways and tunnels from which vapors escaped into daylight. The gatekeeper to the kingdom of Hades was a fierce three-headed dog. Only the dead were allowed to pass through to be judged by Hades. If found worthy, they were allowed to enter the Elysian Fields, the Greek version of heaven. If unworthy, they would be sent to suffer mercilessly in Tartarus. This entire procedure obviously hints at the high price of inner death and the sacrifice necessary to attain transformation, transcendence, enlightenment, and liberation.

Hades seldom came to earth, but when he did, he wore a helmet that made him invisible to all but the initiated. His most-famous adventure into the world of gods and men involved his ravaging and abducting the young goddess, Persephone. After taking her into his kingdom by force, he made her his queen. Persephone remained with her husband and king for one-third of the year; for the other two-thirds she was allowed to ascend to earth to be with her mother Demeter, the goddess of fertility and agriculture. This account helps explain mythologically the barrenness of earth during winter when Demeter was said to roam the earth's surface, moaning for her lost daughter. With Persephone's re-emergence to the earth's surface, spring and new life came to the land. However, the Queen of the Underworld eventually returns not as a youthful virgin, but as a mature, beautiful woman.

Hades was also known by the name of " Pluto. " The latter name stems from the Greek word *plouton*, meaning "wealth or riches." Although he was much feared as the sovereign of the Dark Kingdom, he was also venerated as the carrier of riches. This double nature, found in all deities and archetypes, is perhaps most obvious in Pluto. His dark side warns us of the dangers of approaching him unprepared. His bright side represents what we will encounter once we have successfully integrated his energy into our lives.

Pluto's role in this story is symbolic of the "Shadow" making periodic havoc-and-confusion-causing eruptions into our safe, normal, day-to-day consciousness/life. Here Pluto's role, if correctly understood, is obviously less that of rapist and more that of Divine Initiator.

The dark, mysterious cloak that shrouds this enigmatic god and makes his power so dangerous is in reality our own unresolved subconscious, our own dark side.

The mint and the cypress are sacred to Pluto. In paintings we often see him depicted holding a cornucopia or horn of plenty. He is associated with the double-headed eagle, the scorpion, and the serpent.

Pluto in Astrology

Pluto rules the astrological sign of Scorpio.

His natural house is the Eighth House (joint resources, death and rebirth, personal sacrifices, taxes, inheritance, and legacies).

Pluto is masculine and positive. His astrological symbol is a cross, topped by a crescent moon with a circle in it. This symbolizes matter mastered by the transcendent personality, with the eternal spirit hovering above it all.

Basic key words describing the influence of Pluto are death and rebirth, sexuality, integration, transformation, illumination, control of the inner fire of kundalini, transmutation, and liberation.

Pluto's negative attributes are associated with struggle, destruction, obsession, selfish power, dictatorship, isolation, emotional coldness, cruelty, pride and arrogance.

The basic function of Pluto in the astrological chart involves growth and transcendence through conflict. Pluto is the archetype per se of death and resurrection. He breaks down the old into its component parts only to reassemble them on a newer higher octave. Pluto rules the raising of kundalini, the major driving power of this ongoing process.

In the physical body Pluto rules over the external reproductive organs.

Inner Journey To Contact the Archetype

Sit or lie in a comfortable position and relax by taking several deep breaths. Now count from ten to zero, allowing your body to relax even more with each count.

Imagine you are walking alone in a beautiful meadow. The sun is hot in the deep-blue sky and birds are singing. As insects fly busily among the flowers, the clear air makes the hills in the background appear close and friendly. At the foot of the hills you see a few trees and notice that some of their leaves are already changing, heralding the approach of winter.

You become aware of a very attractive young woman picking flowers nearby. She sings happily to herself as she gathers the blooms and bunches them together in a colorful bouquet. She is tall, slender, and extremely beautiful. Her lustrous black hair is swept up in an elaborate knot and she is dressed in a white tunic worn in the Greek fashion. She wears a necklace of golden fruits with red stones. As it catches the rays of the afternoon sun you recognize the fruits as pomegranates.

The young woman appears sweet and delicate; every movement of her graceful limbs exudes tender femininity. Her presence is so pure and joyful that you feel irresistibly drawn to her. Her graceful features and radiant deep-brown eyes help you recognize her immediately: She is the Greek goddess Persephone who has come to lead you to her husband and king.

As you advance, somewhat hesitant of what may lie ahead, she places her flowers on the grass and welcomes you with outstretched arms. Pulling you towards her into a soft embrace, she remarks:

"Welcome! I am your guide on this journey because it is that time of the year when I rejoin my husband. It is most remarkable that you have come all this way to search the depths of your own nature; the rewards will be plentiful. Do not fear or resist the change and transformation this journey will bring you; rather, make the excitement of this path your own. Identify yourself with me, if only for a little while, and feel my joy and love for the encounter that lies ahead. Experience the thrill and confidence that comes in transcending the safe and known, in exploring and integrating the unknown and concealed! For indeed, changed and transformed you will be on your return."

After these words she takes your hand and gently leads you toward the hills. There you see the opening of a dark cavern and together you enter. It is much larger inside than you had anticipated. You walk quite a distance through a winding passage before you are halted by a heavy stone gate, the symbol of Pluto carved deep and wide into its rough cold surface.

To your right you see a beautiful black dog, its velvety coat gleaming in the darkness. His eyes resemble balls of fire as he approaches you with a growl. You can hear him question you telepathically: "Why have you come here and what gives you the right to cross this gate?" His question feels menacing and you pause for a moment to formulate in your mind your personal answer.

The animal, satisfied with your mental reply, comes forward to welcome his mistress Persephone. They greet each other like long-lost friends, and as the dog licks her ear, an invisible interchange seems to take place. The dog becomes as playful and as friendly as a puppy, pointing with his nose toward the now-open stone gate. You leave the guardian of the gate behind and proceed through the passage with Persephone.

The corridor leads upward now, and suddenly you find yourself outside on a high cliff's edge. It is night and you are surrounded by stars. Still holding tightly onto your guide's hand, you feel lifted up into the night sky. You start flying swiftly away from earth toward the outer regions of the solar system.

Persephone explains: "You are now entering a new dimension of existence, a reality where all things that appear real could be symbolic, and those that seem symbolic may be real. What is reality after all? Who defines it?" asks Persephone.

As your guide speaks these strange and profound words, you see beings of light nearing and surrounding you from all areas of the universe. They form a circle of light and protection as you journey toward the cold planet. Overwhelmed by their presence, by the love and caring they emanate, you weep in gratitude.

After allowing you to absorb their power for some time, they reveal their identity to you:

"We are all those energies you have worked with in your quest for spiritual growth! We are those you have tried so diligently to recognize; we have come across space and time to assist you in this undertaking to kindle the Inner Fire in you once and for all, never to be dimmed again, but to burn eternally in your waking consciousness! We have come to be with you in this act of liberation from the confines of limited space, linear thinking, and ordinary perception; we are the Healers, the Ku, the Shining Ones!"

Traveling safely in the midst of these beings, you pass the planets of the solar system one by one, entering ever-darker and colder realms. Soon the sun appears to be no more than another bright star in the distance.

After a long time you gently land on Pluto. Cold and ice, darkness and desolation surround you. As you hear the screech of a bird above you, you look up and notice that it is a black double-headed eagle. Strange, snake-shaped creatures slither away as you proceed, and on a nearby rock you see a scorpion with raised stinger awaiting its prey.

Although you do not see the golden light of your companions anymore, you can feel their presences near you. Persephone walks ahead, ever faster and more joyful in anticipation of her reunion with her lover, her other half, her king. You feel encouraged by her happiness, but still you wonder how and why such a radiant goddess would choose such a sinister kingdom and still rejoice in it!

At the foot of a big rock formation in the distance you notice an entrance to a big cave. As you approach, Persephone bids you to follow her inside. To your amazement you find yourself in a big hall. In the center, barely visible in the dim light, you see the figure of a tall, dark-haired man.

As you approach this man, a wave of pure power shakes your entire body like a nuclear explosion. The vibration is so intense that you have trouble maintaining your balance. Before you know it, every cell of you body is vibrating to this same rhythm and intensity, as if a thousand snakes had been awakened inside you and were now moving at great speed.

An inner voice tells you not to fear, but to flow with this new energy, to let its immeasurable power permeate and activate you. Following this advice, you surrender and accept.

Suddenly, just as you feel this new energy nearly stabilizing itself in your body and aura and making you shine from within, the entire hall lights up at once, forcing you to become aware of your surroundings. You notice that the walls are made of innumerable gems and precious stones, sparkling in all colors. The entire hall is set up for a banquet, beautiful and richly decorated. The reason for the celebration is the return of the goddess.

Sweet, soft Persephone has joined Hades once again and they are kissing passionately, her delicate body pressed lovingly against the king's hard maleness. As the god raises his eyes, he locks his gaze with yours. With a deep, rumbling voice he poses a question that sends a cold shudder down your spine: "Why have you come to see me?"

Pluto appears much younger than you had imagined. He is tall, handsome, and virile; his eyes are deep brown and warm, but his look is firm. Long black curls and a full beard frame his classic face. A tunic of black silk is draped around his muscular body, leaving one shoulder bare. Above his right shoulder you recognize the double-headed eagle, proudly perched on the back of the royal throne. At his feet peacefully rests the black dog, the guardian of the gate.

You feel magnetically drawn to Pluto by the disarming power of his aura and magnificence. Why has it taken you so long to come here, you wonder? Now you understand why Persephone was so eager to return. Yes, earth was beautiful with its flowers and singing birds, but life was not complete without this other, more-profound side of existence which Pluto personifies and rules.

You had so many requests to ask the god of the Underworld before you started on your journey, but now as you stand here facing him, none seems relevant anymore, except one. Unafraid, you approach Pluto and confess: "I have come here to be reborn! My sacrifice is my old life, my old self. What I wish to receive is the New Life Divine and the power rightfully my own!"

Pluto nods and welcomes you with a smile. You come even closer and kneel at his feet. As he draws his symbol on your head, an incredible wave of power rushes up through your body. This time it seems to originate within you, at the base of your spine. It wells upward along your back and out at the top of your head, making you tremble and vibrate as it passes. It feels like a white-hot fire burning away all impurities and widening the channels and energy centers of your body as it ascends. You remain still and let it happen, totally surrendering to this higher power and trusting its wisdom.

After the greater part of the impurities seem to have been cleared, you feel the current reversing at the top of your head and coming down along the front of your body to the base of the spine. From there up along the spine again it turns round and round like a wheel, empowering you more and more at each turn.

A transformation is happening inside you. Although it is purely on an energetic level at this moment, soon it will become effective on your consciousness, your life, and your environment. Your love and admiration for this powerful being becomes so great, you are overwhelmed by desire to be one with him. While you pour out your love and adoration to Pluto, you see how his features slowly disappear and he himself turns into a dense phosphorescent gas that vibrates with his special energy. The gas flows into you and mixing with your body and energy field, creates a deep communion. Wait some time, savoring the union. Now ask the god to give you a personal message and allow some time for it to appear. Then, when you feel ready, you allow the god to depart and resume his original form.

Now Pluto and Persephone invite you to take a walk outside before you return to earth. The black dog runs ahead and the eagle is soaring high again. You climb a big rock from which you have a good view of the bare and desolate land and the entire solar system that lies essentially at your feet. Pluto powerfully calls out:

"Look below, truthful seeker! This is the solar system, with its planets and the energies and archetypes they represent. You have learned to harness and use their power to your personal advantage. However, it is now time you return all the power and knowledge you have gained to the Great Spirit who is its rightful owner. You must unreservedly dedicate all your power and knowledge to the Great Work, and become completely centered in your own Inner God. You must relinquish all selfish power and desire in order to cross the boundaries of the solar system. Outside this solar system mighty cosmic winds prevail, and none but the strong and righteous shall keep their course and succeed."

"I am the Gatekeeper and the way out is through me. My symbols are the scorpion and the eagle; my toll is death."

"Look at earth and the solar system. Think of the many dimensions within dimensions, and what a small part of all of this is the toll I ask! Connect yourself, if only in spirit, with the indwelling souls of stars and planets, of distant galaxies! Become aware of the bridge of perception and love that exists already now between you the human and the Starlords and Planetary Lords of the other great systems! Transcend the narrowness of linear thinking and allow the greatness of holographic structure and multidimensionality to become part of your daily discipline! I say farewell to you now with the hope that you will bring many more fellow humans to sit on this rock and adjust their inner doors of perception to this wider horizon! God bless you."

With tears in your eyes and great empathy for the important but extremely difficult and lonely task Pluto has set himself to fulfill, you depart toward earth accompanied by the Shining Ones to guide you safely home. Persephone waves to you from a distance and you wave back in tears, longing to return again, to know more of those deep dimensions you have just glimpsed.

After a smooth and swift passage you land gently on the rocky cliff. Retracing your steps, you arrive at the stone gate and soon are outside in the sunny meadow. You feel fresh and rejuvenated, confident about the changes that lie ahead. You feel safe in your new life. The landscape slowly fades away, and gradually you regain your normal waking consciousness.

Kundalini

Kundalini, or Serpent Power as it is also called, is said to be a mysterious archaic force that lies dormant at the base of the spine, waiting to be awakened in each of us. This force cannot be understood intellectually, but must be experienced personally.

Most books written on the subject of kundalini are full of Oriental terminology, making the whole experience seem unfamiliar, obscure, and quite foreign to our Western minds. The reason for this is that metaphysical teachings have always been widely accepted and encouraged in the East. Whereas, in the West they have been banned by religion for many centuries, only to reemerge in the last one-hundred years. Since kundalini has been revered in the East as a goddess, practitioners of Eastern systems of enlightenment are much more familiar with her.

Kundalini, the basic force of creation, is inherent in all manifestation, above and beyond time and space. It cannot be claimed exclusively by any culture or any specific individual. It exists everywhere and can be incorporated into all systems of human enlightenment. In fact, even if many spiritual schools do not inform their practitioners about the power of kundalini and its practical implications, they cannot prevent or protect their students from the shattering encounter with this force by denying, ignoring, or avoiding it. Sooner or later along the Path of spiritual growth kundalini will rise, and there is no power on earth that can stop it.

Kundalini can be voluntarily activated through certain practices, such as Kundalini yoga and Tantra yoga, or it may rise spontaneously. Ideally, when kundalini moves up along the spine, it pierces each chakra until it reaches the crown where an explosion of consciousness occurs and we enter *samadhi.* In this state of *samadhi* the boundaries of the self are dissolved and we experience ourselves as One with the Absolute. Bliss and unity pervade our entire being; we are plunged into divine ecstasy.

Experiencing the inner fire of kundalini is not always as smooth as one might wish. During the ascent of this powerful force, it usually encounters blockages and stagnant energy along the way, which it then proceeds to remove mercilessly. This may bring discomfort and confusion as the energy blocks created by the impressions and conditionings of present as well as past lives are burned and dissolved to facilitate the free upward flow of kundalini. The rising energy may cause bizarre phenomena as it purifies the layers of our being. These phenomena may range from experiencing strange sounds, movements, and lights, hot-and-cold sensations, vibrations, fears, and anxieties to extreme joy and bliss, and ultimately, cosmic consciousness. The occurrences produced by the upward thrust of kundalini are directly related to the attributes associated with the blocked chakra.

The powerful effect of kundalini must not be feared and seen as uncomfortable and obscure, but rather welcomed as the fastest way to purify and liberate our humanity.

Much has been said about the dangers of raising kundalini too early or too quickly in the search for enlightenment. These warnings are correct; however, they should not keep us from striving toward higher spiritual progress.

One reason for caution involves the fact that around each of the chakras we have a protective, built-in screen in the form of an etheric web. If kundalini is forced up abruptly without previous preparation of the human energy field through spiritual practices, these screens may become permanently damaged.

When drugs are taken or when people engage in potent spiritual practices without a true understanding of the mechanisms involved, the delicate nervous and etheric systems are damaged by a sudden overload and the protective screens over the chakras are bypassed or torn, exposing the person to areas of the collective and personal unconscious s/he is unprepared to handle. The person is then plunged into horrible and shocking visions which s/he cannot shut out at will.

The ascent of kundalini, or kundalini-shakti as it is called in its active form, is not a thing to be taken lightly. Nevertheless, this power can accelerate our spiritual unfoldment in such a way that we may develop in a very short period of time what otherwise might have taken us one or several lifetimes.

Kundalini is, in a way, the Essence of all, the fundamental Power of Transmutation. It is a force that never exhausts itself and constitutes the basic energy of the universe, the stars, and our own bodies, regenerating endlessly, forever producing ecstasy without depletion. The experience of kundalini must be sought in complete unconditional surrender to the "here and now" where the subjective "distance" between the different aspects of our being fades away and we fuse into one whole, where past and future are one, and all opposites are resolved.

To reap the greatest benefits from Pluto's energy, we must consciously proceed to clean the central channel from obstructions, which simultaneously clears the mind of distortions. The most-important part of this cleansing-and-integrating action is our work with the Shadow. Then the Serpent of Wisdom can be uncoiled and rise through the central channel along the spine as it is meant to do, and without danger.

The topic of kundalini is so vast that it is impossible to present it all in great detail here. However, I highly recommend you read more about it as well as familiarize yourself with the accounts of the various saints and gurus who have gone through the experience.

The Shadow

The Shadow, or Dweller on the Threshold as he is also called, is depicted as a somber elusive figure who dwells at the edge of our conscious mind and whose nature is composed of our repressed aspects. Our ego or false self habitually disassociates all attributes considered unsuitable, unsocial, or "bad" and throws them into the shadows of our psyche. Subsequently, these rejected aspects organize themselves into a kind of opposite mirror-image of the "nice-and-good self" and become the Shadow.

Pluto's energy works through the Shadow to make us integrate and transcend our duality and separateness. Pluto stimulates the unpurified aspects within each of us dispassionately, aiming toward wholeness, integration, and healing, refining us through the action of the inner fire of transformation. His influence is absolutely impersonal and non-judgmental.

Through your conscious contact with the archetypes you increase the amount of energy running through your system. The Shadow will invariably make itself felt. It will be agitated and empowered, possibly making you experience periods of fear and compulsive inclinations that seemingly appear from nowhere.

But this is very good! And indeed, there is no way around it. Through our inner unfoldment and progress along the path, each of us must sooner or later come face to face with the Shadow. In fact, the appearance of the Shadow is a sign that considerable progress has been made and presents one of the greatest opportunities for inner growth.

A sure sign of the Shadow's appearance is when you feel inner turmoil and confusion, yet in your outer life, all is calm, safe, and loving. Our Higher Self often seems to choose these periods of outer calmness and safety to force us to look inside and do some inner "housecleaning." If this should happen to you, welcome it as an opportunity to take a quantum leap on your road to enlightenment and use the time to its full potential.

The coming to life of the Dweller may manifest in varying degrees of intensity directly related to the degree of stress you are able to handle. If you have a long background of spiritual practices and self-work, a greater portion of the Dweller may appear at once. This emergence is good and justified. It proves that through your practices and wider understanding you have built up a greater resilience and capacity to handle deeper aspects of the Shadow at one time, thus, accelerating the process of integration. Do not resist it; love it.

The encounter with the Dweller is not always as dramatic as one might think; in fact, it can be quite simple. You may at times become aware of a fear or negative quality you are projecting onto someone else, externalizing instead of facing it in yourself. You will then feel things such as "I hate this person" or "This person always does such-and-such a thing and that is bad." What happens is that you have deep within you the need to act exactly in that same way, yet you are not aware of this repressed part, banning it from what you consider your "good self."

Initially, our shadow functions as an automatic filter through which we see the world. It modifies and conditions our perceptions and, of course, dims the amount of light we can receive directly. As we integrate more and more of the Dweller, we start to perceive our environment as it truly is—good and whole in all its imperfections.

Examine yourself honestly whenever you feel discomfort with someone else's attitudes or behavior. If it bothers you, it probably resonates with your own repressed attitudes and beliefs. Allow yourself to feel these repressed emotions. Accept yourself as you are. You are okay as you are now. Recognizing the existence of these fears, unacceptable desires, and beliefs does not mean giving in to them; rather, it means that you label them in yourself instead of projecting them onto someone else. If you reown your projections and start facing your own fears and attitudes without guilt, life will respond very positively.

Remember, no one is perfect. All humans must repress many aspects of themselves in the socialization and civilization process; this is normal and necessary. Now that we are reclaiming our spiritual adulthood, we must be able to choose what may be expressed and what must be sacrificed. By making this conscious choice, we will regain our power and freedom.

Facing our fears will lead us directly to the other side of the Dweller. He is also the Keeper of the Gate to our own true potential. The repressed fears and emotions he represents are precisely those which keep us from achieving what we so long for in life.

The Shadow will not be faced in one big confrontation; it must be integrated gradually in a long process that usually takes several years, if not our entire lives. It is precisely the slowness of this progress that assures thorough integration and assimilation.

Magical Use of Pluto

Preliminaries for the magical use of Pluto's energy involve the following considerations:

• Take responsibility for the new awareness and knowledge this exercise will bring, and commit yourself to applying it to your life for the good of all.

• Open yourself without fear to the forces of change; be ready and willing to grow and mature in all aspects of your life. Above all, be extremely honest with yourself.

• Let the desire for Divine Wisdom and harmony pervade your work.

• Commit yourself to using the power you gain from Pluto's energy for the good of all.

• Don't blame yourself or anybody else for what you might encounter when you approach the Shadow. Don't dwell in anger or self-pity; simply accept what you find and learn to understand and integrate your dark side. It will not be easy, but you are well enough equipped at this point to handle the process safely.

Magical Practice To Integrate the Shadow

To establish communication with your Shadow and gradually integrate it, do the following practice:

1. Sit in a comfortable position and relax by breathing deeply and rhythmically.

2. State firmly that you want to know more about yourself and are now prepared to reclaim all those elements of your psyche you have denied and projected onto your environment and other people. Ready yourself to meet your Dweller on the Threshold. Express your need for help in these matters to the archetype of the god Pluto.

3. Visualize Pluto's astrological symbol as shown at the beginning of this chapter. Build it up with your inner vision until it is large enough to envelop you completely, creating an energetic bond with the power of Pluto.

4. Imagine a building with seven levels or floors. This building represents you. Visualize it either as a simple or elaborate structure; the choice is yours.

5. Center your consciousness on the sixth level, which directly corresponds to your Third Eye. Visualize yourself in a miniature body walking around a big and comfortable living room in the center of this level.

6. Now imagine yourself descending to the first level via a winding double staircase that runs down the center of the building. After reaching the first floor, imagine a dark passage that leads to the basement and follow it.

7. Standing in the center of this dark basement, imagine a blazing white light expanding from your heart center until it reaches the basement and illuminates the entire room. You are literally flooding the basement with the light of unconditional love from your heart, the seat of your spirit.

8. Imagine a hooded figure standing before you. This figure may be a man or a woman, or may change gender with each consecutive meeting.

9. Still maintaining the flow of unconditional love from your heart to all areas of the basement, invite the figure to come to you. Say that you have come to meet and work with it. Assure the figure that you feel ready to see part of its face and to integrate it. Stretch out your hands and welcome the figure.

10. See how the figure approaches and slowly turns back its hood, revealing its face. Prepare to see something frightening, but remember that this shadowy figure is nothing more than part of yourself, one that has lived with you for as long as you have existed and is not new or foreign.

11. Let the figure hold onto your hands and gently guide it up through the dark passage onto the first level, then up the winding staircase to the sixth level, correspondent to your Third Eye.

12. Invite the figure to sit down in your inner living room and communicate with it. Have the figure talk about itself and how it came to be. Let it express its needs and explain how it can integrate itself into your life smoothly and safely. Tell the figure you are just beginning to understand it and you will try to integrate greater portions of it in time, but that for now, you want to take it in slowly.

13. Sit there for some time in peace and harmony with the Shadow. Communicate whatever you feel, if you wish.

14. When you feel ready, again gently guide the Shadow down into the basement. However, now the basement is not dark, but full of light, warm and welcoming, permeated with unconditional love and understanding. It is not a common basement any more; rather, it resembles an elegant, luxuriously decorated apartment.

15. You explain to thc Shadow that soon it will not have to live in this basement anymore, but will share the upper quarters with you. In the meantime it must stay here some time longer until you are completely ready to receive it. Tell the figure it may visit you whenever it needs to communicate and that you will also be watching for it in your dreams.

16. Say farewell to the Shadow and proceed upward.

17. Go up to the fourth level, which corresponds to your heart. From there return to your normal size and reabsorb the building into your heart.

18. Slowly return to normal consciousness.

Advanced Magical Practice To Integrate the Shadow

This advanced version is only to be attempted after you have completed the first practice many times and feel very comfortable with it. No matter how well advanced you think you are, this practice will stir you up quite a bit, so do not take it lightly!

Follow steps one through five, as before.

5a. Before you descend into the basement, you will take an elevator up through the center of the building to reach the seventh level. This level has no roof so that you can see sky all around; directly above your head is the Great Light. Make your unreserved dedication to this Light, stating that you will surrender the power and wisdom to be gained through this exercise to Divine Will, and that you wish to merge with this Divine Will in order to manifest it in your life.

Follow steps six through ten as before.

11. Let the figure hold onto your hands and gently guide it up through the dark passage onto the first level, then up the winding staircase to the fourth level correspondent to your heart chakra.

12. Standing in front of the figure, state that you now feel ready to integrate it. Express your love and desire for this repressed part of your being and accept it and yourself fully as you now are.

13. See the figure slowly dissolving into a gas composed of luminous and opaque particles. Let it enter your body at your heart chakra. Feel how the gas expands and fills your entire being, merging perfectly with what is already there, forming a clear and powerful whole.

14. Renew your unreserved dedication to the Great Light and the forces of evolution. Enter the central elevator and shoot up to the seventh level and beyond into the Great Light.

15. Remain in the Light as long as it feels comfortable.

16. Then return via the elevator to the fourth level correspondent to your heart. Return to your normal size and reabsorb the building into your heart.

17. Slowly return to normal consciousness.

VULCAN

VULCAN

Attunement with the Archetypal Power of Vulcan

To this day the physical existence of Vulcan is uncertain. Some believe he is a small but very hot planet circling the Sun inside Mercury's orbit. Others say he is a "veiled" or hidden planet, existing only on an etheric dimension just beyond physical manifestation and whose influence is only felt indirectly through the moon. However, until further astronomical research is done, esoteric astrologers agree that Vulcan works behind the scenes of physical manifestation, much like the divine blacksmith after whom the planet has been named. We can see Vulcan as a personification of the First Ray or Divine Will energy and of the element of earth in its highest expression.

It is said that the moon veils Vulcan. This means that for the ordinary individual Vulcan's energy is not readily available, but is hidden by the moon's influence. The individual, who is only influenced by the three lower levels of his personality (i. e. , physical, emotional, and mental) and lives a rather self-centered life, is symbolically under lunar influence. As he grows and strengthens him/herself along his/her incarnations, s/he suddenly faces a turning point. The desires and satisfactions of the selfish, personality-oriented life and the enchantment of a successful material existence do not appear in themselves meaningful enough anymore. At this point, a painful longing for something deeper and more lasting sets in, threatening to consume the individual from inside.

The seeker starts to turn inward, crying for his soul, searching for comfort and understanding beyond outer, physical expression. It is here that the Divine Will of his soul, the Will to Wholeness and greater Light, hears his cry and makes itself unmistakably felt, although sporadically at first.

The individual, after feeling and tasting the proximity of the soul, even if only for a few moments, recognizes instantly that this is what s/he had been looking for: Truth, Light, and Meaning, of which physical reality is but a mere reflection. It is at this point that Vulcan comes into play.

The new insight and heightened desire for spiritual reality allows the individual to turn his/her focus away from the physical and lunar influence in a gradual, yet often very painful, process poetically referred to as the "Path. " Along the Path, the individual slowly works his/her way toward the integration of the soul with the personality. It is through Vulcan the blacksmith, who represents the energy of Divine Will and Divine Power, that the personality starts to be forged into a tool suitable for the direct expression of the soul and its purpose.

Vulcan's energy will be most intensely experienced twice along this Path: first, at the shift inward and away from a purely selfish and material existence, and second, much later when the individual goes back over all his/her attachments, then severs them once and for all, opening him/herself to the very abstract and direct inflow of the spirit, the Monad.

On first contact with Vulcan's energy we recognize that we must relinquish much of the comfortable safety of the known and habitual. We realize that even personal power must be sacrificed for awhile until our higher goal (fusion with the soul and then the spirit) is secured. It is nice to feel powerful and aloof at the summit of material existence, but soon that in itself does not bring the expected satisfaction. Discipline and hard work, together with honest introspection, must be applied now with renewed patience. The goal is to be free of the bondage of matter and first fuse the personality with the soul, then with the spirit, permanently filling the two deep and painful gaps (reffered to as the "Gulf" and the "Abyss" in esoteric nomenclature).

The moon represents Mother Nature, her tides and seasons and her very influence in our lives. The moon denotes a very powerful force indeed, deeply ingrained in our subconscious and the memory of our cells. It binds us to the past—personal, racial, and planetary. It connects us to physicality.

The moon stands symbolically for all that is subconscious and instinctive. It stands for our ancestors and ties to living family members. The moon rules the rhythms, automatic responses, and conditioned reflexes of our physical, emotional, and mental vehicles, as the exquisite end product of human evolution. The moon symbolizes Mother Nature's work to fashion us into what we are now, taking all responsibility and all blame. But a time comes during our evolution when we must take back into our own hands responsibility for our lives. At this point we seek out the power represented by the Divine Blacksmith to do the work that follows.

This bondage represented by the moon is very necessary and good to a certain point; it allows us to hold firmly onto our incarnation and provides a safe, solid ground from which to grow upward toward the true light of the soul. However, too much bondage and connection to the safe and natural becomes stifling to the Inner Life Divine. We, like children who eventually leave the safe folds of mother's apron and become responsible adults, must venture forth on our quest to find and express our true self, even if we do not know how or what this is.

There comes a time when the personality is developed enough to feel the fervent pull of its own soul and, suddenly flooded with the passion to be, expands to grow beyond its own boundaries and know its "Father Who is in Heaven." This is the turning point when we must gather all our courage and accept the fact that the lunar influence, which has helped us to grow this far, may now be transcended. We must dare to face the unknown and plunge into the Great Adventure, cutting the umbilical cord that held us safely attached to humanity's womb. We must exchange the warm and nurturing lap of our lunar mother for the unknown challenges of a new life that fully expresses our soul.

After catching first glimpse of our soul, we recognize the moon's influence as a veil or shroud needing to be removed gently. Once this is accomplished, Vulcan's influence pours in, flooding the personality with Divine Will.

Vulcan's power floods us with Spiritual Will, the Power aspect of the Creator. We become spiritually focused as the Great Work of the soul and its life purpose is recognized. Lower desire is renounced as we commit ourselves to fashion the personality into a suitable vehicle for the soul, whose presence and power we now strongly experience.

Symbolically speaking, Vulcan will take us into his forge and lay us on his anvil. He will fashion us into a beautiful but powerful, almost fearsome, weapon of the soul. He will work ceaselessly until his task is accomplished. It will be painful, no doubt, but the end product will be well worth the effort. Our personality will become a gleaming weapon of Light, to be wielded by the Will Divine.

Often this shift or realignment with Spiritual Will is accompanied by the concomitant need for isolation since the new imprint must be secured undisturbed. The result is a new and more powerful commitment to manifest the Spiritual Will rather than adapt to outer expectations. Our work, performed in the dark recesses of our selves, like that of the god Vulcan/Hephaestos, remains hidden to the casual observer.

This first shift from personality-oriented living to soul influence occurs at the time of the first initiation (following the Tibetan Master D. K.'s system as presented in the writings of Alice A. Bailey). Later, as Vulcan's energy becomes active on the mental level, it will start to work on the lunar veil. It will bring it into conscious focus, then burn it away in the fire of Spiritual Will to release the individual from material bondage. This releasing process, which frees up an incredible amount of energy, is closely linked to what has been called by the Tibetan Master D. K. the fourth initiation.

Even though Vulcan's influence seems to come naturally at certain times along the Path, we can contact it anytime to our advantage. However, Vulcan, even though he is the blacksmith of the gods, is also lame and cannot easily leave his forge. We must seek him out in order to reap the benefit of his powerful spiritual thrust and subtle touch.

On the emotional level Vulcan's influence is experienced as the sheer pressure to actualize the soul's purpose. It appears painful at first as Spiritual Will energy surges in and alienates us from what has hitherto been our fortress of safety and habitual behavior. Vulcan storms in and demands immediate detachment from all ways, thoughts, habits, and things superfluous to the soul. At first it appears as if the inrushing Divine Will is destructive and ruthless, severing bonds that have lasted one or several lifetimes, and have taken equally long to build. But after the first wave of cutting and burning, a new and desperate desire sets in, a desire to bring to sublime perfection all those skills and attributes needed to accomplish the soul's mission.

We suddenly realize how much remains to be done and learned. We see, to our regret, how much time we seem to have wasted meandering through the entrapments of the world of forms. It is now through the powerful input of Vulcan that we take on the task of perfecting ourselves to masterhood with the almost fanatical dedication so characteristic of those who are driven by Divine Will.

When Vulcan reaches our emotional level, Divine one-pointed Spiritual Will starts to rush through our veins, throbbing with the desire to express itself unhindered, untamed, unobstructed. No aim seems too lofty, no effort too arduous, no discipline too difficult, and no isolation too harsh to attain the one goal we envision—the ecstatic fusion of our personality with our soul and with Divine Will.

It is here on the emotional level that the battle of the two wills must be fought because it is in water (emotion) that the spiritual sword made by Vulcan (Spiritual Will) must be tempered in order to strengthen the iron and make it truly resistant. Vulcan will hurt on this level until we have cleared out all debris. Spiritual Will must encounter only transparency on its way through the personality to outward manifestation. Spiritual Will pushes and tears at our insides until it can rush through us unhindered to accomplish its task. If we resist it, illness and depression will set in.

Although astrologers are not completely certain if Vulcan is a physical planet or not, Vulcan's effect does have a very physical influence since the Power aspect of God is strongly connected to the base chakra. Vulcan is also intimately linked with the element of earth. However, his effect on our physical lives will not be evident until we recognize that he is behind the veiled influence of the moon. As soon as we set out to pierce that veil and seek him out, he will make his presence felt.

On the physical level Vulcan has an unsettling influence. At first he alienates us from our surroundings. People don't always like the Vulcan energy we emanate and the desperate way we assert ourselves along the Path. They resent the strength and determination they sense in us, which reflects their own impotence. On the other hand, they envy our dedication, discipline, and the purposeful simplicity we use to reach our ideals because it mirrors their own indecision and ragged life patterns.

Once we get used to being different, more assertive, determined, and disciplined than the rest of humanity, Vulcan's influence feels like a blessing on the physical plane. Through our new detachment and purpose we succeed in molding our personality into an almost-perfect vehicle for Spiritual Will to shine through unhindered, guiding and inspiring us at all times.

Proof of Vulcan's effect on the material level will be a smooth but ecstatic physical existence, in constant awareness of our soul (Inner Christ), and with occasional glimpses of our Monad (Father Who is in Heaven).

The God Hephaestus/Vulcan in Mythology

Hephæstus was the son of Zeus and Hera. He represented the benevolent earthy fire which allows humans to work metal and build civilizations. He was at first also closely associated with volcanic eruptions and the volcanic island of Lemnos where his cult is said to have originated.

In contrast to all other Olympian gods, Hephæstus was lame, with both legs deformed at birth. It is said that when his mother discovered her son was malformed, she threw him down from Olympus into the sea. Hephæstus was rescued from the ocean by the goddess Thetis, who took him into a grotto where she hid him for nine years. In his underground abode Hephæstus learned to work metal, fashioning many delicate ornaments and useful weapons.

Hephæstus was taught the art of forging metal by the dwarf Cedalion, who became a close friend. With the faithful guidance of Cedalion, the lame god's craftsmanship, creative genius, and inventiveness was unsurpassed.

After many wanderings and adventures Hephæstus finally made Mount Etna his permanent abode. There he worked ceaselessly on his anvil, fashioning innumerable objects of great beauty. Among these precious articles were Zeus's throne, scepter, thunderbolts, the winged chariot for the sun god Helios, the weapons of Achilles, and the arrows of Apollo and Artemis.

The blacksmith of the gods was a very powerful and virile man despite his handicap. He had strong shoulders and a broad hairy chest. His face was framed by curly black hair and a full beard; his eyes were dark brown, warm, and deep.

Aphrodite was Hephæstus' wife, a considerable mismatch when viewed from an exoteric (meaning "worldly") standpoint. However, if we judge it astrologically, we see that Hephæstus is the esoteric (meaning "inner or hidden") ruler of Taurus, while Venus is its exoteric ruler. The man, the god Hephæstus and the Divine Will he represents, are the driving power behind Venus' influence, so to speak.

Traditionally, however, Venus/Aphrodite was not satisfied with Hephæstus' attentions so that she frequently sought the company of other lovers, Ares and Hermes among the most famous. Here, of course, we see much deep, esoteric symbolism. Hephæstus, being Spiritual Will energy, was mostly at work behind manifestation, hidden inside a cavern, grotto, or volcano. His energy is pioneering but solitary; whereas Aphrodite effects her inspiring influence directly and most strongly in polarity and is never hidden.

Hephæstus was helped and accompanied in his hard work by a number of fire genii. He was very pleased with his work as blacksmith of the gods, difficult and unglamorous though it was.

Things attributed to Hephæstus are all metals and metalworking, subterranean fire, the forge and the anvil.

Vulcan in Astrology

Vulcan, although not really considered in exoteric astrology, is an important influence in esoteric astrology, a branch of astrology mostly based on the teachings of the Tibetan Master D. K. as presented in the books of Alice Bailey.

Vulcan is esoteric ruler of Taurus and his natural house is the Second House (material possessions, money, finance, and objective goals).

The influence of the planet Vulcan is felt as masculine and powerful, once the veil of the moon has been pierced.

Basic key words describing the influence of Vulcan are alignment with Spiritual Will and Divine Purpose, detachment, strength, stamina, endurance, craftsmanship, discipline, creativity, isolation, and a power best described as fire under pressure.

The basic function of Vulcan in our astrological chart is the bringing in of Divine Will, the Power aspect of God.

Inner Journey To Contact the Archetype

Sit or lie in a comfortable position and relax by breathing deeply and rhythmically. Now count from ten to zero, allowing your body to relax even more with each count.

Imagine as your surroundings slowly fade that you find yourself walking along a beautiful beach. It is midnight and the full moon shines brightly in the dark summer sky. You walk along the shore for awhile, pondering the teachings on Vulcan you have just read. After strolling a few yards, you find a small dune and seat yourself on the soft sand.

Looking up at the full moon shining proudly above the sea, you ask yourself how it could be possible that this magnificent, silent body of the night—which is the symbol of femininity and the subconscious mind, of Mother Nature, and even of your own mother— is now something you must release, must let go, must transcend in order to open completely to the realms of the soul.

You have struggled so long to understand your inner subconscious world, your instinctive imprints and urgings. You have worked so diligently to unravel and chart the unseen realms of your psyche. . . and now you are told that these findings are fine and important, but only a preliminary, not an end in themselves. Instead of holding onto them as you might have wanted, you must open yourself again to the uncertain, the unknown, and unpredictable inrush of Divine Will.

To grow and expand even more and become strong enough to fuse with your soul you must sever the deep bonds that connect you to your roots, to your family, to your mother, and your ancestors. You must let go of the past of humanity as a whole since it is but a weight dragging you down on the Path, restraining you from achieving your soul's purpose. You ask yourself again: Can the earth's only satellite, peacefully suspended over the calm waters, truly be a hindrance to the Great Work?

Completely confused and bewildered you start to pray. "Divine God within! Thou Who hast brought me here to the verge of madness in hope meeting my soul. Thou Who hast watched over my tiny body as I was but a little infant, and hast helped me to become the man/woman I am now. Oh, Divine Presence, have mercy on my bewilderment! Show me how and why I should discard all that is sacred and precious to me! Help me see clearly now! My mind has known so many conflicting truths that it has become difficult to know the real from the false."

"Oh, Great Divine Spirit!" you continue. "I have walked the path of the great symbols and archetypes; I have meditated alone; I have healed my emotions and forgiven those who have hurt me. But all through these years I held onto human principle and custom, keeping allegiance to my own kind, being faithful to my roots. Oh, Divine God! How is it that after all this you ask even more? How can I gather the strength and understanding necessary to let go of what has comforted me during all these changes? How can I release the deep connection I hold with my past, the very thing that is my only foothold along this narrow path? Are you asking that I jump off solid ground and venture freely into the dark and unknown, severing my umbilical chord to humanity—past and present? Oh, God! I am determined to walk ahead, but have mercy and ease my journey!"

You remain seated on the little mound for awhile, painfully aware of the empty darkness around you. Not a thing stirs, except for the gentle clashing of the waves on the sandy shore. The moon is still high, oblivious to your sorrow and confusion. Since no help seems to come from your surroundings, you are forced once more to go within.

There you find all your emotions welling up under great pressure. Your love for your family, for all those customs and habits that make up humanity, all those familiar and predictable things and events that have always safely brought you back to reality after your astral wanderings and daily meditations. You must release them now. You must soar past all that your father and mother hold dear and have passed on to you. You must be willing to transcend attachments and instinctual predictability, to face the uncertain, the unknown, and the unforeseeable. You must face your own soul, the accumulation of events and experiences of your entire evolution. Your soul holds it all. Much is unfamiliar to your present personality; nevertheless, you must now face it and integrate it, for with it, with the totality of what you are, Vulcan will forge a new and sacred tool: Your new self, at one with your soul and Divine Will.

There is no turning back now. You have given birth to yourself already. Now you must sever the umbilical cord before it starts to decay. You must step bravely into your new life, the life in the full light of the soul. It is not easy and will hurt you at your most-vulnerable spot. It is, however, a lot better than remaining where you are, allowing energetic stagnation to set in unhindered. Remember that life is change and in the universe nothing remains static.

It is time to turn away from the outer and make the inner your home. You must dedicate yourself to the inner life, understanding that the outer, more-tangible physical reality is a mere substitute for that inner actuality which is your true and only home, your Divine Place of Power.

Having made your decision, you look up at the moon. To your amazement, it does not look the same anymore. It appears as if painted on a piece of cloth suspended in the night sky. The cloth is rippling in the evening breeze and a stark white light seems to illuminate it from behind.

Suddenly the veil of the moon is lifted and a large powerful funnel cloud builds up in its place. It swirls quickly toward you, gleaming in reddish and orange hues. Somewhat afraid, you step back from the shore as the great cloud gently lands before you. Its gaping center facing you, you can see into its depths from which a warm roar is emerging. Slowly a gate forms itself at the swirling center of the funnel. Its knob is shaped in the form of the letter "V." Determined you walk toward it, open, and pass through.

You are immediately pulled upward in a swirling motion by the vacuum inside the shaft. After journeying for some time, you rest on a firm horizontal surface. The light around you grows brighter as you ascend, changing from a dark-and-fierce crimson to a soft-salmon pink, light fuchsia, pale red, and golden orange. You hear the sound of hammered metal and the voices of men at work. Slowly you open your eyes.

You find yourself lying on a table-shaped structure, a dark but attractive man smiling openly into your face. His eyes piercing you with a slightly mocking glance he asks impatiently, "Are you ready?"

Confused, you sit up from your prone position and look around. Now you know! You are in Vulcan's forge, sitting on his anvil. The man in front of you is the god himself, ready to work with Divine Will to make you the perfect vehicle of your soul.

As you lie back he gently brushes your cheek to dispel any lingering fear. He pierces you with his penetrating gaze and insists, "I won't hurt you, you know that. I love you."

With the expertise of a cosmetic surgeon he sets to work on your energy field, reshaping, restructuring, and reforming it. With every stroke of his masterful fingers you feel strengthened and revitalized; with every whisk of his skilled hands you feel more whole, powerful, and compact. After working on you for what seems nearly an eternity, he bids you stand up. You feel incredibly powerful. It is as if Vulcan has healed a thousand inner wounds and tears with his gentle hands. Not until now have you realized how torn and confused you have been all your life. Now you are one in yourself, permeated with a throbbing desire to go out into the world and start the Great Work you had so feared before.

No trace of doubt stirs in you, no anxiety or confusion. All is power; all is directed will to good. The love to manifest this inner Light blazes through your body like an orgasm. The great orgasm To Be, The Divine Orgasm that manifests the universe! You have it! You feel it! Exhilarated and ecstatic you fall into Vulcan's arms and hold him tight, tears of love and appreciation pouring down your cheeks.

After a short embrace Vulcan moves his strong right hand to the base of your spine and holds his left up to your crown chakra. This sends a shiver of power through your body, igniting an explosion in your heart center which breaks down any remaining resistance and fuses your personality to your soul.

You remain this way for a long time, basking in the effect the energy field of the god has on your own, wishing he would always be there when you need this.

Now while still in communion with Vulcan, ask him mentally for a personal message. Allow some time for this message to appear before your inner senses. However, do not worry if you do not get anything. It might come at a later time. The message is only of secondary importance. What truly matters is your contact with Vulcan.

After awhile you separate from Vulcan again, deep love connecting the two of you forever. As you look down at yourself a sword's image keeps flashing in and out of your mental field. You see yourself in your human form. Then suddenly it changes to a sword and back again to your normal body. You raise a questioning look at Vulcan as he insists, "Go ahead. Return home. It's time you take charge of your physical existence! I will be here whenever you need me. But don't forget. You must seek me here; I cannot come to you as easily. "

You give him a last hug and turn toward the direction from which you came. As the surroundings fade slowly, Vulcan and his forge disappear in the mist. Ahead of you is the full moon again, hanging suspended as if painted on a length of silk.

Following a sudden impulse you look down at yourself and, by an act of will, you build up the image of the sword coinciding with your body. You pull it out with your right hand and lash at the lunar shroud in savage determination, cutting it into a thousand pieces, leaving no visible trace of Luna.

The tiny bits snow down beside you, glittering in rainbow colors as they catch the light of the sun against the darkness of outer space. Satisfied, you pause and admire the spectacle, completely absorbed in its beauty. After a few moments you are interrupted in your contemplation by a warm hand on your right shoulder. It is Vulcan! Even behind your back you can recognize his presence easily. "Take this. You know what must be done," he says, holding up a flaming torch, an admiring look gleaming in his obsidian eyes.

Silently you bring back your sword to your body. You blend it with your own shape and it melds with your etheric field. Then you take the flare and hold it to the beautiful flakes now lying scattered at your feet. As the delicate flakes burn hungrily, an enormous smoke cloud rises. It is not a funnel this time, but a large gloomy cloud that spreads all over, entirely covering your surroundings and eclipsing the sunlight for awhile. The darkness and smoky air feel oppressive and foul; nevertheless, you remain still, waiting patiently for the air to clear. And clear it will. That you know. While you wait you give Vulcan one last embrace and say farewell, reassuring him of your return.

As you turn away from the god to resume your journey, you notice that the smoke has cleared and the air is again crisp and clean. Slowly you drift away and down toward the beach. No moon is shining now, only the bright twinkling of the stars to guide your descent. So clean and pure, you think to yourself, so perfect and natural. You feel whole and powerful, one in yourself. Silently you thank the God Within for this opportunity. A new love of life shivers through your body as you set your feet on the delicate sand.

You rest awhile on the sandy shore, allowing the gentle roll of the waves to calm you and kindly rock you back into normal waking consciousness.

The Magical Use of Vulcan

Preliminaries for the magical use of Vulcan's energy involve the following considerations:

• Open yourself to the forces of change. Be ready and willing to see yourself from a completely different perspective. Accept the fact that you might be weird, different, alien—not at all as nice or as human as you have thought yourself to be. Understand and accept yourself this way.

• Commit yourself to using the intuitive knowledge and detachment you have gained through this practice for the benefit of all.

• Accept the fact that you do not know your soul, at least not well, and that you have no idea what it contains.

• Open yourself to it unconditionally and bravely. Do not expect to see only "sugar and spice and everything nice."

• Dedicate yourself to using the newly gained power and piercing contact with Spiritual Will as wisely and lovingly as you possibly can, without forsaking your soul's potency.

Magical Practice To Fuse Your Personality with Your Soul

To fuse your personality with your soul, which is what occurs when you align yourself with pure Divine Will under the influence of Vulcan, do the following magical exercise:

1. Sit or lie in a comfortable position and begin relaxing by breathing deeply and rhythmically. Now count from ten to zero, allowing your body to relax even more with each count.

2. Attune yourself with Divine Will as manifested through Vulcan's power. State firmly that you want to contact your soul and are willing to change.

3. Visualize Vulcan's astrological symbol as shown at the beginning of this chapter. Build it up with your inner vision until it is large enough

to envelop you completely, creating an energetic bond with the power of Vulcan.

4. Allow Vulcan to overshadow you in the following way: Build up with your inner vision the image of the divine blacksmith standing behind you, make his body about seven feet high. Feel his great power and aura extending far beyond his body's limits into outer space. Concentrate on your love and admiration for Vulcan as well as on your gratitude to him for helping you in this matter. Now allow him to step up as close as possible behind you and concentrate on the overshadowing effect of his aura on yours. Still focused on your love for Vulcan, allow him to empower you by blending his great aura with your smaller one. Feel how both your energy fields are strengthened and vitalized by the contact. Feel your aura grow in size and power to coincide with that of the god. Remain this way for awhile before your proceed to the next step.

5. Focus on the tremendous buildup of power and Divine Will for a moment, then proceed to visualize a ball of white light about nine feet in diameter hovering six feet above your crown chakra. This luminous sphere represents your soul.

6. Visualize a shaft of fluorescent light about twelve inches wide, shining in the seven colors of the rainbow. The shaft extends upward from your crown chakra and connects with the center of the ball of white light.

7. Gather yourself together inwardly and concentrate your consciousness inside your crown chakra for about two minutes, or until you feel well centered there.

8. Now travel in your consciousness up through the shaft of light, which stands for the Rainbow Bridge or Antahkarana, into the center of your soul bubble.

9. Once inside, expand yourself all the way to the outer wall of the bubble and fuse with its contents. Note carefully its texture, its zillions of little light particles swirling around inside and now inside you in a well-organized manner. Feel the angelic presence and enveloping unconditional love of your soul.

Understand that all these little dancing particles of light are the experiences of your individuality along the aeons of material existence. They are the essences of the stresses formed during your many incarnations into the worlds of form, neatly coordinated and lovingly organized into one greater luminescent and very sacred whole—your own soul.

Feel the Solar Angel, the Angel of the Presence, overshadowing your consciousness, now fused with your soul. He is a shining replica of your soul's ideal achievement. So familiar to you now that your attraction becomes unbearable, and you fuse together in one big ecstatic explosion. The joy and fulfillment of this fusion runs through your now-spherical body like a lightning flash. You stay quiet for some time, revelling in the nurturing blend of light.

10. You remain in this fusion of consciousness, soul and Solar Angel, as long as it feels necessary, then start to turn your attention downward again.

11. Make certain you are expanded all the way out to the imaginary limits of your soul (the skin of the bubble) and fused with its insides. Then descend down the rainbow-colored shaft into your body, retracting the soul bubble and the shaft with you as you proceed. Once you have reentered your physical body, focus your consciousness at the heart chakra.

12. As soon as you feel well anchored in the heart chakra, rebuild the soul bubble again around your physical body. Allow the soul to expand and fuse with your personality and your energy field all the way to your aura's outer limit.

13. Now extend a shaft of light from your heart chakra all the way to your aura's outer limit and scan through it like the beam on a radar screen, round and round, fusing personality, soul, and consciousness tightly as it passes.

14. Let your scanner run through your entire aura as thoroughly as you can, then remain still for a few minutes to absorb the experience.

Note that the scanner is pure Divine Will burning away any obstacles that might still separate the personality from the soul, fusing the two with incredible power and heat.

15. Retract your imaginary scanner back into your heart center. Take a few minutes to relax. Note that the soul bubble is left intact and fused with your aura and personality.

16. Slowly return to normal consciousness.

Note that in the soul's Light only the essences of your experiences count as they enter into relationship, integrated into a magnificent whole. This is quite different from what your personality might imagine. It is precisely this unpredictability, of what the soul is and how it feels that is so intimidating. Total faithful surrender of the lower personality to the soul is all that can be done.

EPILOGUE

Power Planets shows you how to understand and access the enormous energetic reservoirs of the planetary archetypes. However, showing you "how to" is not enough. To integrate these energies into your personality you must work with discipline and dedication. There are several ways to enhance and accelerate this process.

If you are a beginner, you may want to work with a professional astrologer. Have him or her cast your natal chart. Show the astrologer this book and explain that you wish to work dynamically with the energies of the most-prominent planets in your chart. Once you have mastered those, you may ask the astrologer to show you your transits and progressions and point out the planets involved. Then proceed to work consciously to make the best of their energies, empowering positive aspects between the planets and smoothing out problematic ones with the system delineated in this book.

If you already know astrology, I bet you won't need any encouragement to apply the techniques described in *Power Planets* to your chart and help others do the same.

You may also want to work with the principles and exercises given in *Power Planets* with a group of people that meets regularly. You will be amazed at the amount of power raised in a group formation.

Power Planets is well suited for group work. I suggest that you appoint a leader. You may chose a different leader for each occasion or keep the same one, both ways are fine. Prior to each meeting, have the individual members read the chapter relevant to the planet to be worked with on their own. Then, when you are all assembled, have the leader read the inner journey aloud to the circle to contact the godform as a group. Subsequently, have the leader guide the group through one of the magical practices pertaining to the planet in question.

Most of *Power Planets*' magical practices are well suited to be performed in a group. For some practices, each member may work individually for himself, while still seated within the circle of participants. Other practices may be done collectively. The energy of the group will greatly enhance and empower the experience, making effects more lasting and dramatic.

You may close the meeting with comments, questions and answers. It does not matter if you are not experts in answering queries; what matters is that the questions be formulated aloud. Sooner or later one of the group members, empowered by the archetype, will come up with a satisfactory answer.

I suggest that each group member keep a magical journal, writing down any significant experiences during and after the group work. You may compare notes if you wish, but it is not necessary. However, should any of you decide to lead a group later on, you will find the journal an invaluable help.

For those of you eager to accelerate and intensify the contact with the *Power Planets*, Luis and I have created STAR*LIFE, Instant Access To Cosmic Energies. With STAR*LIFE you can access the *Power Planets* instantly and anytime at will through personal initiations which activate your aura to radiate the energies of the planetary archetypes. STAR*LIFE is powerful and effective. Hundreds of students around the world have taken these Planetary Cosmic Activations and testify how their lives have changed and improved. The quality of empowerment conceded through STAR*LIFE Planetary Activations can only be individually achieved through years of dedicated study and spiritual disciplines. I greatly recommend it.

However, the most-sublime experience of integration with the planetary archetypes comes when a group of people who have already received the STAR*LIFE Cosmic Activations works together. It is impossible to describe the energy and the purity felt in the room, as well as the lasting feeling of plenitude, empowerment, and bliss that lingers long after completion of the work.

It is time to say farewell and I hope you enjoyed reading this book as much as I loved creating it. If you wish to write me a comment on your experiences with *Power Planets*, please do so, especially if you are working with a group. If you are an astrologer and are using *Power Planets* to help your clients, I would love to hear about it. You may reach me through the publisher or through STAR*LIFE, the address is at the back of this book.

May the Kingdom, the Power, and the Glory be with you always.

Luisa De La Lama

APPENDIX A THE CHAKRAS

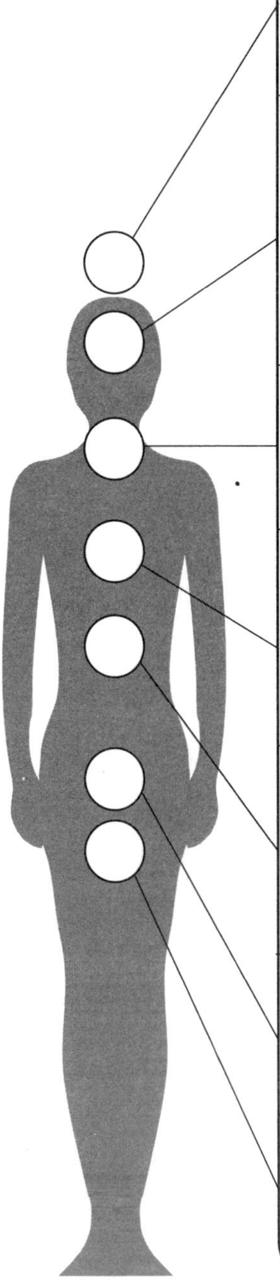

Chakra	Powers
7th Crown	Spiritual will Integration Expansion Universality
6th Third Eye	Soul power Intuition Individuation Vision Perception and actualization of higher ideals
5th Throat	Creative power Expression Sound
4th Heart	Unconditional love Group consciousness Understanding Bliss
3rd Solar Plexus	Astral force Emotion Sensitivity Reserve energy
2nd Sexual	Etheric force Vital energy
1st Basic	*Kundalini*, universal life energy Physical will

APPENDIX B

THE SOUL EXTENDING INTO PHYSICAL EXISTENCE

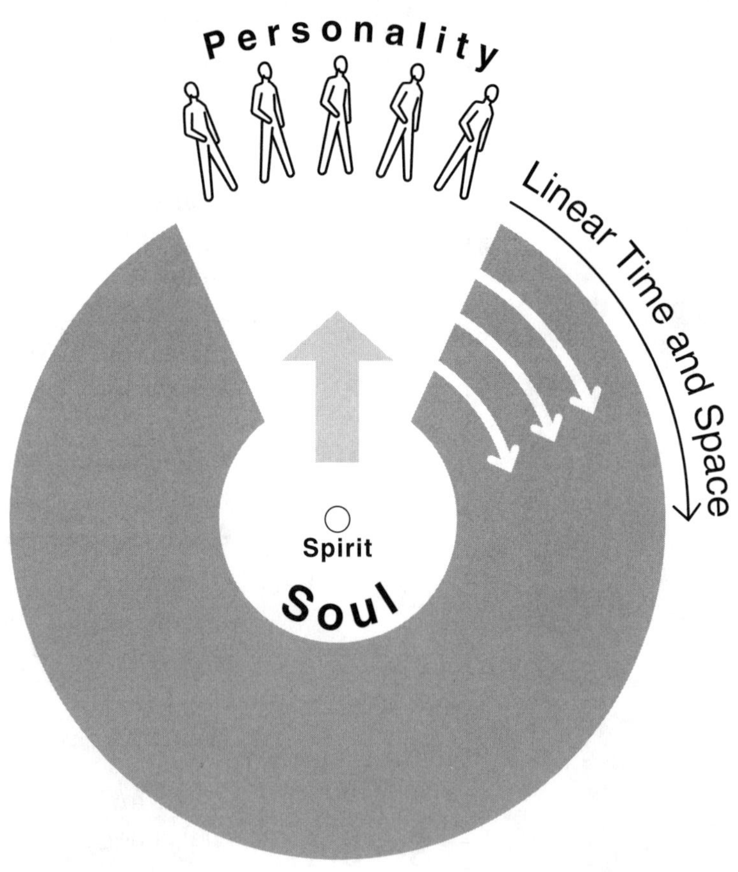

APPENDIX C

ASTROLOGICAL SERVICES

Astro Communications Services, Inc.
P.O. Box 34487
San Diego, California 92163-4487

Bernie Ashman
Innovations Astrological Services
P.O. Box 3314
Durham, NC 27702
1-800-669-0545 and 919-489-0545

If you wish to know how the planetary energies of your natal chart relate to the area where you live, order your Astro*Carto*Graphy from Astro Numeric Services, P.O. Box 336-BJ, Ashland, Oregon 97520 or call 1-800-"MAPPING."

You may also want to subscribe to *The Mountain Astrologer*, P.O. Box 11292, Berkeley, CA 94701. Many professional astrologers list their services in this publication.

BIBLIOGRAPHY

Abraham, Kurt. *The Moon Veils Vulcan and the Sun Veils Neptune.* Oregon: Lampus Press, 1989.

Bailey, Alice A. *The Rays and the Initiations.* London: Lucis Press, 1960.

Bailey, Alice A. *Esoteric Psychology II.* London: Lucis Press, 1942.

Bailey, Alice A. *Esoteric Astrology.* London: Lucis Press, 1951.

Bailey, Alice A. *A Treatise on Cosmic Fire.* London: Lucis Press, 1962.

Ferrier, Loretta, Ph.D. *Dance of the Selves: Uniting the Male and Female Within.* New York: Simon and Schuster, 1992.

Fortune, Dion. *The Cosmic Doctrine.* Great Britain: Aquarian Press, 1976.

Fortune, Dion. *Esoteric Philosophy of Love and Marriage.* New York: Samuel Weiser, 1979.

Green, Jeff. *Uranus: Freedom from the Known.* Minnesota: Llewellyn Publications, 1989.

Green, Jeff. *Pluto: The Evolutionary Journey of the Soul.* Minnesota: Llewellyn Publications, 1990.

Hand, Robert. *Horoscope Symbols.* Pennsylvania: Whitford Press, 1981.

Hope, Murry. *Ancient Egypt: The Sirius Connection.* England: Element Books, 1990.

New Larousse Encyclopedia of Mythology. England: The Hamlyn Publishing Group, 1959.

Oken, Alan. *Soul-Centered Astrology.* New York: Bantam, 1990.

Oken, Alan. *Alan Oken's Complete Astrology*. New York: Bantam, 1988.

Paul, Haydn. *Queen of the Night*. England: Element Books, 1990.

Paul, Haydn. *Phoenix Rising*. England: Element Books, 1988.

Paul, Haydn. *Revolutionary Spirit*. England: Element Books, 1989.

Paul, Haydn. *Visionary Dreamer*. England: Element Books, 1989.

Reinhart, Melanie. *Chiron and the Healing Journey*. London: Arkana/Penguin Group, 1989.

Roman, Sanaya and Duane Packer. *Creating Money*. California: H.J. Kramer, 1988.

Sasportas, Howard. *The Gods of Change*. England: Arkana, 1989.

Silburn, Lilian. *Kundalini: The Energy of the Depths*. New York: State University of New York Press, 1988.

Sullivan, Erin. *Saturn in Transit*. London: Arkana/Penguin Group, 1991.

Temple, Robert K.G. *The Sirius Mystery*. London: Sidgwick and Jackson, 1981.

Weiner, Errol. *Transpersonal Astrology: Finding the Soul's Purpose*. England: Element Books, 1991.

ABOUT THE AUTHOR

Born in Madrid, Spain, the daughter of a Hungarian count and granddaughter of a Spanish marquis, Luisa De La Lama spent most of her life among the European Jet-Set. Luisa speaks fluent Spanish, German, English, and French. She has traveled extensively, lived in five different countries, and graduated from the Hotel and Business Management School in Schloss Klessheim, Salzburg, Austria.

Luisa has trained in eastern and western esoteric disciplines for twenty years. Her extensive knowledge and experience in this field includes Mystical Qabalah, Astrology, Ceremonial Magic, Tarot, Psychology, Mythology, Tantra, and the raising of kundalini.

Together with her husband, Luis De La Lama, she has created STAR*LIFE, Instant Access to Cosmic Energies.

Luisa De La Lama has devoted her life to helping others reclaim their Divine Power and to activate in humanity a deep transformational relationship of love which she calls the Twin Soul Experience.

POWER
PLANETS
Inner Journeys
Audiotapes

With STAR*LIFE you tap directly into the powers of the universe.

The Cosmic Activations given by Luis De La Lama polarize your energy field to receive and radiate specific cosmic energies every time you use simple hand gestures. The first level of STAR*LIFE enables you to apply the powers of the five metaphysical elements to harmonize and fulfill your life as well as that of others.

The STAR*LIFE energies replenish your life force, clear mental, emotional, even physical dysfunctions, and produce spectacular results in self-growth, achievement, and enlightenment. The STAR*LIFE energies are so effective that 96 percent feel their effect right away. They are used professionally by healers, psychologists, chiropractors, massage therapists, counselors, and others in various caretaking roles.

To receive free literature, please call 1-800-441-4111 in the U.S.A. or write to

Workshop conducted by Luis De La Lama

In Life you either stagnate in a meaningless existence trying to fulfill others' models and expectations, or, finding your core power, you become the creator of an exciting new universe.

You know this experiential weekend is for you when

✔ You want to find out for yourself who you are, where you come from, and where you are going.

✔ You have tried *everything* in the self-help market and still feel your life could be better.

✔ You feel ready to face the chaos masking your true self.

✔ You feel ready to challenge your most-basic (and unconscious) assumptions about your parents, God, good and evil, time, and the meaning of life.

✔ You want to assume the responsibility and risk that comes with true power.

For information, please call 1-800-441-4111 in the U.S.A. or write to

STAR*LIFE

1295 South Kihei Rd., Suite 3009

Kihei, Maui, HI 96753

U.S.A.